CHRISTIAN BEGINNINGS

HARPER TORCHLIGHT BOOKS

★

CHRISTIAN BEGINNINGS

Parts I and II

By

MORTON SCOTT ENSLIN

HARPER TORCHBOOKS
Harper & Row, Publishers
New York, Hagerstown, San Francisco, London

First HARPER TORCHLIGHT Edition published 1956

Including Parts I and II of the original edition. Part III
is published as a separate HARPER TORCHLIGHT,
THE LITERATURE OF THE CHRISTIAN MOVEMENT

T. V. E.

A. S. E.

CONTENTS

INTRODUCTION

THERE is no dearth of good *Introductions to the New Testament*. Jülicher, Moffatt, and Bacon—to mention but three—have long been standard, and will continue to be studied with profit for many years to come. In recent years there have appeared several more. It is not unnatural that each scholar wishes, if not to embalm, at least to preserve his own views on the New Testament as a whole. I suppose I must plead guilty to the same desire, at least in part. For many years I have felt a distinct need for a work of somewhat different compass, one that should include between one set of covers a reasonably comprehensive survey of many other matters beside an introduction to each of the twenty-seven books which Christians have long considered of especial value. The New Testament did not produce Christianity. Christianity, on the contrary, produced the New Testament. The student who starts his study of the New Testament with Matthew or even with the earliest of the Pauline letters is under a great handicap. He can truly appreciate these writings only as he understands why Christians felt themselves impelled to write. And Christianity itself did not spring into being full grown like Athene from the head of Zeus. She was the child of Judaism, although an unwanted child and soon disowned. But the Judaism that gave birth to a Jesus and a Paul was not that of the Old Testament prophets. This has often been conceded by Christians who have expatiated on the decay of a once noble religion into a barren and formal legalism. This appears to me an almost total misapprehension. The experiences through which the little nation passed during the five or six centuries before the dawn of the Christian era might well have proved her downfall; instead they made a tremendous and lasting contribution. At once pugnaciously conservative and yet always receptive to new ideas, the Jew exacted his toll from Babylon, Persia, Egypt, Greece, and Rome. The doubts and the fears, the glowing confidence and wistful longings of these eventful years—all these were in the blood of Jesus and his early followers. But within little more than a century after his death the new religion which he had unwittingly begotten had become so completely acclimated to the wider Mediterranean world and had drunk so deeply at wells which no Jewish hand had delved that a Justin Martyr, hard put to answer the pagan charge that Christianity had stolen its rites and teachings, could only account for the obvious similarities by the counter charge that evil demons centuries before had seen what was destined to come to pass, and had frantically but vainly concocted counterfeits to discredit the genuine when it should appear. It is only as the student gains

vii

some inkling of all this that he can hope to understand these writings, for as some nameless wit has well said: "The simple gospel is not nearly so simple as simple people sometimes think." Then when these writings had been produced, what happened to them? Did they become canonical overnight? Do we have them today precisely as they left their authors' hands? Surely these questions are of consequence not only to the minister but to "Everyman," if he would call himself educated, for the Bible has long since ceased to be simply a book of religion.

For thirteen years I have sought to introduce my students to the New Testament in this fashion. Each year I have found, as every other teacher does, the time seems shorter. One purely selfish purpose in writing this book was to free my conscience when I dallied in pleasant fields and talked "more and more about less and less." At least my class would have the opportunity of reading a reasonably complete and balanced statement. Thus the volume is severely practical in its scope. It is intended really to introduce the New Testament. It makes no claim to be exhaustive despite its size, which is larger than I could wish. Every one of the forty-six chapters could be, and has been, expanded into a sizeable volume. While I have not entirely forgotten the expert and have made occasional suggestions intended principally for his consideration, I have tried never to forget the reader who is not and never will be a professional scholar. Accordingly, I early decided to omit, so far as was practicable, the reference to works other than in English, for, unfortunate though it is, most American students are limited to one tongue. Whenever possible, standard foreign works have been cited in translation, even though later and better German editions are available. Thus I have regularly referred to Schürer's and Jülicher's works in their English dress, although occasionally adding a reference to the latter's seventh edition. I have resolutely kept Greek out of the volume. Only in a very few cases have a few words trickled in, generally in footnotes, and almost always with an interpretation. This has not been easy; to describe the task of the textual critic without use of Greek is a task to try one's ingenuity and add grey to one's hair. I have finally decided not to include a bibliography. This was not done solely to save space. Most teachers, I believe, prefer to suggest their own collateral reading. Furthermore, I am firmly convinced that one of the chief disciplines a student has is to work out his own bibliography. Many of the more important works are referred to in the text and notes. The rest the student can find for himself; the general reader will probably not want them.

It is quite impossible to express adequately my obligation and indebtedness to the countless scholars whose works I have freely used. I have tried to be punctilious in expressing specific indebtedness in the footnotes; it may well be that I am under even greater obligation than I realize. There is little originality, after all, in scholarship. The newest and most spectacular "discovery" oftentimes turns out to have been discovered and then forgotten a century or more ago. I have tried to present a fair picture of the various views on this problem or that, when competent opinions differ. On the other hand, I have not hesitated to express my own opinions; even if, as occasionally is the case, the voice of the majority is contrary and the matter is highly debatable. I think in every such case there is ample indication that no unwary reader may be tempted to follow blindly, thinking he is running with the main herd. Regularly I have quoted from the text of the American Revised Version of the Bible, copyrighted 1919 by the International Council of Religious Education, and wish to express my indebtedness to them for this permission. While many of the translations of the classic authors are my own, I have not hesitated to make use of the many and admirable renderings which have been made available by the industry of many scholars living and dead to whom I would make this grateful, if general, acknowledgment.

I feel it a real obligation—but much more than a mere obligation, a sincere joy—to express my indebtedness to Frederick Lincoln Anderson, for many years professor of New Testament Interpretation at the Newton Theological Institution. For nearly twenty years I can count him a respected teacher and a generous friend. He is not responsible for the views expressed; none the less, it was he who aroused in me the love for this book and the desire to know more about it.

PART I
THE BACKGROUND

Chapter I

UNDER FOREIGN DOMINION

At the death of Solomon (933 B.C.) the united kingdom split, and gradually, to the ire of the Chronicler, the northern kingdom, Israel, gained the ascendancy. Foreign powers were making themselves felt. By location Israel and Judah formed the buffer between Syria on the north and Egypt on the south. Due to complex causes, both within and without, their strength became lessened and in 722 came the so-called fall of the northern kingdom before Sargon of Assyria. Although Judah's time was not for 136 years, this is not to be interpreted as due to her superior strength, but rather to Israel's more exposed location and greater value as plunder.

As the war clouds of the rising Assyria and Babylonia are reflected in the sky the prophets raise their voices anew. And a strange note it seems to us. With our knowledge today we can see how Israel had come to a worship of one God. Apparently each local shrine had originally had its own Baal; gradually, however, Jehovah[1] had increased and had come to stand alone. Still, however, he was the Lord God of Israel. But more was to follow. After the northern kingdom had fallen and the southern could see all too plainly the handwriting on the wall a taking stock was necessary. If Judah fell, did that mean that Jehovah was impotent? that the gods of the other nations were more powerful? The prophets refused such an answer. By no means. Jehovah was all-powerful. He was merely using these foreign foes as whips with which to scourge Israel for her sins. Think of that faith—almost impudence it seems to us—for this little tottering nation to declare that Assyria and Babylonia were but instruments in the hands of her god. While this impending peril was not the only cause, it must not be disregarded in an attempt to account for the elevation of Jehovah.

And then in 586 came the collapse of the southern kingdom, after two unsuccessful attempts to throw off the Babylonian yoke. The lenient treatment of Nebuchadnezzar in putting down the first revolt was not repeated; this year saw the burning of the temple and the breaching of the city walls.

Then followed a period of "captivity," but not of imprisonment. Although Jerusalem was apparently laid waste, only a small fraction of its inhabitants were transported to Babylonia, and many of them soon found life by no

[1] The conventional spelling of the name will be used in these pages, since it has seemed pedantic to print the tetragrammaton and since the present writer has no desire to perpetrate a fresh guess as to the original pronunciation.

means intolerable. None the less, although all did not spend their entire time weeping by the rivers of Babylon, hatred of the conqueror was real. In the sudden rise to power of Persia, following the spectacular conquest by Cyrus of the Medes and Lydians, Israel saw her hopes rise once more. Babylon would fall next, and in 538 the triumphal entry of Cyrus into Babylon fulfilled these hopes.

Jehovah hath broken the staff of the wicked, the sceptre of the rulers; that smote the peoples in wrath with a continual stroke, that ruled the nations in anger, with a persecution that none restrained.[2]

The next two hundred years saw Persia's sway. In accord with Cyrus' general policy the Jews were free to return home and to rebuild their temple. Later Judaism with its emphasis on the omnipotence of Jehovah in this saw Cyrus as Jehovah's agent.

Now in the first year of Cyrus king of Persia, that the word of Jehovah by the mouth of Jeremiah might be accomplished, Jehovah stirred up the spirit of Cyrus king of Persia so that he made a proclamation throughout all his kingdom, and put it also in writing, saying, Thus saith Cyrus king of Persia. All the kingdoms of the earth hath Jehovah, the God of heaven, given me; and he hath charged me to build him a house in Jerusalem, which is in Judah. Whosoever there is among you of all his people, his God be with him, and let him go up to Jerusalem, which is in Judah, and build the house of Jehovah, the God of Israel (he is God), which is in Jerusalem. And whosoever is left, in any place where he sojourneth, let the men of his place help him with silver, and with gold, and with goods, and with beasts, besides the freewill-offering for the house of God which is in Jerusalem.[3]

It is to be doubted if Cyrus would have appreciated this description. Some Jews returned, but the universal return as described by the Chronicler in Ezra 2 cannot be accepted. Persia had no intention of restoring Israel. The administration of her vast empire demanded a highly developed organization and clear-cut centralized policy which gave little or no opportunity for even such nominal independence as, as we shall see, Rome granted. On the whole, Persian control was far less irksome than had been slavery to Babylonia; on the other hand, it appears highly probable that many sanguine hopes for restored independence were blasted. The temple was not rebuilt for years, and even when that was finally accomplished at the insistence of Haggai and Zechariah the expected good times failed to appear. National hopes as centred in Zerubbabel met with short shrift. Persia's general attitude toward the administration of her Empire is epitomized in the Behistun inscriptions of Darius: "By the grace of Ahuramazda these lands have conformed to my decree; even as it was commanded unto them by me, so was it done." And the kings kept paid officials, called the King's Ears or King's Eyes, whose duty it was to keep a sharp watch for incipient uprising or rebellion.

[2] Isa. 14:5,6.
[3] Ezra 1:1-4.

Although the Jews soon realized that whatever part Jehovah had had in elevating Cyrus, there was to be no opportunity for a restored monarchy, and that it was easier to obtain permission to erect a temple than to build city walls, there was ample opportunity for religious development. The not unnatural result was an increased emphasis on religion. The high priest became the head of Judaism; now that there was no king to overshadow him he enjoyed far more power than had the priests in the days of the monarchy. It was not, however, a political power. In Breasted's happy phrase: "The Jewish state was . . . a *religious* organization, a church with a priest at its head."[4]

This development was at least partially due to the fact that Persian religion was as favourable to Judaism as her political policies were hostile to local independence. That both Persian and Jew worshipped one supreme God gave a ready bond of sympathy; in addition, a bitter hatred of idolatry and a keen expectation of a glorious age in the future were common to both. Consequently, in these two centuries of Persian control Judaism underwent many changes, and changes which were no less real because they were less the result of conscious borrowing than of stimulation. Ideas were in the air; and Judaism accumulated a good deal which was alien to her early inheritance.

Persian dualism with its notions of the powers of good as personified in the Supreme Being in ceaseless clash with the forces of evil under their prince gives us the New Testament devil, the god of this age,[5] who thus became identified with the totally different Satan of the Old Testament. A belief in future life, with its recompenses and punishments, usurps the older view, that "there is no work, nor device, nor knowledge, nor wisdom, in Sheol, whither thou goest,"[6] which appears to be presupposed by the almost fanatical desire for a son and the resultant institution of levirate marriage. With the increasing confidence that only one place (and that Jerusalem) could serve as a sanctuary for sacrifice there developed the institution of the synagogue as the actual centre of the nation, in practice if not in theory. Discussion of these developments, which can be but listed here, may profitably be postponed to the study of Judaism, as such, in a subsequent chapter. It is important, however, to realize that these long years of exile and captivity, which might easily have become a flood in which they perished, became in reality a bath of regeneration.

It may be wondered how it was that Judaism with its tough-bitted insistence on its own supremacy and its growing confidence that God had revealed his complete and entire will could have acquired these alien strains. Again it is to be emphasized that it was not so much conscious borrowing as almost imperceptible stimulation from forces which did not seem so

---

[4] J. H. Breasted, *Ancient Times*, p. 216.
[5] II Cor. 4:4.
[6] Eccl. 9:10.

strange. They were living in the world, and simply went further than they knew. There are many more things than vice which we "first endure, then pity, then embrace." And again, Judaism always laid its emphasis on action. God's supreme and complete will had been revealed. Israel was to keep his law; that was as well their joy as their task. It was breaking the law that constituted sin; a generous latitude was always left to individual notions, and it is hardly an exaggeration to say that throughout Israel's history there have been as many opinions as there have been individuals to hold them. Many are our heritages from Judaism; heresy-hunting, however, is not one of them. Many mistaken notions to the contrary notwithstanding, as we shall later see, it was not distinctions of belief which aroused Jewish hostility toward Jesus. Without always realizing it, Judaism has ever been receptive to new ideas and new notions. Because of this she has survived through the centuries, herself the veritable century plant, often dying, but always to blossom anew. And it was during these years, to us years of almost complete silence, that she gained a by no means negligible access of strength.

But now a star appears in the western sky in the person of the young Alexander of Macedon, and two years after the battle of Issus (333 B.C.), which had made him master of all western Syria, he met and signally defeated Darius at Gaugamela, a little town near Arbela (331 B.C.), in what justly merits the name, one of the fifteen decisive battles of the world, and put to an end for ever the Persian supremacy.

The ephemeral rise of the young Macedonian has been so often and ably reviewed that it need not be repeated here. At the age of twenty-two he dealt the western satraps of Darius III a crushing defeat at the Granicus River (334 B.C.) in Asia Minor, near the site of ancient Troy—the first blow in his successful attempt to overthrow the kingdom of Persia, then mistress to the Ægean, and to make good his title, Master of Greece. Two years later (333 B.C.), having followed the track of Xenophon's immortal Ten Thousand, he pushed through southern Asia Minor and met the main Persian army under the personal direction of Darius III. The two armies clashed at Issus, and again Alexander was victor. Darius in terror offers terms of peace. He is even willing to surrender all his territory west of the Euphrates. Alexander refuses; why accept half the loaf when the whole was his for the taking? The vision of world empire is before his eye. Though young in years, his was the genius of the wise tactician. Before pushing east he wished to reduce the seacoast of the Mediterranean, in order to bring about the collapse of the Persian fleet, the unrivalled mistress of the Sea.

In accord with this determination he proceeded at once against Damascus and Tyre. The latter city stood siege, and for seven months held out. When it finally fell, his vengeance was terrible. Next he turned south to Gaza on the coast road to Egypt. After a two-month siege this city too fell, and received the same severe treatment.

Josephus preserves a romantic and edifying tale of Alexander's awe and reverence before the Jewish high priest, whom "God had honoured with the high-priesthood," who stays him on his way to Jerusalem to exact vengeance for the failure of the Jews to obey his peremptory demand to sever their allegiance to Persia and send him aid against Tyre. The story is highly coloured, and reminds us of the picture of Cyrus presented by the Chronicler in Ezra 1. Whether, in fact, Alexander visited Jerusalem at all is a moot question. At any rate, he did not destroy it. Judea was apparently incorporated into the satrapy of Cœle-Syria, with Samaria as the capital city. Later the Samaritans got into trouble with Alexander and were severely punished on his return from Egypt. Judea, however, Josephus tells us, was left in quiet. This treatment of Judea was in keeping with his aim of welding East and West together, rather than of annihilating the East. His aim was frankly a world empire. His teacher, Aristotle, had urged him to treat the Greeks as freemen, the Orientals as slaves. Wisely he sought the better way of uniting all. To achieve this he sought to use Greek civilization, with its language and culture, both so dear to him, as the medium. In him the earlier dreams of Xenophon and Isocrates found their fulfilment.

In 332 he was master of Egypt, which capitulated without struggle, and thus gave the last blow to the once proud Persian fleet, now deprived both of its harbours and of all contact with the army. Now he could turn east for the final conflict with tottering Persia. And the next year saw the end of the Persian power, so long the mistress of the East. At Gaugamela, near Arbela, on the Tigris West and East met (331 B.C.). The Persian force was hopelessly outclassed; even the scythe-wheeled war chariots with which Persia sought in vain desperation to check the Macedonian advances were unavailing. Darius III fled, soon to fall by an assassin's hand. Alexander's dream was realized. Persia was finally his. Although his untimely death—he was but thirty-three—in 323 prevented the realization of his world ambition, he had effectually removed the barrier between East and West, and had brought the magic of Greek civilization into the Oriental world.

Unlike the eastern war lords, his advance was marked by something more lasting than desolation and ruin. An Assyrian monarch might inscribe:

With battle and slaughter I assailed and took the city. Their possessions I carried away. Many of their soldiers I carried away. Of some I cut off hands and limbs; of others the noses, ears, and arms; of many soldiers I put out the eyes. I devastated the city, dug it up, in fire I burned it; I annihilated it.

Instead, wherever Alexander went, Greek culture took root; in Egypt had been founded the city of Alexandria, destined to receive from Athens the torch of Greek learning and in her stead become the schoolmistress of the world. His empire cracked—there was none able to succeed their impetuous master—but Greek kingdoms appeared throughout Asia, destined to endure for centuries; and far more significant than his battles were the strides in knowledge that resulted from his campaigns. East and West had become united. Writing in the middle of the second century of our era the Greek historian Arrian piously remarked of this prince of generals, he, "who was like no other man, could not have been given to the world without the special design of Providence." Nor do his words seem an entire overstatement.

At the death of Alexander the great empire crumbled overnight. He had left no heir,[7] but there were many claimants. One of his generals, Perdiccas, had received his signet, and sought to maintain the imperial interests until the birth and growth of the expected heir. His rivals combined against him, and in 321 his own soldiers murdered him at Memphis, whither he had proceeded against Ptolemy.

The empire fell into the hands of a group of men known to us as the Diadochi or Successors, among whom were Ptolemy, Antigonus, Seleucus, Lysimachus, and Antipater. Ptolemy had received Egypt, but not content had determined to gain Cœle-Syria, in which lay Palestine, as a buffer against his rivals to the north and east. This with Cyprus he soon secured (320 B.C.). He is said to have entered Jerusalem on a Sabbath, thus meeting with no resistance—on the plea of desiring to sacrifice—and to have carried off many Jews to Egypt as colonists.

This maritime plain became the theatre of war between the armies of Ptolemy and Antigonus, as Palestine, like a veritable shuttlecock, passed back and forth from the one to the other. Antigonus easily regained Syria in 315, but three years later lost at least the southern half as a result of the battle of Gaza, only to regain it the next year. Suffice it to say, this ancient Alsace-Lorraine changed hands at least five times in less than ten years.

Antigonus, who had been confirmed in his possession of the kingdom of Phrygia in the nominal agreement at Triparadeisus in 321, was the ablest and most ambitious of the Diadochi, and accordingly in the most dangerous position. He gradually made his power felt. Eumenes, who had been appointed by Perdiccas to the district south of the Black Sea, had always been hated by the rest, and had been declared a public enemy. By 315 Antigonus had brought about his death and appropriated his domain. It became perfectly patent that his ambitions would stop at nothing short of Alexander's whole domain.

Naturally this ambition resulted in a coalition against him of the rest of the successors. Lysimachus of Thrace, Cassander (who had succeeded his father Antipater in Macedon and Greece), and Seleucus, the able general to whom

---

[7] Later a posthumous son was born to his widow, but he plays no part in our story. In his thirteenth year he was murdered by Cassander. Than his there have been few more pathetic stories in history.

had fallen Babylon, combined, and finally Ptolemy joined them on the promise that while Seleucus should gain Syria, he would receive Cœle-Syria[8] including Palestine, that is, apparently the territory south of Damascus. The combined force was finally successful against him and his able son Demetrius at the battle of Ipsus in Phrygia (301 B.C.). Seleucus gained all of Syria from the Mediterranean to the Indus. Some twenty years later he wrested almost all of Asia Minor from Lysimachus who had gained the western half as his part of the spoils. Seleucus settled in Syria and built his capital city, Antioch, on the Orontes, with its harbor Seleucia. This was the start of the Seleucidæ[9]—the ruling house of Syria—destined to play such an important part in the affairs of Palestine.

Alexander's empire was now in four parts: Lysimachus had Thrace and a part of Asia Minor; Cassander, Macedon and Greece; Seleucus, Syria and all east to the Indus; Ptolemy, Egypt and the southernmost part of Syria, including Palestine. Because of Ptolemy's but indifferent help in the campaign against Antigonus, the other members of the coalition had assigned Palestine to Seleucus. Ptolemy, however, had proceeded to occupy it, and apparently it remained in the control of his house until the victory of Antiochus the Great at Panium in 198, although some historians, as Schürer, maintain that it was not until some twenty years later that it passed definitely into Egyptian control.

Geographically Palestine should have belonged to Northern Syria since the desert to the south is the real frontier between Egypt and Syria. On the other hand, Ptolemy had at once realized its peculiar importance as a buffer, while in addition the timber of the Lebanons was by no means to be despised by a land as poor as Egypt was in this respect. Accordingly, it is no wonder that this little land should have been the cause of constant trouble between the two rivals. Of the actual history of Palestine during the years of Egyptian control we know very little. The external history of Palestine during the years of Egyptian control appears to have been limited to a passive survey of the

---

[8] Strictly speaking, Cœle-Syria means the hollow between the Lebanons and Anti-Lebanons. Polybius refers to it as "a cañon called Marsyas, which lies between the skirts of Libanus and Anti-Libanus, and is contracted into a narrow gorge by these two mountains. Just where the valley is narrowest it is divided by marshes and lakes, from which the scented reed is cut" (*Hist.* v,45). The term is, however, popularly employed by Polybius as well as others to indicate all Palestine and Phœnicia to the Egyptian frontier. The Jewish commonwealth itself, to use Schürer's convenient term, was limited to Judea, that is, the district south of Samaria, which was essentially a distinct province. It did not embrace Galilee, the Perœa (land east of the Jordan) which was made up both of Hellenistic cities and native communities, nor the seacoast cities. Thus the sway of the high priest was over a decidedly limited district. Cf. Schürer, *History of the Jewish People*, Div. I, Vol. I, pp. 186-192.

[9] Seleucus' return to Babylon in 312 B.C. (following the repulse of Antigonus at Gaza) was later regarded the beginning of the Seleucid empire and the moment from which subsequent dates were to be reckoned. Cf. "Thus the yoke of the heathen was taken away from Israel in the hundred and seventieth year" (I Macc. 13:41). This hundred and seventieth year was 143 B.C. A convenient table for the conversion of dates may be found in Schürer, *op. cit.*, Div. I, Vol. II, pp. 393-398.

struggle between the Ptolemies and Seleucids, and even the details of this struggle in the first decades are very meagre. Of her internal development we know correspondingly little. Apparently her lot was comparatively easy. Aside from the appointment of governors and the imposition of taxes, she appears to have been given practical independence. Josephus[10] preserves a highly coloured story of the difficulties which arose during the high-priest-hood of Onias II, when the latter, due either to his inability or perhaps to his pro-Syrian leanings, failed to pay his taxes. The story is not without diffi-culties with regard to chronology and is also replete with the gossipy details which Josephus was wont to employ when his sources ran dry. It gives a vivid picture of what may well have been the method employed to farm the taxes out. Such a power as we are told this Joseph and his son Hyrcanus as tax farmers enjoyed for more than twenty years could hardly have failed to result in the rise of a wealthy class in Jerusalem vastly more interested in the Hellenistic culture of Alexandria than in the strict Jewish piety. Egypt, so far as we know, never employed coercive measures to hellenize Palestine as did the Seleucids later, notably as we shall see Antiochus IV. None the less, she was in every respect a Greek kingdom, and her century of suzerainty can hardly have failed to leave its impress.

But changes far more drastic were coming. The power of the Ptolemies in the compact and easily protected Egypt had increased during the long reign of Ptolemy II Philadelphus (285-246); while under his successor, Ptolemy III (246-221), real inroads had been made into the territory of the Seleucids, which was so large as to be unwieldy, if not actually inchoate. For a time a large section of North Syria had been under Egyptian control, while Pales-tine had remained firm in the latter's grasp, although Syria had made at least three definite attempts to wrest it away. During the reign of the dissolute Ptolemy IV (221-204) a decline, however, set in. Two years before the latter's accession to the throne, Antiochus III, popularly and rightly surnamed the Great, had succeeded his brother Seleucus II as sixth in the Syrian line. Within a few years he turned his attention to a systematic attempt at the conquest of Palestine. His chief seaport, Seleucia, now in the hands of Egypt, was regained and he turned south. Following varying fortunes, a wearisome negotiation was entered into by the two kings, which failing of its purpose gave way to further warfare. In 217 came the decisive battle of Raphia, a little south of Gaza. Ptolemy was successful and Antiochus withdrew to Syria. A few years later Ptolemy died, and in the resultant weakness of Egypt—the heir was but five years of age and a series of regents was disas-trous—Antiochus saw his chance. With Philip V of Macedon he made a con-certed drive against Egypt, this time successful. As a result of his victory at Panium (198 B.C.), near the head waters of the Jordan, later to be the site of Cæsarea Philippi, Cœle-Syria passed into the hands of Syria. Egypt was never

[10] *Antt.* 12,4,1 ff.

to regain it. Many of the Jews hailed Antiochus as their saviour. They had been ill-treated by Scopas, the Egyptian general, and remembered that after Raphia Ptolemy had sought to push his way into the holy of holies.[11] Antiochus appears to have treated the Jews kindly. Thousands were settled in Syria as colonists; taxes were remitted; Antiochus, in contrast to Ptolemy Philopator, is said to have been most scrupulous in his observance of the niceties of the Jewish law. But changes were in store, and the enthusiasm of the hour was destined soon to wane.

Coincident with the transfer of Palestine to Syria we see the rise of a Hellenistic party in Jerusalem. The Seleucids were far more enthusiastic in their attempt to foster Greek culture than had been the Ptolemies. Syria had been eager to accept the latest fashions in civilization, and she was equally eager to impart it. In this respect she was a true child of Alexander the Great. In the days of Egyptian control Greek must have become familiar at least to a measure in the upper classes in Jerusalem, although Palestine as a whole was not then bilingual, nor did she ever become so. Now with Syria in the saddle the Hellenists—Greek apers—increased in number and influence, to the disgust of many Jews. They could see the handwriting on the wall. For many others this new, freer civilization was becoming highly fascinating. This group naturally became coincident with the pro-Syrian element; the anti-Hellenists, on the contrary, became increasingly pro-Egyptian as a natural reaction, although Egypt was Hellenistic to the core. Although Hellenism was thus becoming increasingly fashionable among the gilded youth of Jerusalem, there was no forcible attempt to promote the spread of foreign ways throughout the reign of Antiochus the Great or of his elder son and successor, Seleucus IV. But this was soon to change.

In 175 B.C. Seleucus IV, who had succeeded to the Syrian throne twelve years before on the death of his father, Antiochus the Great, was murdered by his prime minister, Heliodorus, who ostentatiously put the infant crown prince on the throne. This was a gesture which deceived no one. The elder prince, Demetrius, later to ascend the throne, had been sent to Rome as a hostage. He was thus free from Heliodorus' plottings, but was powerless to claim his rightful position. His arrival at Rome as a hostage had freed his father's younger brother, Antiochus, from that position. The latter had left Rome for Athens, where word came of the confusion in Syria. With an armed force he appeared in Antioch; Heliodorus vanishes from history, and the newcomer soon sits on the throne of the Seleucids with the title Antiochus IV (175-164). It is hard to estimate him dispassionately. Hatred of him instantly blazed up. He chose the title Epiphanes ("the illustrious"); some nameless wit in his court parodied it to Epimanes ("the mad man"), which must have seemed to many most apt as they looked askance at his playboy practical jokes and theatrical absurdities. He was greatly enamoured of Hel-

[11] At least this story is dramatically recounted in III Macc. 1 and 2.

lenism, without apparently having any very deep appreciation of the real values of this culture. On the other hand, he was an astute politician and a clever trickster. He was by no means the weak demagogue that has often been pictured. Of all the Syrians he was the most hated by the Jews. Even yet we can sense this fury in the book of Daniel with its mention of the "little horn, before which three of the first horns were plucked up by the roots" and which had "eyes like the eyes of a man, and a mouth speaking great things."[12]

His accession in Syria secured the triumph of the pro-Syrian party in Jerusalem. Previous to his advent there had been no studied attempt at hellenization; now this changed and the initiative was taken in the highest quarters where we might least have expected it. Joshua, the brother of the high priest, Onias IV, was the acknowledged leader of the Hellenist party. This precious Joshua or, to give him the name he preferred, Jason by gifts to Antiochus contrived to get himself appointed high priest with *carte blanche* to turn Jerusalem into a second Antioch. Now Greek customs were openly introduced into Jerusalem. The gymnasium, without which no Greek town could feel itself a city, rose before the citadel. Young bloods of Judea contended with Greeks in the games. Many to avoid ridicule submitted to operations to remove the stigma of circumcision;[13] they affected Greek garb, in particular the petasus, or broad-brimmed hat, and were eager to get themselves enrolled as citizens of Antioch. Jerusalem received a Greek constitution, and afforded Antiochus a cordial welcome with "torch light and much shoutings"[14] on the occasion of his visit to the city, much to the satisfaction of the monarch, who rejoiced in Hellenism not only for its own sake, but also because of its effectiveness as a means of breaking down local peculiarities and aloofness and of making possible the unity in his kingdom which he so desired.

As can be easily imagined, all this aroused deep resentment in the hearts of the more conservative. Their attitude stands revealed in II Macc. 4:11-15:

He (*sc.* Jason) brought up new customs against the law: for he built gladly a place of exercise[15] under the tower itself, and brought the chief young men under his subjection, and made them wear a hat. Now such was the height of Greek fashions and increase of heathenish manners, through the exceeding profaneness of Jason, that ungodly wretch, and no high priest: that the priests had no courage to serve any more at the altar, but despising the temple, and neglecting the sacrifices, hastened to be partaker of the unlawful allowance in the place of exercise, after the game of Discus called them forth; not setting by the honours of their fathers, but liking the glories of the Grecians best of all.

[12] Dan. 7:8.
[13] Josephus, *Antt.* 12,5,1.
[14] II Macc. 4:22.
[15] *I.e.*, gymnasium.

Harsh words these, but there were undoubtedly many saying them. We would err if we drew the contrast too sharply. It is probably true that the particular brand of Hellenism that became popular in Syria was not always of the highest sort. The desire for a strong mind in a strong body was highly commendable; the gymnasiums and the revival of interest in the Greek classics no doubt met real needs. On the other hand, it is undeniably the case that often what was intrinsically wholesome became quite the reverse and tended to fill Syrian cities with arrogant and insolent braggadocios, contemptuous of the earlier simplicity and homely morality. It was not wholly this phase, however, that awakened opposition in Jerusalem. It was not the opposition of outraged godliness to godlessness. Rather it was essentially a deep-seated abhorrence towards new and foreign notions and practices. The Jew was different from other people, and was proud of it. This outward sign which was causing the Jerusalem youth to feel countrified before their city friends was God's own seal, betokening the fact that they were different. Their customs, which they fondly believed were hallowed by centuries of almost universal observance—nay which had been instituted by God himself in the very beginning—their proudest birthright, were being wantonly discarded by these misguided Esaus, hungering for the red pottage of Syria. It is easy to stigmatize such an attitude intolerant conservatism; such a label does not free the student of history from the necessity of understanding it, nor should it blind his eyes to the fact that it was precisely this intolerant conservatism which enabled Judaism to weather the many hurricanes that beset her course.

Soon fresh fuel was heaped on the flames of discontent. In 171 a certain Menelaus (Menahem) was sent to Antioch by Jason. He improved this shining opportunity to offer Antiochus three hundred talents more than Jason was paying, could he become high priest. Such piety could not go unrewarded. Menelaus received the appointment. To raise the promised tribute, he helped himself to some of the temple treasure. A riot of indignation resulted. Jason fled to the other side of Jordan to bide his time, and Menelaus "who had the fury of a cruel tyrant, and the rage of a wild beast"[16] was seated in his holy office.

These efforts by Antiochus and his creatures to hellenize—which meant essentially to heathenize—tended to drive the disgruntled Jews still closer to Egypt. As has been already pointed out, some of them had at first turned to Syria with enthusiasm. Antiochus the Great had seemed their saviour. The results of a hundred years' contact with Egypt, however, were not easily broken, and Syria's now intolerant attitude and rapacity disabused their earlier sanguine hopes. Syria needed money to pay Rome, who had already made herself felt in the days of Antiochus the Great. Accordingly, her greed in the matter of taxes. Taxes on the salt mined at the Dead Sea; taxes amount-

[16] II Macc. 4:25.

ing to a third of the grain harvested, to a half of the all too scanty fruits; poll taxes, crown taxes, temple taxes, to say nothing of the sovereign right to seize cattle and stores in the name of military conscription—all this fomented unrest.

In 170 war broke out again between Syria and Egypt over the vexed question of Palestine. The sympathies of the Jews were with Egypt. A rumour came to Jerusalem that Antiochus had been slain. This was a signal for Jason to attempt an unsuccessful *coup de main* to regain his old position. Antiochus, however, was not dead, as Jerusalem soon realized, and on his return to Syria stopped at Jerusalem, entered the holy of holies, carried off the golden altar of incense, the table of shewbread, and everything else he could lay his hands upon, even stripping the gold plating from the front of the temple.[17] In the spring of 168 he made another attempt on Egypt, ostensibly to regain Pelusium, and Egypt appealed to Rome, who had already interested herself in matters Syrian. In 190 Scipio had checked Antiochus the Great at Magnesia and had wrested all of western Asia Minor to the Halys River from the Seleucidæ. Rome's answer was decisive. Antiochus must withdraw at once. Polybius preserves the incident in all its dramatic setting. Popilius, the Roman legate, handed Antiochus the Senate's decree.

On the king (*i.e.,* Antiochus), after reading the dispatch, saying that he desired to consult with his friends on the situation, Popilius did a thing which was looked upon as exceedingly overbearing and insolent. Happening to have a vine stick in his hand, he drew a circle round Antiochus with it, and ordered him to give his answer to the letter before he stepped out of that circumference. The king was taken aback by this haughty proceeding. After a brief interval of embarrassed silence, he replied he would do whatever the Romans demanded. Then Popilius and his colleagues shook him by the hand, and one and all greeted him with warmth.[18]

Disappointed in his hope of recouping his waning fortunes—the vast kingdom of Seleucus had now shrunk to little more than Syria itself—Antiochus cast wrathful eyes on Palestine and the strong pro-Egyptian party that his policies had fostered in Jerusalem. Their joy at his recent discomfiture was more real than politic. Those who "kept the Jewish superstition alive" were to be exterminated, for Antiochus now clearly saw that the Jewish opposition was religious. Instead of refusing to allow this to take a political aspect, as was later to be the policy of Rome, he made a systematic effort to crush it. A Syrian officer—II Maccabees calls him Apollonius—came to Jerusalem with a large force and treacherously attacked on the Sabbath after proffering terms of peace. Then followed terrible scenes of carnage. The walls were breached; a citadel on the Acra was built up, to be a menace for nearly thirty years; women and children were sold into slavery, and drastic prohibitions of

[17] I Macc. 1:20-24; II Macc. 5:11-21; Josephus, *Antt.* 12,5,3.
[18] Polybius, *Hist.* xxix,27(11).

Judaism were enacted: Sacrifice to Jehovah was to cease; Sabbath observance was prohibited; circumcision was a capital offence; possession of a copy of the Scripture meant death. The most galling act of all took place a short time later. On Dec. 15, 168, a heathen altar to Zeus was erected on the top of the great altar of sacrifice, and ten days later a hog was sacrificed upon it. The temple sanctuary was smeared with blood; in the general riot soldiers committed the grossest indecencies in the revered courts. The "abomination of desolation" still throbs in the passionate hatred of such contemporary writings as Daniel and Judith. Nor were these measures restricted to Jerusalem. Strict ɔarch in all Jewish communities was inaugurated. Many in terror gave allegiance. For others the mask was now torn off; such was the true nature of the vaunted culture. The issue was clear. If Judaism was to live, she must fight.

Chapter II

THE MACCABEAN REVOLT AND THE HOUSE
OF HASMON

For the moment the scene of our story shifts from Jerusalem to the little hill town of Modein, twenty miles northwest of Jerusalem. To his farm in this town the old priest, Mattathias, had withdrawn with his five sons during the profanation and the resultant confusion.[1] Mattathias, as a prominent resident, is called upon to set an example of obedience, and is promised immunity. His answer and the consequences of the refusal are best told in the word of I Maccabees:

> Then Mattathias answered and spake with a loud voice. Though all the nations that are under the king's dominion obey him, and fall away every one from the religion of their fathers, and give consent to his commandments: yet will I and my sons and my brethren walk in the covenant of our fathers. God forbid that we should forsake the law and the ordinances. We will not hearken to the king's words, to go from our religion, either on the right hand, or the left. Now when he had left speaking these words, there came one of the Jews in the sight of all to sacrifice on the altar which was at Modin, according to the king's commandment. Which thing when Mattathias saw, he was inflamed with zeal, and his reins trembled, neither could he forbare to shew his anger according to judgment: Wherefore he ran, and slew him upon the altar. Also the king's commissioner, who compelled men to sacrifice, he killed at that time, and the altar he pulled down. Thus dealt he zealously for the law of God, like as Phineas did unto Zambri the son of Salom. And Mattathias cried throughout the city with a loud voice, saying, Whosoever is zealous for the law, and maintaineth the covenant, let him follow me. So he and his sons fled into the mountains and left all that ever they had in the city.[2]

This was the Sarajevo of the Maccabean uprising. Soon joined by others, they lurked in the passes and defiles of northern Judea—a more ideal spot for such activities could hardly be imagined—to sally forth to destroy all signs of heathenism and to kill apostate Jews. A veritable wave of terror set in.

The revolt was supported at the beginning by an influential group of the devotedly religious who called themselves, or were nicknamed, Hasidim or Asideans, that is, "the pious." Their interests were not political; they took to arms in desperation solely because they believed their religion was

[1] Gruesome stories of the scenes may be read in II Macc. 6 and 7.
[2] I Macc. 2:19-28.

at stake. When once the revolt was successful, with the altar reconsecrated and worship restored under a high priest of undoubted Aaronic descent, they lost further interest. It was a vastly different thing to use arms to gain political independence; such a course lay outside their interests. Their accession to the Hasmoneans, as the patriots were dubbed since Mattathias was a descendant of Hasmon, brought both strength and prestige.

After a few months, in 167, Mattathias died, and the active leadership fell to the third of his five sons, Judas. These five—John, Simon, Judas, Eleazar, and Jonathan—are popularly known as the Maccabees, from the nickname *Maccabæus* ("hammerer") which Judas received. The story of the dramatic successes of the band under Judas' leadership against far larger and highly trained Syrian armies reads like a fairy tale until one realizes the difficulties these soldiers met, trained as they were to open fighting on the Syrian plains, when they were forced to chase these Judeans back and forth through the unfamiliar defiles of rocky Judea. In addition, political difficulties were constantly arising in Syria which compelled withdrawal of the royal forces at critical moments. All of these difficulties Judas capitalized. At first Apollonius, the governor of Samaria (who had oversight of Judea), sought to check the disturbance. His defeat and the subsequent discomfiture of Seron, military commander of Cœle-Syria, alarmed Antiochus. Three generals with 40,000 foot and 7,000 horse[3] were dispatched post haste to Judea and were defeated near Emmaus (166). The next year Lysias, who had been left in charge of the whole southern domain during the absence of Antiochus in the east, changed the plan of military tactics, which had been so uniformly unsuccessful, and, circling Judea, attacked from the south at Bethsura, near Hebron, but with no better success. "Then said Judas and his brethren, Behold, our enemies are discomfited: let us go up to cleanse and dedicate the sanctuary."[4] Although unable to drive out the garrison in the Acra, he cleansed the sacred area, demolished the hated altar, and constructed a new one. Whether the consecration which the original stones had received at the time of the erection of the altar, centuries before, was powerful enough to overcome the defilement of hog's blood and the resultant heathenish idolatry was quite beyond him. He was a fighter, not a lawyer. With commendable common sense he built his altar of new stone, carefully laying the dubious ones aside "until there should come a prophet to shew what should be done with them." Thus three years to a day after that first hateful sacrifice to Olympian Zeus, the smoke of sacrifice ascended once more and worship was restored. This success has been perpetuated in the annual Feast of Lights or, as it is often called, of Dedication.[5]

[3] I Macc. 3:39.
[4] I Macc. 4:36.
[5] Cf., for example, John 10:22.

Then followed expeditions led by Judas and his brothers against neighbouring tribes, terrified by his success. These were soundly trounced, but
the loyal Jews in these remoter districts were finding themselves in a most
precarious position. Judas sensibly determined to centralize his supporters.
While he proceeded across the Jordan to Gilead, he sent Simon to Galilee.
Both were successful, and brought back those Jewish colonists to greater
safety in Judea. The significance of this de-judaizing of Galilee and the
Perea should not be overlooked. We shall have occasion later to consider
its consequences.

Now started a campaign to restore Jewish independence. This was made
possible by the timely civil strife in Syria. Antiochus had died (164), not,
as the author of Daniel[6] had expected he would, on the coast road between
Syria and Egypt, but in the Persian city, Tabæ.[7] At once strife over the
succession arose. Philip, a friend of Epiphanes, had been appointed regent
during the minority of the young heir, Antiochus V, but Lysias had been
left in control in Syria. He at once appointed himself Antiochus' guardian.
This is but one of many cases which give us the clue to the surprising advances the Jews made. The Maccabeans were skilful enough to turn these
moments of civil unrest in Syria to their own advantage and to play one
leader against another.

At once Judas made a determined attack on the thorn in Judea's side,
the Acra. This brought Lysias back from Antioch. A crushing defeat for
Judas was the result. His brother Eleazar was slain, and his force retreated
to Jerusalem. Fortunately for Palestine, Lysias could not make effective
use of the opportunity. Philip had returned to Syria and was marching
against Antioch. Lysias must return to Syria; accordingly, he offered terms
of peace whereby they might "make use of and live according to the laws
of their fathers."[8] Although Jerusalem had fallen, although the citadel still
remained a menace, the battle for religious liberty had been successful.
Menelaus, the high priest who had been so largely responsible for the
whole disturbance, was exiled and later executed, and Alcimus, a zealous
Hellenist, although of unimpeachable Aaronic descent, was installed in his
stead. Enforced Hellenism from the outside was over; its presence from
within was by no means dead.

Changes had taken place in Antioch. The young Antiochus V (Eupator)
and his general, Lysias, had been successful against Philip, but soon found
themselves confronted by Demetrius, the son of Seleucus IV. During his

---

[6] Dan. 11:40-45. Indeed this sudden error in "prophecy"—Antiochus' career is sketched with
the utmost fidelity in 11:21-39; then suddenly an alien note is sounded—provides decisive evidence with regard to the date of the "prophecy." It is, unfortunately, far harder to achieve
accuracy when one essays to "prophesy" before an event than afterward!

[7] Polybius, *Hist.* xxxi,11.

[8] Josephus, *Antt.* 12,9,7.

enforced stay in Rome as a hostage he had grown to maturity, and twice had sought to gain the Senate's support in his claim to the Syrian throne. Despairing of success in this direction, he had fled from Rome, and suddenly appeared in Antioch, got into power, and executed both of his rivals (162 B.C.).

To him Alcimus appealed for help against Judas, who was causing him decided difficulties. Bacchides was dispatched by the new king to install Alcimus and to punish the traitors. At this moment a significant change in the temper of the Jews is seen. The Asideans had rallied to the side of Judas when religious liberty was at stake. That, however, had now been secured; Alcimus' promises were fair, his Aaronic descent undoubted. Accordingly, they lost interest in further warfare. Political independence or aggrandizement held no attraction. They turned from Judas and accepted the new régime. According to I Maccabees, Alcimus slew sixty of them. Whether this disillusioning treatment alienated them or not we cannot say, for they disappear from the pages of history. Whether, as has been often maintained, they make their appearance later in the Pharisees or the Essenes or both we can reserve for later consideration.

Alcimus soon found himself in difficulties. Bacchides had enjoined obedience to him and had made gestures against the recalcitrant, but upon his return to Syria, although deprived probably of the support of the Asideans, Judas had at once got the upper hand. In this unequal struggle Alcimus was obliged once more to seek protection from his Syrian master. Demetrius felt he could not afford to disregard Judas, who had become far too powerful, and accordingly sent Nicanor into Palestine to end this difficulty once and for all. To his amazement, however, Nicanor fared no better than had his predecessors: first an unsuccessful manœuvre to get Judas by trickery, then a repulse near Jerusalem, finally a crushing defeat at Adasa (161). Here he lost his life, and his head and hand were hung up as trophies on the temple gates. The anniversary of this happy event—"Nicanor's Day"— was celebrated as an annual festival.

For the moment Judas had a breathing space. However, he knew all too well the inevitable result. Another army would soon appear to avenge Nicanor. He had been remarkably successful: superior knowledge of the Judean hills, complications in Syria's political household, amazing good luck—all these had aided him; but if he was not to be defeated in the end by the sheer force of fresh troops, outside help was imperative. In this crisis, according to I Maccabees he turned to the rising power of the West, which had thwarted Antiochus Epiphanes' dreams for Egypt, and which thirty years before had checked Antiochus the Great at Magnesia—Rome. Judas was no prophet, nor was he enough of a statesman to see that this queen of the West was destined to exercise great power in Palestine, eventually to achieve its destruction. He needed help, and Rome was the archenemy of Syria. His appeal to the Senate for confederacy and peace was successful. The ambassadors were returned with the treaty emblazoned on bronze shields. Each was to help the other in war.

All this, however, took time, and time was precious. No sooner had Demetrius learned of the discomfiture of Nicanor's forces than he sent Bacchides with a fresh army to the south. By the time Rome's peremptory order to Syria reached Antioch, the army had left. With his present force Judas was powerless; of the three thousand (I Macc. 9:5), all but eight hundred deserted. Judas could not be restrained. With this tiny remnant he held his ground at Eleasa—the Jewish Thermopylæ—and there fell (161). For seven years he had fought bravely. He had brought the struggle for religious liberty to a successful conclusion, and had also encouraged a desire for political independence. At his death it appeared that this latter hope could never be realized. His army was routed; many of his erstwhile supporters failed to share his dreams of a restored Israel; Syria had been finally aroused to the seriousness of the situation. Yet these dreams were to be realized—not through force of arms, for his successors must pursue a different course of action—but through the sagacious policy of the later leaders who cleverly turned Syria's extremity into Palestine's opportunity.

Now the ground was clear for Alcimus to be high priest in more than name. Judas, his archenemy, was dead; his forces had been routed. Championing Alcimus, the Hellenists sought to strike while the iron was hot and to root out the rest of the Hasmoneans. Of the five sons of Mattathias three were still alive, John, Simon, and Jonathan. In this crisis Jonathan was appealed to. He was the crafty politician rather than the warrior. During the eighteen years of his leadership (161-143) Israel was to make great seeming advances, not due so much to her own strength but through the clever way that Jonathan and his successors turned the weakness of Syria with its ever-present rival claimants for the throne to the advantage of Palestine.

Wishing to avoid Alcimus, who had returned with Bacchides on the latter's expedition which had accomplished the death of Judas, Jonathan first retreated to the wilderness of Tekoah, and then sent his baggage with his eldest brother, John, across the Jordan to the Nabateans, who had been friendly to Judas. These plans, however, miscarried. The party was attacked by a robber clan, and John was killed. Jonathan went across Jordan to avenge his brother, but found himself confronted by Bacchides. It was a critical moment, but Jonathan rallied to it:

Then Jonathan said to his company, Let us go up now and fight for our lives; for it standeth not with us today, as in time past: For behold the battle is before us and behind us, and the water of Jordan on this side and on that side, the marsh likewise and wood, neither is there place for us to turn aside. Wherefore cry ye now unto heaven, that ye may be delivered from the hand of your enemies. With that they joined battle.[9]

The Jordan was crossed, and Bacchides repulsed. But greater dangers faced the new leader. As has already been pointed out, Syria had consistently allowed herself to be outmanœuvred by the rebels. Bacchides appears now to have become convinced of the sheer folly of attempting to chase this band of outlaws from pillar to post. On the contrary, he threw a ring of heavily fortified cities around Judea (Jericho, Emmaus, Bethhoron, Bethel, Timnath, Pharathon, Tephon, Bethsura, and Gazara,[10] and sent as hostages the sons of the leading men to the citadel in Jerusalem.

This common-sense procedure successfully throttled opposition. For the moment the Hellenists were free to move as they pleased. In this Alcimus played a prominent part. It is perhaps not precisely clear what is to be understood by the reproach: "he commanded that the wall of the inner court of the sanctuary should be pulled down; he pulled down also the works of the prophets";[11] at any rate it aroused bitter resentment, and his sudden death in agony appeared heaven sent.[12] More important than the death of Alcimus is the fact that for six years (159-153) the office of high priest remained vacant until the crafty Jonathan himself appeared in his pontifical robes, the appointee of an ambitious pretender to the throne of the Seleucids.

Shortly afterward Bacchides returned to Syria. The girdle of Syrian fortresses had paralysed resistance; there was no longer a high priest to defend: "the land of Judea was in rest two years." Later the opponents of Jonathan, now inclined to be a bit too confident in their supremacy, sought to eliminate him entirely. Word was sent to Syria that the rebel leader could be taken. Bacchides responded to this overture and came south. He soon found his task was greater than he had anticipated, since Jonathan had got wind of the plan. Bacchides quickly tired of the thankless task of pursuing the will-o'-the-wisp natives through their own haunts, concluded some sort of a treaty with Jonathan, and returned to Syria, after wreaking his displeasure on many of the Hellenists who had involved him in the débâcle. The next few years are passed over in silence by I Maccabees. The sword had ceased in Israel. Jonathan appears to have resided in Michmash as a sort of privileged freebooter, like David had before him in Hebron. The one comment that we hear, *viz.,* that Jonathan "began to govern the people" and that "he destroyed the ungodly men of Israel," would indicate that during these years he was gradually gaining more and

[9] I Macc. 9:44-47.

[10] I Macc. 9:50,52.

[11] I Macc. 9:54. Cf. Schürer, *op. cit.,* Div. I, Vol. I, p. 236, n. 5.

[12] It is perhaps not out of place to observe that most of those of whom ancient writers disapproved died "with great torment."

more power at the expense of his rivals in Jerusalem. But more was soon to follow.

As has been already indicated, the clue to the surprising advances of Judea lies in the story of Syria's weakness. It is difficult to find an instant in the later years of the Seleucids when there were not several rival claimants to the throne. In 153 serious difficulties arose. An unknown adventurer, named Alexander Balas, claimed to be a natural son of Antiochus Epiphanes, and established himself in Ptolemaïs as a rival to Demetrius. He received support from the latter's rivals, even from Ptolemy Philometor of Egypt. In the resultant civil war in Syria Demetrius was no longer able to interfere in Palestine. On the contrary, he sorely needed Jewish support, and Jonathan became essential. Overtures were made and accepted. Jonathan entered Jerusalem as chief of the native state; the garrisons in the neighbouring towns fled. Only the office of high priest failed; even that was soon to be his. Balas, too, needed supporters, and proceeded to overbid his rival. He appointed Jonathan high priest, and enrolled him as among the "king's friends." At the Feast of Tabernacles Jonathan made his appearance in the robes of office, high priest, as Wellhausen sardonically remarked, by the grace of Balas.[13] It need hardly be emphasized that his ambition to hold this office was not due to any humble or pious desire to offer sacrifice to Jehovah. From the days when religious toleration had crowned Judas' early efforts the consistent aim of his followers had been to achieve independence and temporal power.

Demetrius sought, but in vain, to bring Jonathan back to himself. Larger offers, even the promise of surrendering the Acra, failed to lure the crafty Jonathan, who was now convinced that Balas would be successful, favoured as he was by Rome. Nor was he disappointed. Soon Balas triumphed; Demetrius fell in battle. During the short usurpation of Balas (150-145) Jonathan was highly honoured as one of his "first friends." A nominal tribute was paid, but save for the Acra in Jerusalem Judea was to all intents free. But Balas was not without rivals. In 147 the young son of Demetrius, Demetrius II, came from Crete "into the land of his fathers," and at once received support from those disgusted with the utterly worthless usurper. Jonathan alone of the erstwhile foreign supporters remained firm. He defeated Apollonius, the governor of Cœle-Syria, who was now championing Demetrius, at Azotus, and burned the city. The routed force of Apollonius fled for refuge into the temple of Dagon, which temple Jonathan without compunction set in flames. For this act of fealty Balas rewarded him with the town of Ekron. Two years later, however, Balas was worsted and murdered. It might have seemed that Jonathan would have been undone by the failure of his patron, especially as he had ventured to besiege the Acra. Demetrius II summoned Jonathan to Ptolemais. Jona-

[13] Wellhausen, *Israelitische und Jüdische Geschichte*, p. 253.

than went boldly and apparently convinced the new monarch that it was for his interest to overlook his erstwhile zeal for Balas. At any rate, Jonathan returned to Jerusalem with three frontier districts in Samaria and with the promise of subsequent exemption from tribute. The Hasmoneans were increasing as the Seleucids were tottering.

Soon Jonathan found opportunity to repay his new patron. Trypho, an officer of the murdered Balas, sponsored the latter's young son as claimant for his father's throne under the title Antiochus VI. Demetrius' cruelty and the insolence of his Cretan henchmen had already aroused great opposition to him. Jonathan promised assistance on condition that the Acra be surrendered. Demetrius readily promised, "for he lied in all that ever he spake," and Jonathan with a force of three thousand relieved him in the nick of time. Demetrius rashly failed to keep his promise. In anger Jonathan swung to the side of Trypho, who was soon successful against the quite incompetent Demetrius. The young Antiochus confirmed Jonathan in his governorship of Judea, while Simon was named military governor of the coastal plain from the Ladder of Tyre to the Egyptian frontier.

Jonathan turned this power to his own advantage. He was expected to fortify those outposts which had been won from Demetrius; he took pains, however, to man them with Jewish troops. He also started a new wall in Jerusalem to cut off the hated Acra from the upper market and to starve it into submission. His plan was clever; it was also transparent, and Trypho had no illusions regarding Jonathan's unselfish devotion to himself or to his young master Antiochus. It may be, as I Maccabees represents, that Trypho had personal grounds for fear of Jonathan, namely, that since his sponsoring of the dubious claims of the young Antiochus had been due to his desire to gain the crown for himself, he feared Jonathan might seek to thwart him. However that may be, as soon as he had a breathing space, he turned towards Judea. Jonathan came to meet him with an equal force. Trypho was shocked. Why this armed force? He had come to hand over to his loyal colleague those districts between Judea proper and the seacoast territory of Simon. If Jonathan would accompany him to Ptolemaïs, this should all be accomplished. And, amazing as it may seem, the crafty Jonathan actually was deceived. Yielding to the tempting offer, he followed Trypho, who promptly imprisoned him.

In this crisis (143), Simon, the last of the five sons, steps into the breach. Jerusalem was strengthened; Joppa, already nominally under the command of Simon, was manned by Jewish troops. Trypho attacked, but was repulsed. He persisted in veiling his true purpose, and represented that Jonathan was being held captive simply because he had failed to pay the promised fees for the many concessions he had received. Simon patiently met all these overtures, and paid the sums demanded. Trypho meanwhile sought to outflank Simon and get to Jerusalem before him. Failing in this, he slew Jonathan in rage and retreated to Syria through the region east of the Jordan.

Simon struck while the iron was hot. He flatly demanded from Demetrius absolute independence, with complete freedom from taxation. Syria was in no position to refuse. We can still read the note of exultation, "Thus the yoke of the heathen was taken away from Israel in the hundred and seventieth year (143)."[14]

Gazara, the fortress on the road to Joppa, was taken; Judea's strongholds were increased; and finally in the May of 142 the Acra, which for so many years had been the thorn in Jerusalem's flesh, was starved into submission. In 141, in grateful recognition of his ability, Simon was confirmed by popular vote high priest and governor—Demetrius in the preceding year had bestowed these offices upon him—with the double position to be hereditary until a faithful prophet should arise and direct otherwise. Even more significant than the capture of the Acra was this conquest of popular support. Simon had achieved the goal that Judas had longed for twenty years before. The struggle of the Maccabees had been successful.

Then followed a short time of peace and prosperity for the Jews. Demetrius was too hard pressed by Trypho, who had now appeared in his true colours, as claimant of the throne, after having had his young protégé Antiochus treacherously murdered, to interfere in Judea. The Hellenists were forced to accept the new régime or to vacate the land. Joppa had become a Jewish post; convenient access to it from Jerusalem had been gained through the capture of Gazara. Judea began a lively trade, and for the moment Jerusalem was flourishing.

The treaty which Jonathan had made with Rome soon after his break with Demetrius I was now renewed. Simon felt secure enough to coin his own money, although his own name did not appear upon it. This privilege was later "granted" to Simon by the new claimant of the Seleucid throne; Simon, it may be observed, however, had been busy coining his money for more than a year before this privilege was conferred.

This new figure in Syrian politics is of interest, for he was, as Wellhausen remarked, "hewn of entirely different wood" from his brother Demetrius II.[15] Demetrius had pushed east against the Parthians (140 B.C.), seeking to recover certain provinces which this new and threatening power had seized. After varying fortunes he had been imprisoned, and for ten years (138-128) drops from history. His younger brother, Antiochus VII, surnamed Sidetes, was appealed to in this crisis by Cleopatra, wife of the captured Demetrius. She, hard pressed by Trypho, who had gained control of the army, invited her brother-in-law to wed her and to ascend the throne. Nothing loath, the ambitious young Antiochus had hastily returned from

[14] I Macc. 13:41.
[15] Wellhausen, *Israelitische und Jüdische Geschichte,* p. 258.

Rhodes to Syria. Even before landing he had sent word to Simon confirming him in all his power and specifying his right to coin money with his own stamp.[16] Trypho was routed, and later decisively defeated at Dora, whither he had fled and had stood siege. Though he escaped for the moment, he was overtaken at Apamea, where he lost his life.

Simon had responded to Antiochus' initial friendly overtures, and had even sent a strong force to Dora to assist his new friend against Trypho. In the course of the months following his arrival on the Phœnician coast, the new king's confidence had rapidly increased. Now he considered himself able to dispense with Simon's friendship. The troops were curtly refused, and word was sent to Simon that he was to relinquish his unlawfully acquired extra-Judean territory, including the seaport Joppa, the citadel Gazara, and the Acra in Jerusalem. Should Simon refuse, the Syrian legate was empowered to accept the sum of a thousand talents as a *quid pro quo*. Simon refused the terms as exorbitant, but was willing to pay a hundred talents. Antiochus sought to enforce his demand, but Simon's sons—he himself was too old to lead his forces in person—so signally defeated the enemy that no further attempt was made during Simon's rule.

Then came his tragic end. His position had become a tempting prize for ambitious rivals. His son-in-law, Ptolemy, who held an important military command in the Jericho plain, plotted to murder Simon and his sons and thus to clear the way for his own accession. Simon and his two elder sons Mattathias and Judas, were victims of this treachery. The plan, however, miscarried, since John Hyrcanus, the third son, received word of the plot in time to refuse the dinner invitation and to escape. For thirty years he was destined to rule over Judea.

So ended the family of the Maccabees. In the little more than thirty years that had passed since Mattathias had boldly flung down the gauntlet in Modein, much had been accomplished. Not only had the danger of forced apostasy been averted, but the yoke of thralldom to Syria had been thrust aside, and a Maccabean prince—that is, a prince in all but name—had been made at once hereditary ruler and high priest of an enlarged Judea. But mighty changes were in store in the near future. Like Cæsar, the Hasmoneans were ambitious; like Cæsar, they reaped the inevitable harvest.

Hyrcanus at once claimed his inheritance and hastened to Jerusalem, arriving, fortunately, before Ptolemy. In disappointment the latter retreated to Dagon near Jericho. Here he would undoubtedly have fallen into the hands of his irate brother-in-law save for his threat to murder Hyrcanus' mother, whom he had in his power, unless the siege was abandoned. Hyrcanus' unwillingness to cause his mother's death and the

[16] I Macc. 15:6.

fortunate arrival of a Sabbatic year enabled the disappointed Ptolemy to escape to Philadelphia across the Jordan, where he drops out of sight.

Antiochus Sidetes had neither forgotten nor forgiven Simon's effective resistance to his desire to regain control of Joppa and Gazara, and early in Hyrcanus' reign he came in person against him. Instead of meeting him in the mountains, as Judas had so often done, Hyrcanus stood siege in Jerusalem and was finally forced to make terms, entailing the breaching of the Jerusalem walls, the payment of tribute for such towns as Joppa and Gazara, and the payment of five hundred talents indemnity. These terms, while by no means satisfactory, were far better than had been feared, and are probably to be explained as due to the intervention of Rome, whose aid had been sought in keeping with the existing treaty.

But even this indignity was of short duration. Soon Sidetes was involved in fresh difficulties with Parthia. At first successful, he was later defeated, and to avoid becoming a prisoner committed suicide (128 B.C.). His brother Demetrius, whom the Parthians had freed to embarrass Sidetes, returned to his throne. With him came chaos. Foolishly he sought to meddle in Egypt. Ptolemy VII countered by sponsoring Alexander Zabinas, who speedily worsted Demetrius, compelling him to flee for his life. Although Demetrius was soon murdered (125?), Zabinas found himself opposed by the king's son, Antiochus VIII Grypsos (125-113, 111-96),[17] who soon (123) vanquished Zabinas. After nine or ten years Grypsos was attacked by his cousin Antiochus IX Cyzicenos, who for two years (113-111) was master of Syria. Although Grypsos soon regained the greater part of his domain, and ruled it till his death (96 B.C.), Cyzicenos settled down as ruler of Cœle-Syria (111-95), and, weak and theatrical as he was, served as a buffer between his more ambitious kinsman and Hyrcanus. Thus it was that soon Hyrcanus was able to disregard the Syrian claim, and that he and his successors were free from further overlordship from the north. Syria had received her death blow. It was only a question now of giving her decent burial.

Following the death of Sidetes, Hyrcanus, now freed from the need of following his Syrian master in fruitless campaigns against Parthia, turned his attention to matters in Palestine, in the hope of enlarging his domain. He was the first of the Jewish princes to employ foreign mercenaries, and with them extended the bounds of his state. First he appears to have pushed across Jordan and to have taken, after a lengthy siege, the redoubtable fortress of Medeba; then into Samaria, where Shechem soon fell. The Samaritan temple on Gerizim, always a thorn in the flesh of every pious Jew, was destroyed—a deed highly acceptable to all save the Samaritans. Flushed with this success, he turned south to Idumea, a dis-

---

[17] His elder brother, Seleucus V, had claimed the throne, but had been assassinated by his own mother, Cleopatra (125?).

trict which had caused Judea much difficulty and was destined to play an important rôle in the later story through her greatest son, Herod. Here in Idumea his success continued, and the inhabitants received the choice of becoming Jews or exiles. They accepted circumcision. This enforced marriage of Jacob and Edom was to be fraught with tremendous results, for thereby the Hasmonean dynasty was to be first dominated and eventually overthrown. What a story could be written of the "If I had only known's" of history! It was from this people, whom the proud Jewish aristocracy contemptuously styled "half Jews," that the most capable and strongest king the Jews ever had was to appear, Herod, son of Antipater, the Richelieu of Jewish politics. Here we have but one more example of history's seemingly eternal jest: The conquered is ever conqueror.

Hyrcanus was the first of Jewish rulers to have his own name stamped on his coins. In all but name he was king. This was reserved for his son and successor, Aristobulus. The last campaign of Hyrcanus revealed the weakness of Syria, now split into two parts, as mentioned in an earlier paragraph. According to Josephus, the inhabitants of the city of Samaria, a Macedonian colony,[18] had aroused Hyrcanus' ire by interfering with a Jewish colony, Marissa. Using this as an excuse, Hyrcanus proceeded against it. Samaria appealed to Antiochus Cyzicenos for aid. This was promptly given, but was unsuccessful. A second time Cyzicenos appeared, this time with some Egyptian troops, which he had gained from Ptolemy Lathurus, co-regent of Egypt. In spite of this help Hyrcanus eventually triumphed, and Samaria after a lengthy siege was annihilated. During the same campaign Scythopolis came into his control. Thus Hyrcanus' territory extended from Carmel to Scythopolis in the north, south through Judea and Idumea. Most of the seacoast of this territory was his; slight gains had been made across the Jordan. It is even possible that a portion of southern Galilee had fallen into his hands,[19] although we have no record of campaigns here. Judea was now a nation among nations. Under his successors, Aristobulus and Jannæus, the boundaries might be still extended, but at the cost of internal strength. Under Hyrcanus the peak of prosperity for Israel was realized.

Troubles, however, were brewing, and their causes are not far to seek. The simple piety and religious fervor that had characterized the brave stand of Mattathias had given way to a desire for conquest. Enthusiastic memories of the palmy days of David and of Solomon—memories which had lost nothing in the lapse of years—had been revived. Once again a Jewish king was perhaps to rule over a reunited Israel. The prophecy was

---

[18] Samaria the city is to be differentiated from the territory of Samaria, which Hyrcanus had already conquered, and whose capital was Shechem.

[19] The reason for this assumption will appear later.

fulfilled: Jehovah had visited the sheep of his flock and had made them as his goodly horse in the battle.[20] Joel too might have rejoiced: ploughshares had been beaten into swords, and pruninghooks into spears. The weak had said, I am strong.[21]

Nothing succeeds like success. The phenomenal advances of a half-century must have tended to allay the disquietude of many a saint who might well have had qualms of conscience at the sight of the high priest leading armies of mercenaries. Yet after all Hyrcanus was high priest, and he was proud of it. For his successors it was to become a stepping-stone, a political job; all desire to sacrifice humbly before Jehovah had departed. Not so for him. As Wellhausen rightly remarks, the balance between state and church still remained undisturbed. Josephus praises him in most appreciative fashion. In the Talmud he is spoken of with reverence and appreciation. Had he not destroyed the abominable Samaritan temple on Gerizim? Had not circumcision been forced upon the Idumeans? Many of the pious must have found sweet consolation in those thoughts.

Yet although the nation supported its leader enthusiastically, there appeared even during his reign a growing dissatisfaction. Josephus recounts the story replete with the gossipy details he so much enjoyed.[22] The story is certainly legendary; yet it may well be of value to the historian. According to the tale, Hyrcanus gave a dinner party, partly to allay growing opposition on the part of the Pharisees—a group Josephus here mentions for the first time. Hyrcanus graciously expressed the desire that should his conduct be open to reproach they might feel free to point it out. All flattered him until finally a Pharisee named Eleazar remarked that he lacked one thing. He should resign his office of high priest and content himself with the civil government. It is one thing for a ruler to ask for criticisms, another to get them. Pressed for an explanation, Eleazar replied that it was noised about that Hyrcanus' mother had been a captive in the reign of Antiochus Epiphanes, perhaps intimating not too delicately that his paternity was not certain, or at least that he was obviously ineligible to the sacred office. At this gratuitous insult, the Pharisees as well as Hyrcanus were angered. Their rivals, however, the Sadducees, used the occasion for their own ends. The Pharisees, they told him, might outwardly condemn Eleazar; inwardly, however, they approved, as Hyrcanus could see if he demanded that the Pharisees set Eleazar's punishment. Incensed at the mildness of the penalty, "stripes and bonds," Hyrcanus broke with them and joined the Sadducees.

Essentially the same story is preserved by the rabbis,[23] although in this recension Jannai (Alexander Jannæus) replaces Hyrcanus. That the story

[20] Zech. 10:3.
[21] Joel 3:10.
[22] Antt. 13,10,5 f.
[23] Kiddushin 66a.

is historical in the sense of explaining the real reason for the break between the Pharisees and Hyrcanus (or Jannæus) is most improbable. That such a story came to be told, however, attests the fact, independently substantiated, that during these years the political aspirations of the high-priest rulers, actually kings in all but name, were arousing fears and discontent. We can reserve a detailed discussion of the Pharisees and Sadducees as such until a later chapter.

John Hyrcanus was succeeded by his eldest son, Aristobulus, of whose short reign we know very little. Josephus, our chief source of information, preserves little beside the lurid story of his cruel treatment of his mother and brothers and of his consequent remorseful death in agony. On the other hand, he concludes this sorry statement with the contradictory remark:

He was naturally a man of candor, and of great modesty, as Strabo bears witness in the name of Timagenes, who says thus: "This man was a person of candor, and very serviceable to the Jews, for he added a country to them, and obtained a part of the nation of the Itureans for them and bound them to him by the bond of the circumcision of their genitals."[24]

It is, accordingly, not improbable that the distressing story of domestic unhappiness reflects the growing antipathy of the Pharisees to their Hasmonean masters.

Apparently Hyrcanus had intended that Aristobulus should succeed him as high priest; the widow was to administer the government. Aristobulus, however, thought differently and promptly imprisoned his mother and brothers,[25] thus assuming full control over Palestine. Josephus states he assumed the title king; Strabo,[26] on the contrary, asserts this of his successor, Alexander Jannæus. The only other bit of information we have about his short rule is also perplexing, namely, his partial conquest of the Itureans. As has been often pointed out, the Itureans were the Arabians in the Lebanons, a district remote from the apparent northern boundary attained by Hyrcanus. Hence it has often been assumed that the term is inaccurately used for the inhabitants of northern Galilee. The matter is perhaps impossible of solution. At any rate, it would render probable the suggestion in an earlier paragraph that Hyrcanus' northern conquests may well have extended into southern Galilee, since it is highly improbable that his successor attempted the conquest of a district separated from his own domain by territory as yet unsubdued. Whoever the Itureans were,

[24] *Antt.* 13,11,3.
[25] Wellhausen (*Israelitische und Jüdische Geschichte,* p. 262, n. 4) assumes that these were his stepmother and stepbrothers, since he was so much older than Alexander Jannæus and because he was at first so kindly disposed to Antigonus, who would thus be his own brother.
[26] *Geogr.* xvi,2,40.

they were compelled to become Jews, even though their conversion was scarcely more than skin-deep. Thus during his short reign of but a single year (104 B.C.), Aristobulus seems to have contributed his share in extending the boundaries of the Jewish state.

No sooner was Aristobulus dead than his widow Alexandra released from prison his brothers and married the eldest, Alexander Jannæus.[27] Of the marriage Wellhausen[28] tersely comments: "He was twenty-four, she thirty-seven; from this fact the nature of the marriage is evident." Thus in 104 B.C. both civil and religious power were vested in the capable if ruthless young grandnephew of Judas the Maccabee. He was by nature a warrior, and his long reign (104-78 B.C.) was entirely devoted to extending his domain; he was successful in this endeavour, but his was a losing battle. The territory he gained at such terrible cost was to be wrested from his house within a score of years after his death.

Upon his accession to his brother's throne the interior of Palestine from the Lebanons to the desert south of Idumea was nominally his. East of the Jordan the territory was but partially subdued; furthermore, the majority of the seaboard towns were outside his domain. To these latter he first turned his attention. Again came foreign complications which came near to thwarting his designs at the start. During his siege on Ptolemaïs, north of Carmel, the inhabitants in their extremity appealed to Ptolemy Lathurus, who was then in Cyprus awaiting an opportunity to attack his mother, Cleopatra III of Egypt. Ptolemy accepted the invitation and repulsed Jannæus. Thereupon Jannæus played the risky game of pretending allegiance to Ptolemy while at the same time urging Cleopatra to proceed against her unfilial rival. In rage Ptolemy revenged himself by a ruthless campaign in Galilee until checked by his mother's forces. As it was, Cleopatra is said to have considered the suggestion of seeking to reunite Palestine with Egypt, but was fortunately dissuaded by her Judean generals as well as by influential Jews in Alexandria.

This initial disastrous campaign by no means damped Jannæus' ambitions. Better success awaited him in the south, whither he now proceeded after a partially successful campaign east of the Jordan, during which he had subdued Gadara, just south of the Sea of Galilee, and the strongly fortified Amathus. Raphia and Anthedon in the Philistine plain capitulated. Gaza, which had incurred his wrath through its alliance with Ptolemy, was next attacked, but seems to have withstood him nearly a year, confident that it would receive aid from the Nabatean king, Aretas. Finally, however, through treachery the city fell into his hands and received the full brunt of his rage for its long defiance. Apparently these campaigns in the east and south occupied the first nine years of his reign.

---

[27] Josephus does not refer specifically to this marriage, but it is clearly implied.
[28] *Israelitische und Jüdische Geschichte*, p. 263.

During these years the opposition against him was increasing in violence. The dissatisfaction which had arisen in the days of Hyrcanus against a high priest whose real interest lay in leading mercenaries rather than in humble adoration of the true King had gone on apace. And the fact that Jannæus had not been over-successful in his initial campaigns as a warrior from choice may well have swelled the discontent. Stories are told which, while they are themselves of little import, illustrate the growing antipathy. For example, one year during the celebration of the Feast of Tabernacles, he was pelted with lemons as he was officiating at the altar, and is said by Josephus to have had six thousand of his subjects executed in revenge. To protect himself from further insult he had a wooden screen built about the altar. The time was ripe for rebellion; nor was its coming long delayed.

A year or so after his conquest of Gaza he had crossed the Jordan and in an encounter with Obodas, son of the former Nabatean chieftain Aretas, had lost his army, as a result of pursuing the wily Arabian into a ravine, where, hemmed in on all sides, his soldiers were crushed to death by camels which the enemy drove over them. This débâcle caused many of his erstwhile supporters to join the opposition. His prestige was gone. Jerusalem on his return was the scene of a civil war which raged for six years (94-89 B.C.). We know nothing of the details of the rebellion save that Josephus asserts that though the king slew more than 50,000 of his rebellious subjects, they refused all overtures of peace and even appealed in their extremity to Demetrius III, one of the five sons of Antiochus VIII, who had been in conflict with one another since their father's death. Demetrius, true Syrian incompetent that he was, was only too ready to meddle in Jewish affairs, and dealt Jannæus[29] a crippling blow near Shechem.

It was a critical moment. The rebels had been ready to invoke foreign aid, but now that the Syrian seemed about to become supreme, they weakened. They remembered Antiochus Epiphanes and the bloody years of struggle to free themselves from the Syrian yoke. Better to have a worthless high priest who was a Jew—and Jannæus had been that; circumcision had always followed victory—than to be subject once again to a Syrian king. Six thousand Jews deserted to Jannæus. The tide turned and Demetrius departed. The rebellion was soon over. In revenge and as a warning for the future, Jannæus is said to have had eight hundred of the leaders of the opposition crucified while he dallied openly with his con-

[29] That Josephus' figures cannot always be relied upon is evidenced by the discrepancy between his two statements of Jannæus' force in this encounter. *Wars* 1,4,5 states he had 1,000 horsemen, 8,000 mercenaries on foot, and "that part of the Jews which favored him, to the number of 10,000." *Antt.* 13,14,1 gives the figures 6,200 mercenaries and 20,000 Jews of his party. Josephus' phrase, "his party," has usually been understood to signify the Sadducees, who aided him against the Pharisees, who were the instigators of the civil war. That the Pharisees may properly be regarded in this light is by no means clear.

cubines, and to add to the terror had his soldiers cut the throats of the wives and children before the eyes of the dying wretches on the crosses. Many fled in terror from Jerusalem that dread night, and Jannæus received the nickname *Thracida*, that is, "son of a Thracian," akin to our epithet, "Hun."

Though now free from opposition at home, Jannæus became once more involved in foreign affairs. Antiochus XII of Syria, the youngest of the five sons of Antiochus VIII Grypsos who had been in constant conflict among themselves since 95 B.C., sought to check the rising menace of the Arabian Aretas who was striving for Damascus. Antiochus tried to head him off by a hasty march through Judea. This Jannæus sought to prevent, and even built a wall and trench from Joppa to Antipatris. The Syrians broke through, but were worsted by Aretas, who quickly became master of Cœle-Syria. Soon Jannæus, whose land extended into territory desired by Aretas, felt his power. He was forced to retreat into Judea, and though standing siege in a town on the road between Joppa and Jerusalem was soon defeated. Just what his relations with Aretas were is not clear, for soon he was engaged in another campaign across Jordan, seeking to subdue those communities which still opposed him. In this campaign he was largely successful. Several important towns capitulated, among them Dion, Heshbon, Pella, Gerasa, and Gamala. When he returned to Jerusalem, flushed with victory, his reception was far different from that a dozen years before. Nothing succeeds like success.

The whole district from the Lebanons to the Egyptian frontier and from the Mediterranean to the desert was nominally in his control, although probably several of the seacoast towns were not his. That this domain was thoroughly loyal is not for a moment to be thought. Many of the towns must be conquered again and again. Nor were his subjects all loyal Jews. The rough-and-ready tactics of forcing all the vanquished to become circumcised, which he zealously practised as his father and brother had done before him, could hardly be expected to achieve very lasting results. As a matter of fact, the land across the Jordan, to mention but one example, was and remained gentile territory in spite of Jewish zeal. One of the first reforms that the Roman general Pompey instituted after his conquest of Palestine was to free these east Jordan cities from their irksome bondage to Jerusalem. This is but one example of the artificial and fragile nature of the expanded kingdom of Hyrcanus' two successors. The game had not been worth the candle, and the silly attempt to bring unwilling converts into the Jewish fold was to reap its proper reward.

Jannæus, who had died in the field attempting to bring Ragaba, one of the transjordanian fortresses, into subjection, was succeeded by his widow, Alexandra. She, doughty woman that she was, completed the destruction of the city and then returned to Jerusalem to rule in her husband's stead for nine

years (78-69 B.C.). With the aid of the army and the strong outposts established by Jannæus little opposition from outside was to be feared. One crisis
occurred, but was weathered successfully. Tigranes of Armenia had made
himself master of Syria several years before Jannæus' death and had forced
Aretas to withdraw. He apparently had hopes of pushing south into Palestine. Fortunately for Alexandra, however, Lucullus the Roman had become
such a menace in his Armenian campaign that Tigranes was compelled to
abandon his hopes for further conquest and to turn homeward. Alexandra
seems also to have attempted the subjugation of Damascus, but without
success.

The most significant aspect of her rule was the change in policy at home.
Josephus, with his happy knack of composing appropriate deathbed speeches,
recounts that during his fatal illness Jannæus had counselled his wife to seek
the favour of the Pharisees who were so hostile to himself. That this was the
case is perhaps improbable. Nevertheless, the canny widow, sensing the popular dissatisfaction that had so menaced her husband and had been paralysed
but not removed, at once sought to make her position secure through overtures to the opposition. Accordingly, she gave vastly more authority to the
local Jerusalem council than it had enjoyed during the previous reigns. In
addition to the nobles and priests who had apparently formerly constituted
this council, she introduced a new group, the Scribes. Her brother, Simon
ben Shetach, a Pharisee, seems to have been her confidant. As a result of
these tactful modifications she weathered the storm that must otherwise
have broken as soon as the dread figure of Jannæus was removed. Josephus,
an ardent Pharisee himself, complacently remarks: "While she governed
other peoples . . . the Pharisees governed her,"[30] and again, "So she had indeed the name of the Regent; but the Pharisees had the authority."[31]
Schürer[32] and most modern historians accept his statements unqualifiedly.
Rather, it would seem to me probable that her policy was not quite so completely passive, but, as suggested above, that she sought to strengthen her
precarious position by permitting to a greater degree the voices of her non-
imperialistic subjects and by recognizing the scholarly, that is, the scribal,
group who had already displaced in the popular eye the less highly educated
priests as the real religious leaders of Israel. In consequence of this increased
recognition the actual leadership in things religious became confirmed to the
Scribes and to their supporters, the Pharisees, so that Josephus might well say,
"The Pharisees have the multitude on their side."[33] During these nine years
of freedom their leaders achieved the position to which their learning entitled them, and from which they were never displaced. This, however, does

[30] *Wars* 1,5,2.
[31] *Antt.* 13,16,2.
[32] "During these years the Pharisees were the real rulers in the land," *op. cit.,* Div. I, Vol. I,
p. 309.
[33] *Antt.* 13,10,6.

not mean that either the Pharisees or the Scribes became the political dictators of Israel, as has often been implied from the statements of Josephus. This period, during which the reins of absolute rule were to a measured degree slackened succeeding the tyrannical Jannæus and preceding the days of the absolute Herod and the later procurators, may well have become idealized in the eyes of later Pharisees. "Under Simon ben Shetach and Queen Salome (*i.e.,* Alexandra)," ran the tradition, "rain fell on the eve of the Sabbath, so that the corns of wheat were as large as kidneys, the barley corns as large as olives, and the lentils like golden denarii; the scribes gathered such corns, and preserved specimens of them in order to show future generations what sin entails."[34]

Since the office of high priest could not be hers, she caused the appointment of her elder son, the weak-minded and thoroughly incompetent Hyrcanus. The younger, Aristobulus, a true son of his father, was occasionally used by the queen as a general, but was kept out of actual power as a dangerous rival. Accordingly, he was obliged to bide his time until he might swing into the saddle. Eventually his time came. All had by no means sympathized with Alexandra's moderation. Prisoners had been released; many who had fled from Jerusalem in terror at the collapse of the rebellion had returned. Customs and traditions had been revived; new educational advances were made. While all this was highly satisfactory to those whose chief delight lay in the law of the Lord, it was highly distasteful to the real supporters of Jannæus and his predecessors. Their lot was made the more unpleasant by the zeal their opponents showed in wreaking whatever vengeance was possible upon their erstwhile war lords. These latter, accordingly, got themselves appointed to the various fortresses through the land.

Alexandra's fatal illness proved her ambitious son's opportunity. The already disgruntled nobles were ready to support him; they were now strategically placed throughout Palestine. Without difficulty he became a most menacing figure overnight. Before the outbreak of actual hostilities Alexandra died and the harmless Hyrcanus II, already high priest, was in nominal command. He was no match for his brother, and was speedily defeated near Jericho and deprived of his twofold position as high priest and king. Quite placidly he retired to the former house of Aristobulus as a private citizen, while his energetic young brother took up his residence in the palace.

At this stage of the story a very important figure comes to prominence, Antipater the Idumean. His father had been military governor of Idumea under Jannæus. To his command the son had succeeded. This man more than any other was responsible for the upset of the Hasmonean dynasty, and by his scheming brought to the Jewish throne its greatest king, his own son, Herod. Antipater was the Richelieu of Palestine. His policy was always to

[34] Ta'anit 23a, quoted by Schürer, *op. cit.,* Div. I, Vol. I, p. 311.

be the directing influence, to hold all the threads in his hand, to be the power behind the throne, but to allow another to sit upon it.

At the victory of Aristobulus he felt the time ripe. Recognizing that Hyrcanus would be far more easily controlled than his impetuous and able brother, he sought to arouse his injured friend to action. Finally he convinced him that his royal brother was plotting his death, flattered his vanity, and prevailed upon him to hasten to Petra, the capital of Aretas the Arabian, from whom he had already received the promise of assistance. Once here, it was easy to persuade Hyrcanus to attempt to regain his position. Aretas promised assistance on condition of the return of twelve cities to the south and east of the Dead Sea which Jannæus had captured. With the strong support of the Arabians Aristobulus was repulsed, many of his followers deserted, and he was forced to retreat to Jerusalem, where he stood siege in the temple, supported loyally by the priestly faction. Eventually the besieged, untrained though their attackers were in besieging a city, must have surrendered had it not been for the intervention of the power before whom Judea was to bow and lose forever her independence—Rome.

Since 88 B.C. Roman legions had been in the East attempting the subjection of Mithradates of Pontus, who had been ever anxious to invade the Roman province of Asia, and of his ofttime ally, Tigranes of Armenia. Although Sulla had defeated Mithradates, the latter had recouped his fortunes, and the struggle had gone on. In 69 B.C. Lucullus had checked the two kings—in the course of this campaign, it will be remembered, he had ended Tigranes' hope of the conquest of Palestine—and had wrested Syria from Tigranes, who had held it since 83 B.C., and had set up Antiochus XIII as nominal king. Shortly after this the direction of eastern affairs was transferred to Pompey, due largely to Cicero's eloquent championing of the bill presented to the Senate by Manilius. To Pompey thus fell the credit of finally crushing the power of Rome's archenemy, Mithradates. This he soon accomplished (66-65 B.C.). He recognized Tigranes' position in Armenia, but refused him Syria, which he organized as a new Roman province. His aim was to extend Roman rule to the Euphrates. In this reorganization he intended to include Palestine as a part of this newly created province, since he considered it virtually a province of the old Seleucid empire which had revolted and had gained temporary freedom. His general, Scaurus, who was in Damascus, saw in the civil war between the two priest-kings, Hyrcanus II and Aristobulus II, his opportunity, and hastened south. Although both sides made overtures to him, he wisely considered it easier to disperse the Arabian rabble than to take Jerusalem by storm. Accordingly, he raised the siege and ordered the Nabateans to leave the territory under the penalty of Rome's wrath. Thus Aristobulus was temporarily reinstated in his position, pending Pompey's arrival and final decision. Apparently Hyrcanus' erstwhile supporters returned their allegiance to Aristobulus, now that Rome had spoken, for Josephus records that after Scaurus' departure Aristobulus "with a great army" dealt the combined forces of his brother and Aretas a crushing defeat at Papyron.[35]

For two years Aristobulus remained undisturbed. Upon Pompey's arrival in Damascus to make definite arrangements for the administration of Palestine both brothers sought him, each to defame the other and to seek his support. Along with them came a third group who did not wish either, but desired the restoration of the hierocracy. This latter protest was the consequence of the growing dissatisfaction with the royal form of government of which the later Hasmoneans with their desire for conquest had given them their fill. The interpretation often put upon their protest that it was due to the fact that the priests had usurped the throne of David and were thus no legitimate kings is quite unfounded.

At the moment Pompey was busy with plans for a campaign against the Nabateans, and accordingly reserved his final decision. Aristobulus now lost whatever chance he may have had of gaining a favourable verdict by leaving Pompey at Dium, whither he had accompanied the Roman legions, and hastening to Alexandrium. This brought matters to a crisis. Pompey at once proceeded against him, and forced him to flee to Jerusalem. Pompey followed. When Aristobulus saw the Roman eagles before his gate his courage failed—so great was the dread of Rome—and coming to Pompey, promised to open the gates. Gabinius, a lieutenant of Pompey's, came to receive the city, but found it ready for resistance. Now only one course was open to Pompey. Summarily arresting Aristobulus, he started the siege of Jerusalem. Through the aid of Hyrcanus' followers the city was gained without bloodshed, but Aristobulus' forces retreated to the temple mount. To gain that meant a three-month siege. Finally, on a Sabbath in the June of 63 B.C. a breach in the temple wall was made, the temple was captured, and in the resulting massacre twelve thousand Jews are said to have lost their lives. Out of curiosity Pompey entered the holy of holies, and to his amazement found it empty.[36] Pompey's act was not one of wanton insult, but nevertheless the Jews never forgave it. The temple treasure remained untouched; next day saw the temple purified and the regular service of worship in full swing. It is an interesting commentary upon the place religion bore in Judaism that during the dreadful days of the siege itself the daily sacrifices had still continued uninterrupted.

Aristobulus and his two sons were sent to Rome to grace Pompey's triumph; Hyrcanus was restored as high priest and as ethnarch of Judea, but the independence of Palestine was forever past. The year 63 B.C. marks the end of

[35] *Wars* 1,6,3; *Antt.* 14,2,3.

[36] This may well account in part for the curious notion which the Romans always seem to have had that the Jews were atheists.

Jewish history. From now on Palestine was a tributary to Rome. Herod the Great and Agrippa might later be styled king; they were simply agents of Rome. Her territory shrank overnight. The important seacoast towns which had been gained at such terrific cost were taken from her and added to the Roman province of Syria. Samaria, the many Hellenistic towns and strongholds in Galilee and especially east of the Jordan, were set free from the hated Jewish yoke of servitude. Only the non-Grecian Idumea was left to the extra-Judean territory. And Judea herself was no longer a kingdom even in name. Hyrcanus now bore the title ethnarch, not king, and was responsible for good order to the Roman governor of the province of Syria

All this was in line with Rome's sensible *laissez faire* policy for the administration of her provinces. With actual local governments she never sought to interfere. Her aim was to have strong and steady control, and she realized this could usually be best accomplished by native princes who knew and understood the peculiarities of their own peoples. Accordingly, Pompey's arrangement was a distinct blessing to the peoples of the East. Jewish pride and desire for domain were offended, but the instability and top-heaviness of such a kingdom as Jannæus' gave way to a solid and common-sense administration. The regions which Jerusalem had lost were not Jewish, but predominantly gentile. There could never be peace so long as these unnatural and decidedly arbitrary conditions remained. The petty princes of Syria who had appeared as a consequence of the crumbling of the Seleucid empire and the ambitious sheiks like Aretas now gave way to a firm administration of the peace.

Chapter III

THE RISE AND RULE OF HEROD

For several years after Pompey's departure peace reigned in Palestine. The conquest had been a blessing, since it had introduced a strong hand to hold all over-ambitious princes in order. Hyrcanus II was now both high priest and ethnarch, under the general oversight of the governor of Syria. The real power, however, lay in the hands of his able and ambitious self-appointed adviser, Antipater, who had emerged from the débâcle with increased strength, and whose policy—later to be followed scrupulously by his son Herod—was: keep in favour with Rome, and in Rome stand always with the victor.

The dashing of the hopes of Aristobulus and his following of swaggering aristocrats was highly satisfactory to the Pharisees and their sympathizers. To be sure, they had lost their freedom, but their political interest was never large and had been more or less thrust upon them. Their general attitude is expressed by the ideal: "Love work, eschew domination, and hold aloof from the civil power."[1] They were well rid of the hated Hasmonean line. No high priest with hands reeking with the unholy blood of conquest would again sacrifice at the altar. The nation had once again been chastened for her sin. This attitude is well seen in a psalm coming from this period:

God laid bare their sins in the sight of the sun; all the earth hath learned the righteous judgments of God. . . . The holy things of God they took for spoil; and there was no inheritor to deliver out of their hand. They went up to the altar of the Lord when they were full of all uncleanness; yea, even in their separation they polluted the sacrifices, eating them like profane meats. They left not a sin undone, wherein they offended not above the heathen. For this cause did God mingle for them a spirit of error, he made them to drink of the cup of unmixed wine until they were drunken. He brought him that is from the utmost part of the earth, whose stroke is mighty; he decreed war against Jerusalem and her land. The princes of the land met him with joy; they said unto him, Blessed is thy path! come ye, enter in with peace. They made the rough paths even before their entering in, they opened the gates that led into Jerusalem; her walls they crowned with garlands. He entered in, as a father entereth into his sons' house, in peace. He established his feet and made them very firm. He occupied her strongholds, yea, and the wall of Jerusalem. For God led him in safety, because of their blindness. He cut off their princes and every wise councillor; he poured out the blood of the dwellers in Jerusalem like the water of uncleanness, he carried away their

[1] Abot 1,10.

sons and their daughters whom they had begotten in their defilement. They had done according to their uncleanness, even as their fathers did, they polluted Jerusalem and the things that had been dedicated unto the name of God.[2]

Although many of the liberated cities in Palestine reckoned their independence from the year of Pompey's conquest, and the Pharisees and their followers rejoiced in the collapse of the Hasmonean line, this sentiment was by no means universal in Judea. Much as they honoured the Scribes, they prized their freedom higher. The fact of being once again a subject nation was galling, although Rome's demands were not excessive. This dissatisfaction was naturally fanned by the war party of Jannæus and Aristobulus. The result was that party strife was forgotten; Rome was seen as the common foe.

For five or six years there seems to have been no overt acts. Scaurus and his two successors in Syria, Marcius Philippus and Lentulus Marcellinus, were involved in intermittent warfare with the Arabians, but Palestine seems to have been comparatively quiet. But following these years of quiet came five years (57-52 B.C.) of rebellion with no less than four distinct revolts. Aristobulus and his family had not been executed by Pompey, but had been sent to Rome to grace the latter's triumph. There they had been settled on the right bank of the Tiber. The elder son, Alexander, however, had escaped and finally made his appearance in Palestine. Getting together a force of some ten thousand of his disgruntled fellow-patriots, he made an ill-omened attempt to regain the throne. Hyrcanus was powerless, but Gabinius, who had been sent to Syria a few months before, quickly put down the insurrection, and to avoid similar outbreaks sought to destroy the spirit of national unity by dividing the Jewish territory into five mutually independent districts, with Jerusalem, Jericho, Gazara, Amathus, and Sepphoris the respective centres, each with its own council. Hyrcanus was deprived of the little civil authority he had formerly had. The land was thus actually a part of Syria. The two succeeding years each saw another fruitless attempt—the first led by Aristobulus and his second son, Antigonus (56 B.C.), the second by Alexander (55 B.C.). Both attempts were but flashes in the pan, but they had one highly significant result, increased prestige for the ambitious Idumean, Antipater.

During the whole period Antipater had been playing his cards well. First of all, he had been of decided help to Scaurus in his campaign against the Nabateans which Pompey had earlier planned. Then in these insurrections he had aided Gabinius so wholeheartedly and efficiently that he became the Roman governor's chief adviser in Judea. Apparently as a reward for loyalty Gabinius at this time reappointed Hyrcanus ethnarch at the request of Antipater, but the real power was in the hands of his minister. Never did the latter make the mistake of trying to thrust himself to the fore. Though in

[2] Psalms of Solomon 8:8-26 (ed. Ryle and James).

complete control, his deference and courtesy to his master were scrupulously maintained.

The fourth of these revolts was the result of Rome's own greed. The famous triumvirate—Pompey, Cæsar, and Crassus—was now in control. To Crassus, following his consulship of 55 B.C., fell Syria, where he hoped to gain military glory by taking Mesopotamia from the Parthians. Such an expedition required money. In shameful violation of his word he stripped the Jerusalem temple of its treasure, a deed which both Pompey and Gabinius had shunned, although the latter had exacted heavy tribute. This act fanned the popular hatred to a fury which Crassus' death in Parthia the next year (53 B.C.) did not abate. On the return of Cassius, his lieutenant and successor, strong measures were necessary to put down the revolt which had broken out. This time the moving figure was neither Aristobulus nor his sons, but one of their henchmen, Pitholaus. This fourth uprising came to a sorry end near Taricheæ on the Sea of Galilee; Pitholaus was executed at the request of Antipater, and thirty thousand of his followers are said to have been sold into slavery.[3]

Shortly after came the dreadful period of civil war in Rome. It is impossible to overemphasize its significance. As Schürer acutely remarks: "From Cæsar's crossing the Rubicon down to the death of Antony, B.C. 49-30, the whole Roman history was reflected in the history of Syria and also in that of Palestine."[4] The death of Crassus had dissolved the triumvirate; the long series of disagreements between Pompey and Cæsar came finally to a head. Rome was too small a place for them both. The Senate decreed that Cæsar must retire from office on July 1 or be declared a public enemy. Mark Antony, Cæsar's friend then tribune, vetoed the bill. Cicero sought a compromise. It was of no avail. A week later the Senate passed its famous "last decree," throwing the government into the hands of the military power in spite of the tribune's veto. Cæsar no longer delayed, but crossed the Rubicon[5] onto Italian soil and proceeded at once against Rome.

In Palestine Antipater continued on the side of his erstwhile patron, Pompey, as did all the East. At first it looked ominous for him, for one of Cæsar's first acts was to aid Aristobulus to regain Palestine in order to hamper Pompey. This danger was averted since Aristobulus was poisoned before he could leave Rome, and his son Alexander was beheaded in Antioch. Pompey's star was setting. Within sixty days Cæsar had become master of Italy; then following his brief campaign in Spain he hastened into Greece. The two armies finally joined battle on the plains of Thessaly near Pharsalia, Aug. 9, 48. Pompey's army, though twice the size of his rival's, was no match for the veterans who had so often routed hordes vastly greater than their own,

[3] Josephus, *Antt.* 14,7,3; *Wars* 1,8,9.

[4] *Op. cit.,* Div. 1, Vol. 1, p. 376.

[5] For the account of this dramatic incident with the famous words: "The die is cast," see Plutarch, *Cæsar* 32.

and was utterly defeated. Pompey fled to Egypt and soon was murdered by the treacherous Egyptians, who feared that they would be drawn into the conflict.

In this crisis Antipater at once changed sides, and made himself extremely valuable to his next patron. Not only did he give most efficient assistance to Cæsar's ally, Mithradates of Pergamum, at Ascalon, as the latter was hastening to Egypt to aid him, but he actually saved the day for Cæsar in Alexandria, by relieving him in the nick of time from the attack of the Egyptian mob. Furthermore, he was able to win the large Jewish population of Alexandria to Cæsar's side. For all this Cæsar was grateful. The divisions of Gabinius were abolished; the claims of Aristobulus' younger son, Antigonus, were contemptuously dismissed; Hyrcanus was confirmed in his position as hereditary high priest, reëstablished ethnarch of Judea, and elevated to senatorial rank; Antipater became authorized as Hyrcanus' prime minister, was granted Roman citizenship, and freed from tribute. Once more Jerusalem became the capital of the land and Jews were again in control of Jewish affairs. To be sure, the boundaries were not extended to embrace the territory gained by John Hyrcanus and his two sons, for the Greek cities retained their freedom. But the rich Esdraelon plain and, even better, the seaport Joppa were returned; Jerusalem's walls, demolished by Pompey, were now rebuilt. In addition to this, Jews were exempted from military service in the Roman legions and their religious prejudices were respected. Cæsar's assassination three years later (44 B.C.) was a source of genuine sorrow throughout all Jewry.

Shortly after Cæsar's departure from Syria, where he had acted the munificent patron of Antipater, another figure destined to play an important rôle in the history of the Jews makes his appearance. This was Herod, the younger son of the crafty Antipater.

Firmly established in favour with Cæsar, Antipater made it perfectly clear that if the nationalists sought to displace him they would bring upon themselves the wrath of Rome as well as that of himself and Hyrcanus. Further to strengthen his position he appointed his two sons, Phasaël and Herod, governors of Judea and Galilee, respectively. It is upon the latter that our interest is centred. No more ideal spot for the imperious young Idumean—he was but twenty-five at the time of his appointment—could be conceived. Galilee was a turbulent place, seething with discontent. Its past history had made it largely gentile. Centuries before, at the time of the fall of the northern kingdom, it had been colonized from the East. In the early days of the Maccabean uprising the bulk of the remaining Jews had been withdrawn to the south by Simon. Later it had been conquered by Aristobulus and Jannæus, and perhaps also, as we have seen, by John Hyrcanus. Yet distinct from some of the conquered territory it had become distinctly Jewish. As is often the case, the new converts seem to have exhibited an enthusiasm immature but almost fanatic in its intensity. As we shall see, this district was to remain the hotbed of incipient rebellion. At once Herod found himself in conflict with a group headed by Hezekiah. Josephus, with his pro-Roman interests and the desire to minimize all Jewish opposition to the empire, gives a one-sided picture of this group, which he dismisses as a band of robbers. Herod inflicted drastic punishment upon them, and executed the ringleader, Hezekiah, along with many of his followers. Instead of being rejoiced to see the outlaws discomfited, the Sanhedrin in Jerusalem prevailed upon Hyrcanus to summon the young leader to account. Although at first abashed by his appearance—he came as no penitent—the council started proceedings against him. Hyrcanus, however, warned by Sextus Cæsar, the governor of Syria, adjourned the council and urged Herod to flee. On his return to Galilee he was appointed by Sextus military governor of Cœle-Syria. All of this reveals that the group in Galilee was certainly no mere group of mountain brigands, but militant nationalists who saw in Antipater and his sons the actual representatives of the hated Rome. Not only Sextus' championing and later rewarding Herod for crushing them, but also the attitude of the Sanhedrin in seeking to punish Herod for his drastic actions—the claim was that they alone were empowered to pronounce the death sentence—becomes intelligible. The affair nearly had disastrous consequences. Determined to wipe out the disgrace he had suffered at the hand of the Sanhedrin, Herod soon returned with an armed force, and but for the pleas of his father and brother would have ousted Hyrcanus. Thus the only result of the Sanhedrin's action was to seat Antipater and his sons the more securely in the saddle. But fresh difficulties soon arose.

Two years later, on the ides of March (44 B.C.) Cæsar was assassinated. Cassius, one of the conspirators, fled to Syria. Indeed, shortly before his death Cæsar had himself appointed him to be governor of this province which he had defended so successfully against the Parthians a few years before. Soon he made himself master of the province, gained the support of the legions of Cæcilius Bassus, an erstwhile supporter of Pompey, who had wrested Syria from Sextus Cæsar in the spring of 46, and thus had forestalled his rival Dolabella, whom Antony had contrived to have appointed.

For the maintenance of his army money was necessary. From Judea seven hundred talents were demanded, and when Emmaus, Lydda, Gophna, and Thamne failed to contribute their share, the luckless inhabitants were sold as slaves. Seeing the way the wind blew, Herod threw in his lot with Cassius, aided him in collecting the tribute, and for his zeal was confirmed in his office as governor of Cœle-Syria.

A few months later an unhappy circumstance contrived to thrust him even more to the front. Antipater was murdered through the cunning of a certain Malichus, who apparently hoped to supplant him. Herod with the aid of his brother and the connivance of Cassius avenged his father's death.

Now Judea, too, was in the hands of Herod, for while at the departure of Cassius there had been incipient rebellion, incited by Antigonus, the two sons of Antipater had triumphed although apparently at the loss of some territory in Galilee. About this time Herod sought to strengthen his position by becoming betrothed to Mariamne, the daughter of Alexander and thus the granddaughter of both Hyrcanus and Aristobulus. Though the marriage did not take place for five years, the alliance tended to make his position less obnoxious to Jewish sensibilities.

Once more came fresh complications and the need of changing sides. Cassius had joined his fellow conspirator, Brutus, and with him had proceeded to Macedon. In the late autumn of 42 B.C. they had met the combined forces of Antony and Octavian at Philippi and after the hopeless rout had committed suicide. To the victors belonged the spoils. Octavian took the West; Antony became absolute master of the Roman East, and with it, of course, Syria. This might well have spelled disaster for Herod, and so his enemies hoped. No less than three delegations for the purpose of defaming Herod were sent to Antony during his leisurely march to Egypt (41 B.C.). They were quite unsuccessful. Antony had been an intimate friend of Antipater's during his campaigns under Gabinius, and well knew the effective support he could count on from his able son. Furthermore, Hyrcanus had himself championed the claims of Herod and Phasaël. As a consequence, Antony disregarded the attacks, overlooked the fact that Herod had supported Cassius, and appointed him and Phasaël tetrarchs with full political power. Hyrcanus remained high priest; his political power had, however, passed to the sons of his former minister.

The one force in the East which Rome feared was Parthia, and not without reason. During his stay in Syria Cassius had entered into negotiations with them to aid him against the partisans of Cæsar. Now while Antony was disporting himself with Cleopatra in Egypt their menace had become real. Pacorus of Parthia, incited and aided by the fugitive Titus Labienus, had crossed the Euphrates and gained possession of Syria. Antigonus, the archenemy of Herod, seized this opportunity for his own advantage. Supported by many disgruntled Jews, he proceeded against Herod and Phasaël, having previously entered into negotiations with Pacorus for the latter's support. Soon the Parthians arrived. By trickery they got possession of Hyrcanus and Phasaël, who too late awoke to the fact that the invaders were but creatures of Antigonus. The only course open to Herod was flight. Leaving his family in the fortress on Masada, he first turned for help to Petra. But the Arabian king, fearing the Parthians, would not receive him. In disappointment Herod hastened to Alexandria to his master, Antony. Here again he was disappointed. Finally alarmed by affairs in Syria, Antony had stopped his lovemaking and had hastened to Tyre, one of the few cities that had remained loyal. But here word reached him that his presence in Rome was imperative.

His wife Fulvia—according to Plutarch, in order to stir up such a commotion that her wandering spouse must return—had precipitated a crisis between himself and Octavian. With two hundred ships he hastened to Rome. Though a civil war now seemed imminent, mutual friends of Antony and Octavian succeeded in patching up a peace. This was made the easier since Fulvia had opportunely died, thus making a marriage between Antony and Octavian's sister, Octavia, possible. To her credit, it may be remarked in passing, for three years Octavia kept her husband in Athens, where with commendable zeal he attended to his duties without dallying with the siren of the Nile.

Disappointed at not finding his patron in Alexandria, Herod had refused Cleopatra's offer to command an expedition of hers, and had set sail for Rome. He arrived in the nick of time (40 B.C.). Antony and Octavian, once more friends, were parcelling out the Roman world. Herod had little difficulty in enlisting their aid, for both realized his ability. He would be a loyal ally against Antigonus who had not only aided the Parthians but was flouting Roman authority by his royal claims. Within seven days after his arrival in Rome as a fugitive Herod had left it again, having heard himself lauded in the Senate and, best of all, having received the title "King of the Jews." All that he needed now was his kingdom!

Early in the spring of 39 B.C. Herod arrived in Ptolemaïs with the intention of making his new title a reality. He soon found his task was to be a very difficult one. During his months of absence the rebellion had increased. Antigonus was established in Jerusalem with the title high priest and king; Phasaël had committed suicide; Hyrcanus had been deprived of his ears by Antigonus to render him for ever ineligible to the sacred office[6]—one account of this deed was that Antigonus had actually bitten them off with his own teeth!—and had been carried off as a prisoner to Parthia by the departing allies of the newly established king. To be sure, Ventidius, who had been sent by Antony to the East to take the place of Decidius Saxa, who had fallen before Labienus, had driven Labienus and his Parthian troops back to Taurus, and thus had become master of Syria and Palestine (39 B.C.). Antigonus had been forced to pay a heavy tribute, but had not been displaced.

Herod's position was difficult, but hardly desperate. He proceeded at once to Galilee, got together an army, and with nominal help from Silo, the lieutenant of Ventidius, took Joppa, hastened to Masada, where his relations were hard pressed by the enemy, relieved them in the nick of time, and proceeded to Jerusalem. Had he had any real support from the Romans, he would probably have succeeded. This, however, he did not receive. Silo, as a result of bribes from Antigonus, suddenly refused to

[6] Lev. 21:16-24.

continue the campaign, although victory was about in their hands, and insisted upon going into winter quarters. In disgust, Herod, obliged to postpone his plans for the capture of Jerusalem, sent his brother Joseph against the Idumeans, and himself hastened to Galilee. Soon Sepphoris was his. After a lively campaign against the insurrectionists who had retreated to inaccessible caves—the whole dramatic account is vividly told by Josephus[7]—he succeeded in subduing Galilee.

Early in the next year (38 B.C.) Ventidius had been obliged to check a new invasion by the Parthians. In this he was successful. Pacorus, who with Labienus had been the moving spirit, was slain, and Ventidius now felt free to move against Antiochus of Commagene, whom he besieged in Samosata. During this time Herod had received no help from Rome. To be sure, just before leaving for his campaign against Antiochus, Ventidius had sent Herod a force under Macheras. The latter was, if anything, worse than Silo and yielded to Antigonus' bribes. In disgust Herod decided the time had come for action. Antony himself was now at Samosata, directing the siege. To him Herod determined to go. Disregarding the plea of the faithless Macheras, who apparently dreaded Antony's wrath, Herod departed, was cordially welcomed by Antony, and returned with the assurance, this time actually fulfilled, that he should receive real assistance. When Herod reached Syrian Antioch bad news awaited him: his brother Joseph had disregarded his explicit instruction and had been slain near Jericho; in Galilee the insurrectionists had again risen, had regained the territory, and had drowned many of Herod's supporters in the lake. Herod did not delay. With two Roman legions and the promise that Sosius—the successor of Ventidius—would himself speedily follow, he hastened south, regained Galilee, and pushed into Judea. After an indecisive battle near Jericho he destroyed Antigonus' force under Pappus at Isanas, and, had it not now become necessary to postpone further operations on account of the approach of winter, would have marched at once against the demoralized Antigonus in Jerusalem.

With the advent of spring he prepared for the siege, and then, perhaps as a foretaste of his coming victory, left his army to go to Samaria to consummate the marriage with Mariamne, contracted nearly five years before. It was an opportune time, for Sosius, though on the march, had not arrived. On his return to his army, Herod started the siege in earnest with the efficient aid of Sosius and his strong forces. Within two months the first two walls had been taken—the attack, of course, was from the north—but the upper city and temple court were still in the hands of Antigonus. Although there could be but one outcome, the besieged fought with a fury almost fanatic. As Wellhausen well remarked, "It was actually less faith than hate which inspired the Jews and blinded their eyes to the obvious madness of opposition

[7] *Antt.* 14,15,5; *Wars* 1,16,4.

to the superior power."[8] Soon came the end; the temple area was theirs. Infuriated by the mad resistance of the city, both the Romans and Herod's forces started a carnival of blood. Antigonus in terror came out of his hiding-place and threw himself a suppliant at the feet of Sosius. The sneering Roman with the gibe, "Antigone," put him in chains. For a time Herod must have feared the victory would be more costly than defeat. He did not want his capital destroyed, nor did he desire to add unnecessary fuel to the hatred of his subjects. Well did he realize the consequences of the earlier siege when Pompey had entered the holy of holies. This must at all costs be prevented. Finally he prevailed; the temple was saved, and the looting ceased, although to attain the latter, Herod had to promise to indemnify from his own purse the soldiers for the spoils which were rightly theirs. In fact, all through the siege—and, for that matter, through his entire reign—Herod seems always to have sought in a blunderbuss fashion to placate his people who would not be placated. Just before the temple fell he had allowed animals to be taken in to the enemy on the false plea that they were necessary for sacrifice.

Finally the Romans left the city and returned to meet Antony at Antioch. Antigonus went as a captive. Herod took no chances. Remembering the civil strife which Aristobulus and his two sons had fomented after they had been carried to Rome by Pompey, he had no desire to see such history repeated. He prevailed upon Antony to end the danger. In answer to his request the head of Antigonus fell beneath the ax of the Roman executioner.

And thus did the government of the Asmoneans cease, a hundred and twenty-six years after it was first set up. This family was a splendid and an illustrious one, both on account of the nobility of their stock and of the dignity of the high-priest-hood, as also for the glorious actions their ancestors had performed for our nation: but these men lost the government by their dissensions one with another, and it came to Herod, the son of Antipater, who was of no more than a vulgar family, and of no eminent extraction, but one that was subject to other kings. And this is what history tells us was the end of the Asmonean family.[9]

Herod, like his father Antipater before him, had ruled in the name of Hyrcanus. This was, however, in the past. Now not only was he actually king, but called himself so. The act of the Senate three years before had become fact. He was one of the *reges socii*, a king who owed his coronet to Rome, and kept it only as long as pleased her. He need pay no tribute, but must provide troops in time of war. He might keep an army, but it must not be so large as to arouse suspicion that he was seeking to cut loose from the empire. He might coin money. Herod, curiously enough, although enjoying Augustus' favour and confidence, seems to have been restricted to copper. The one paramount requirement—and no excuses for failure were ever ac-

---

[8] *Israelitische und Jüdische Geschichte*, p. 303.

[9] Josephus, *Antt.* 14,16,4.

cepted—was that he administer his territory efficiently and keep the peace. And this Herod did. For more than thirty years Herod administered his district so efficiently that not only did he continue in favour at Rome, but received large accessions of land. In fact, not only did he rule a territory larger than had ever before been subject to Jerusalem, but he was, in spite of the oft-expressed contempt of the disgruntled Jerusalem nobility for this "insolent king who is not of the race of the priests," far and away the most able and competent ruler the Jews ever had. His reign has been compared with that of Solomon. Actually it far surpassed it. His borders were again and again extended, and the newly added districts were put in thorough order. But his was not so much an age of conquest as of building. Though an Idumean by birth, he was in spirit a Hellenist. He did not make the mistake of striving to thrust Hellenism down his people's throat, as had Antiochus Epiphanes. Nevertheless, he introduced it in no less degree. Theatres, amphitheatres, chariot races, gladiatorial shows, games—all these made their appearance. Not only within his borders but as far west as Athens and Rome evidences of his lavish hand and purse were to be found.

To understand Herod it is necessary to observe that his political life was an ellipse: the two foci were Herod and Rome.

Herod made no initial false gesture of conciliation. Forty-five nobles of Antigonus' court were summarily executed and their wealth confiscated. The advent of Herod meant the downfall of the Sadducees, who had become more and more the dominant factor in Jewish politics. They might and did continue to exert an influence, but they had received their deathblow, and their numbers rapidly dwindled. When the new Sanhedrin convened, it soon found itself shorn of most of its power; not until after the deposition of Archelaus did it again become a dominant force in Jewish politics. Nor did the other leading party, the Pharisees, fare much better; although always inclined as they were to "hold aloof from the civil power," they came into less conflict and accordingly suffered less loss than did their rivals. It is unwise to over-emphasize the fact that Pollio the Pharisee and his disciple Sameas advised the besieged to open the gates to Herod. This they probably did, and it is not unlikely that others of their group assented, but not because of any affection for Herod. Rather, they apparently saw in him the scourge of God, the opponent of Antigonus and the Sadducaic aristocracy. Once more it was the old story of bitter opposition to the incestuous marriage of religion and politics. If David might not even build a temple to God since he was a man of war with hands stained by blood, how much less tolerable was it when those who claimed to be his successors and occupied his throne dared to usurp the holy garments and minister in the temple! With the death of Antigonus this outrage was never repeated, for the gentile Herod could not become high priest.

This brings us to the crux of his difficulties. First, last, and all the time

Herod's chief trouble lay with the women of his acquaintance. Three of them ultimately caused his downfall. Of these three one hated him with cold and calculating intensity; one blew now hot, now cold; one passionately loved him. They were respectively his mother-in-law, Alexandra, proud Hasmonean princess and daughter of the exiled Hyrcanus; Cleopatra of Egypt, who stole his choicest lands and sought to entice him into adultery with her; and Salome, his unscrupulous but devoted sister.

When Herod married Mariamne during the siege of Jerusalem, he was brought into a somewhat more friendly relationship with the Hasmonean line. After all, he had always shown the highest respect for Hyrcanus II and had protected him against his younger brother and the latter's son. Now he brought the old man back to Jerusalem—the Parthians had long since freed him from actual bondage and allowed him to live comfortably in Babylon—and showed him the greatest deference. Since, however, the old man had lost his ears, he could not resume his sacerdotal office. In his place Herod appointed an obscure Babylonian priest, Ananel, making the choice apparently to avoid the danger of giving such authority to the none too friendly Jerusalem hierarchy.

Alexandra realized perfectly that, in spite of his deference to her father, Herod had effectively overthrown the dynasty of her house. Her wrath was all the more intense because her seventeen-year-old son, Aristobulus, had not succeeded his grandfather as high priest. At once she sought to enlist the aid of Cleopatra, who had the ear of Antony. Cleopatra, who was trying to oust Herod and gain his territory, was willing. Herod sensed his danger and effectively checked it. Deposing Ananel, he installed his wife's brother. This sealed the youth's doom, for he had now become a real menace to Herod. A strict watch was set on Alexandra. Finding this irksome, she attempted to flee with her son to Cleopatra, but the scheme miscarried. In his first year of office the young high priest was drowned at Jericho, where he had retreated after officiating at the Feast of Tabernacles (35 B.C.). Although Herod expressed the keenest grief at the tragedy, Alexandra was not deceived. Through Cleopatra's help she got Antony to summon Herod to account for the murder.

Herod was in suspense. Well did he know the hatred of Alexandra and her friends; Cleopatra, too, was only too eager to accomplish his downfall and would spare no pains to insure his disgrace with Antony. It was with heavy heart that Herod left for Laodicea. Just prior to his departure he made his uncle Joseph, who chanced also to be Salome's husband, regent and instructed him, should the worst occur, to slay Mariamne lest she fall into the hands of another man.

Contrary to his fears, he was exonerated by Antony. The opposite report, however, came to Jerusalem. Just as Alexandra had persuaded Joseph to let her and Mariamne flee to a near-by Roman garrison, another report, this time favourable, came, and the scheme for flight fell through. On Herod's return his sister Salome informed him of the plan, and further to prejudice him against Mariamne—for the proud Salome hated the beautiful queen because of the latter's thinly veiled contempt for "the Idumean woman"—charged Mariamne with adultery with Joseph. At first, Herod disbelieved it; later, learning that Mariamne knew of his command to Joseph, he refused to believe that it had been told merely to show the queen how her husband loved her, and summarily executed Joseph, but permitted his wife to live.

Though Cleopatra had not succeeded in ousting Herod, she received shortly after nearly all the Palestinian seacoast, a large grant of land in Arabia, and, worst of all, Herod's prize possessions, the district around Jericho rich with palm and balsam, and the salt and pitch rights. Herod thus had to lease back from her his own lands and collect—or pay himself—the corresponding fees from Malichus the Arabian. This lavish series of gifts was but part of Antony's madness. In 37 B.C. the triumvirate—Antony, Octavian, and Lepidus—had been renewed for five years. Shortly after, Lepidus had been ousted by Octavian, and Antony, forgetting his good resolution, left Octavia and returned to Cleopatra. Matters went from bad to worse. He sought to make Alexandria his capital, celebrated a triumph there to the scandal of the Romans, gave his mistress—he now posed as her husband—not only the districts already mentioned but other Roman domains, including Cyprus and Cilicia, on the absurd claim that they had formerly belonged to the Ptolemies, and even bestowed the title "kings" upon the two sons he had had by Cleopatra, settling by secret will certain provinces over which they should reign. Octavian got wind of this; the secret will was opened and the treason came to light.

Since the end of the five-year period was now at hand (32 B.C.), the Senate intervened; Octavian, who had brought the West into peace and quiet, felt the time was ripe, and bitterly denounced his erstwhile associate. The next year, Cleopatra was formally proclaimed a public enemy and war was declared. The decisive battle was at Actium (31 B.C.). Octavian was victor. Cleopatra's ships fled in the midst of the encounter, and Antony, demoralized by this defection, soon followed. During the next few months Cleopatra played her trumps. She sought to ingratiate herself with Octavian, but learning that she was to be exhibited in Rome at his triumph, she committed suicide, as had Antony a short time before. The West had again conquered. Octavian was in the seats of the mighty.

This downfall of Antony might well have spelled doom for Herod. He had not been personally involved, for, though he had wanted to come to Antony's assistance, Cleopatra had prevented it. She had forced him to go against the Nabatean Arabs to collect her taxes. Her desire was twofold: first, to prevent Herod from establishing further claim upon the gratitude of Antony; second, she hoped that by embroiling Herod and the Arabs to

wear them both out and to appropriate their domains. To further this scheme
she actually aided Malichus. Her plans, however, totally miscarried. Herod
was successful. Antony, whom she had confidently expected to triumph, was
routed. The one man upon whose fidelity Antony had counted was prevented thus from aiding him. Herod saw the collapse of Antony with horror.
He is said to have counselled him to cut himself loose from Cleopatra and to
try again. When Antony refused, Herod wisely decided to quit before it was
too late. As he had turned from Pompey to Cæsar after Pharsalia (48 B.C.),
to Cassius after Cæsar's assassination (44 B.C.), to Antony after Philippi
(42 B.C.), so now he switched allegiance to Octavian and gave most efficient
aid to Didius, governor of Syria, in preventing a company of Antony's
gladiators from sailing from Cyzicus to Egypt to the aid of their now desperate master.

Now Herod wants to go to Octavian at Rhodes. Two preliminary steps
were necessary. The aged Hyrcanus was executed. Most historians roundly
condemn Herod for this act. To be sure, Hyrcanus was an inoffensive old
man whose whole life had been one long tragedy, forced as he had been into
the political limelight against his will; yet he could be a very real danger in
the hands of the unscrupulous Alexandra at such a critical hour. If we
cannot applaud, we can at least appreciate Herod's dilemma. The other task
involved his wife Mariamne. The story is told that again he gave secret
instruction—this time to Sohemus—to slay the queen should Herod fail with
Octavian. This command with its sequel is so similar to the earlier incident
that many consider it a doublet.

Now Herod appears before Octavian; he proudly admits his earlier loyalty
to Antony. Will Octavian receive him as a supporter? Indeed yes. Octavian
confirms him in his rank. A little later, as Octavian proceeded to Egypt to
complete the destruction of Antony, Herod showed him the greatest attention. Then a few months later came the glad news. Octavian was supreme;
Antony and Cleopatra had both committed suicide (Aug., 30 B.C.). Herod's
wise choice had been justified. He hastened to Egypt, proffered his felicita-
tions; they were graciously accepted and rewarded. His rich lands around
Jericho were returned, the Phœnician seacoast and the cities of Gadara,
Samaria, and Hippos were granted him. Thus the whole overturn of Roman
politics had been greatly to Herod's advantage. In the place of Antony, fast
coasting to destruction, stood the popular Octavian, hailed as the saviour of
the world. And Cleopatra, always a thorn in his side and a real menace, was
removed. With hopes high, Herod returned to Jerusalem from Antioch,
whither he had gratefully accompanied his munificent patron.

On his arrival home his joy turned to gloom. His beloved Mariamne
showed no joy at his success; on the contrary, she openly reproached him for
the murder of her grandfather and brother and made it perfectly clear that
her love for him was past. This was a bitter disappointment to the proud

king. Though at a later date he had nine wives living side by side in his palace and turning it into a perfect Bedlam with their plots and jealousies, during Mariamne's life there was no rival. Even Doris, his first wife, and her son Antipater, had been dismissed. Salome, however, was overjoyed at the rupture and did all in her power to bring it to a crisis to rid the palace of the presence of this coldly disdainful favourite. Soon she succeeded. She bribed Herod's cupbearer to say that Mariamne had prepared a poison drink for her husband; the queen's eunuch confessed under torture that his mistress hated the king because she knew of the secret word to Sohemus. Herod was convinced of his queen's unfaithfulness, and soon both the indiscreet minister and the lovely Hasmonean were executed (29 B.C.).

For several months it seemed as if Herod's star had set. Forgetting his cares of state, he sought to drown his grief in hunting and drinking. Soon he fell sick in Samaria, and word came to Jerusalem that he was dying. Alexandra felt the time had come to rid herself of her detested son-in-law. To achieve this end she sought to get control of the two citadels in Jerusalem. Word came to Herod. Sick though he was, he roused himself; all his grief and remorse changed to wild rage against this detestable woman whose plottings had brought him so often to destruction's door. The pleasure of her execution (28 B.C.) was far more effective than the doctor's physic in restoring Herod's strength and reason.

Two years later the last step in rooting out possible rivals was taken. The incident is worth telling, for it gives a good picture of the plots and counterplots in the Herodian court during these early years. Following the disgrace and execution of Joseph, Herod had appointed Costobarus, an Idumean, as governor of Idumea (34 B.C.). Not only was Costobarus Joseph's political successor; he, too, married Salome. In his first years of office he had sought to weaken his patron's power by negotiations with Cleopatra. Although Herod had learned of it, Salome had persuaded her brother to forgive the treason. Now, however, Salome had tired of her husband and sought to rid herself of him. She told Herod that her husband had hid and protected the two young sons of Babas, distant kin of the Hasmoneans, whom Herod had sought for in vain. Costobarus, she said, had never given up his plan to gain Idumea for himself. These two youths were to be his tools. With the death of the treacherous Costobarus and the two princes whose existence had always been a source of apprehension for Herod, he felt at last free from outside danger.

There were now none at all left of the kindred of Hyrcanus; and the kingdom was entirely in Herod's own power, and there was nobody remaining of such dignity as could put a stop to what he did against the Jewish laws.[10]

Now with Herod firmly established on his throne we must look for the

[10] *Antt.* 15,7,10 (end).

moment to Rome to see what was happening there, for the history of Herod—save for the sinister family disorder of his last years—is but a miniature of that of Augustus.

Julius Cæsar had been assassinated—Shakespeare to the contrary notwithstanding—for his imperial longings. Octavian had them in a lesser degree, but was wise enough to study the causes of his uncle's downfall. Since the end of the second triumvirate in 32 B.C. his power had rested on no constitutional basis, but rather upon his prestige, his annual consulship, and the readiness of the Senate to grant him whatever he wished.

Finally in 27 B.C. he declared that it was his wish that the republic be restored; laid down voluntarily the extraordinary powers he had received, including command of the armies and control of the provinces; and signified that the Senate was now supreme. At once ,the Senate voted him proconsular power over all the frontier provinces which required armed support, voted him the name Augustus with the title, *princeps senatus,* and changed the name of the month *Sextilis* to *Augustus* in his honour. Thus his position was secure. He had surrendered all claims to dictatorship, had disabused all fear that he desired to restore the hated kingdom, and had secured in a most regular and legal fashion command of the army.[11] Apparently sincere in his wish that the Senate become the responsible body, he left Rome for the West and it was not until 24 B.C. that he returned. The Senate in the meanwhile had shown itself incapable of independent action—their almost invariable answer to his every request was that his will was law without their action. During his absence his fellow-consul Murenas had plotted to remove him. Accordingly, his return saw drastic changes. Resigning his perennial consulship, he received the *tribunicia potestas* for life. Now he was doubly fortified. The Senate's grant in 27 B.C. assured him control of the standing army through his proconsular authority over the frontier provinces; the people had now invested him with the control of legislation and the veto. The net result was that he held all the reins of authority in his own hand, yet without the onus of having stolen prestige from the Senate. Thus the term "dyarchy" is more apt than "monarchy."

This access of power was especially applauded by the provinces, which rightly preferred a strong ruler like Augustus to the rival cliques in the Senate and the irresponsible magistrates who regularly had retired from their short tenures of office with ill-gotten fortunes. A full discussion of the new arrangements for provincial adminintration may be reserved for a later chapter. Here it may suffice to say that Augustus had no intention of carrying out Cæsar's and Antony's scheme of an empire extending beyond the Euphrates. That was to be the eastern boundary of an empire not

[11] Cf. Tacitus, *Annal.* i,i ". . . *et Pompei Crassique potentia cito in Cæsarem; Lepidi atque Antonii arma in Augustum cessere, qui cuncta discordiis civilibus fessa nomine principis sub imperium accepit." Idem* i,9 ". . . *non regno tamen neque dictatura, sed principis nomine, constitutam rem publicam."*

too large to be efficiently controlled. The key provinces were naturally those along the frontiers. These were now in his own hands, and their governors were responsible solely to him and retained office during his pleasure. While in a province such as Syria an experienced veteran was usually governor, in some of the smaller and more difficult provinces—such, for example, as Palestine—native princes, who knew the temper and peculiarities of their subjects and yet were loyal to Rome, were preferred, so long as they were strong enough to keep the peace and sensible enough not to kick up insurrection.

This explains Herod's favour in the eyes of Augustus. Absolutely loyal to his new master, he sought in every way to advance the Augustan plans. As Augustus planned and built, so planned and built Herod. His favour with Augustus continually rose. During his long reign his territory was practically doubled, so that the little land embraced a territory far larger than that of the palmy days of David and Solomon.

Actually he was an excellent ruler. He was generous to a fault; in times of famine he relieved the resulting distress, at one time buying eight hundred thousand measures of corn which he distributed free. He is said to have clothed whole villages in winter. On at least two occasions he made drastic reductions in the taxes: thirty-three percent in 20 B.C., twenty-five percent in 14 B.C. Following the lead of Augustus, his building activity was carried on with a lavish scale—temples, gymnasiums, cloisters, amphitheatres, and aqueducts. Samaria was rebuilt under the name Sebaste and furnished with a temple in honour of the emperor. Other cities were built and named in honour of his relatives and friends. Among them were Antipatris, Phasaëlis, and Agrippium. New citadels—one at Jericho in honour of his mother, Cypros; two named after himself Herodium and set in strategic places, Geba in Galilee, Heshbon across the Jordan—encircled his domains with efficient garrisons.

Trade flourished. A satisfactory harbour was the need of the day. On his whole inhospitable coast Joppa was the only port south of Tyre. On the site of Strato's Tower a new and magnificent city, Cæsarea Stratonis, arose with a splendid harbour protected by huge moles two hundred feet wide. At its entrance stood twin statues, the one in honour of Rome, the other of Augustus. This city, which took twelve years to build, became the most important in Judea; years later, when Roman procurators had succeeded to Herod's power, this was their capital city, although Jerusalem continued to share the nominal honour.

Nor did he stand as patron of architecture solely in his own domain. Far from Palestine his munificence was reflected. Temples, baths, porticos, and monuments were erected not only in the seacoast cities of Syria, *viz.,* Tyre, Sidon, Berytus, Tripolis, but in Damascus and Antioch. The Pythian temple at Rhodes; a restored portico on the island of Chios, whither he had accompanied Agrippa; numerous public buildings at Nicopolis, a city built by Augustus on the site of his victory over Antony at Actium—these are but examples of his zeal. In his list of benefactions Josephus records: "And are not the Athenians, and Lacedemonians, and Nicopolitans, and that Pergamus which is in Mysia, full of decorations that Herod presented them withal!"[12] Even today fragments of inscriptions provide tangible proof of the accuracy of the stories.

The chief glory was, however, the new temple in Jerusalem. The actual labour on the shrine itself lasted but eighteen months, although eight years were required on the surroundings. The last detail, however, of this gem of all Palestine was not completed until the days of Albinus (62-64 A.D.). And then, less than a decade later, it was fired by the conqueror's torch! Its magnificence—white marble with its overlay of gold and precious stones—gleaming high on the summit of Zion, and bursting into sudden view as pilgrims came over the top of Olivet on the Jericho road, gave rise to the rabbinical saying: "Whoever has not seen the temple of Herod has seen nothing beautiful."[13]

No better illustration of the relation between Herod and his subjects can be found than is afforded in the story of the construction of the temple. Not only would it be a crown for his realm; it would also tend to placate the people, for Herod passionately wanted to be known as a popular sovereign. Suspicion rather than gratitude met his plan. Rumours spread that the religion of Jehovah was to be stamped out; the promise to build a new temple was a mere subterfuge to allow the old one to be torn down. Soon the actual building showed the rumours false; still suspicion persisted, in spite of Herod's scrupulous care not to offend religious sensibilities. Priests were taught the trades of mason and carpenter that no unconsecrated foot need defile holy ground. No attempt was made to blot out the distinction between Jew and gentile.

When you go through these first cloisters, unto the second court of the temple, there was a partition made of stone all round, whose height was three cubits: its construction was very elegant; upon it stood pillars, at equal distances from one another, declaring the law of purity, some in Greek, and some in Roman letters, that no foreigner should go within that sanctuary.[14]

[12] Josephus, Wars 1,21,11. This whole chapter should be read.

[13] Cf. also Josephus, Wars 5,5,1-8; Antt. 15,11,1-7.

[14] Josephus, Wars 5,5,2. In 1871 one of these pillars was excavated, bearing the following inscription:

ΜΗΘΕΝΑΑΛΛΟΓΕΝΗΕΙΣΠΟ
ΡΕΤΕΣΘΑΙΕΝΤΟΣΤΟΥΠΕ
ΡΙΤΟΙΕΡΟΝΤΡΥΦΑΚΤΟΥΚΑΙ
ΠΕΡΙΒΟΛΟΥΟΣΔΑΝΛΗ
ΦΘΗΕΑΤΤΩΙΑΙΤΙΟΣΕΣ
ΤΑΙΔΙΑΤΟΕΞΑΚΟΛΟΥ
ΘΕΙΝΘΑΝΑΤΟΝ.

"No foreigner is to enter within the balustrade and embankment around the sacred place; whoever is caught will be responsible for his death which will follow."

Nor did Herod himself ever transgress it, although, says Josephus, he caused a secret passage to be built underground from the Antonia to the inner temple to guard against possible insurrections.

Yet this scrupulous care was at once forgotten when over the great east gate of the temple was placed a golden eagle. This perfectly natural gesture of courtesy to Rome aroused deep resentment. Indeed, one of the last deeds of Herod was to execute some forty pious thugs who tore it down as an insolent gesture to the dying monarch.

Not only building, but other forms of Greek culture were enthusiastically championed by Herod. Both in Cæsarea and Jerusalem games were celebrated every fourth year; his munificence in aiding the restoration of the famed Olympic games resulted in his name being inscribed as one of the perpetual managers of those games. Culture and learning were zealously fostered. He surrounded himself with a group of literati, chief among whom was his faithful adviser and friend, Nicolas of Damascus, to whose prolific writings—Athenæus says Nicolas' history contained 144 books—Josephus was so indebted. It was to this group that Eurykles, the rascally Lacedemonian, joined himself with such baleful results.

Nor was his activity restricted to the purely ornamental. Jerusalem had received a new and adequate water supply; his domain was at peace. Banditry had been put down with a firm hand. The circle of fortresses checked inroads from predatory neighbours. His secret police and a strict curfew legislation may well have been irksome; at least it checked the looting of orderly citizens as well as secured the government. In spite of the fierce resentment that could only see Edom grafted upon Rome, the office of high priest used to the alien's own advantage, and an ancient Sanhedrin stripped of its power, if not its prestige, Herod's moderation seems almost surprising. No replica of himself appeared on his coins. Again and again his influence with Roman dignitaries secured justice for Jews who dwelt outside his domain.

The highest tribute to his ability is the fact that his reputation grew so steadily in the eyes of Augustus that from time to time the latter added troublesome frontier districts to Herod's domain, confident that under his oversight the peace would be secure. One example may suffice. After Antony had mastered Iturea and executed Lysanias, he had given the territory to Cleopatra. She in turn farmed the territory out to Zenodorus. The latter weathered the storm which sank Antony and Cleopatra, and was confirmed by Augustus as tetrarch of the "house of Lysanias." Later, however, he not only failed to check the brigands in the neighbouring Trachonitis, but shared their spoils. This endangered the stability of the eastern frontier and made the caravan route from Damascus to the East insecure. Augustus at once intervened, and to secure the peace handed over the three districts, Trachonitis, Batanea, and Auranitis, to Herod (23 B.C.), much to the wrath of Obodas and his Nabateans. Zenodorus protested, but in vain. Three years later, when Augustus visited the East, Zenodorus renewed his complaints. Augustus not only refused to hear them, but added Zenodorus' own domain, which extended south to the Sea of Galilee and thus included Ulatha and Panias, to Herod's kingdom (20 B.C.). Nor did Augustus stop there. Josephus' statement may be a bit fulsome, but the facts he records are undoubtedly substantially correct:

He also made him one of the procurators of Syria, and commanded that they should do everything with his approbation; and, in short, he arrived at that pitch of felicity, that whereas there were but two men that governed the vast Roman empire, first Cæsar and then Agrippa, who was his principal favorite, Cæsar preferred no one to Herod besides Agrippa; and Agrippa made no one his greater friend than Herod beside Cæsar: and when he had acquired such freedom, he begged of Cæsar a tetrarchy for his brother Pheroras, while he did himself bestow upon him a revenue of a hundred talents out of his own kingdom, that in case he came to any harm himself, his brother might be in safety, and that his sons might not have dominion over him.[15]

Perhaps the climax of his whole reign was the visit of this Marcus Agrippa, high commissioner of the East, in 15 B.C. Agrippa is said to have been amazed and delighted at what he saw. In Jerusalem Agrippa "offered a hecatomb of sacrifices to God." Such a signal compliment to their king from the illustrious Roman could not fail to impress Herod's subjects, even against their will. This triumph of Herod's was followed by his trip the next year in Agrippa's retinue north. The journey was one triumph after another. Again and again native Jews embraced the opportunity to appeal to Herod to use his influence for redress of wrongs. Nor did Agrippa refuse his requests.

Thus in many ways Herod's reign were halcyon days. Outside of Judea proper, where religious prejudices did not run so high, Herod appears to have been eminently popular. But dark and bloody days were in store for this truly unfortunate monarch, who could hold his realm secure but whose palace was a seething inferno of plotting and murder.

The tragedy of domestic misery which took place during the last years of Herod's reign has been often told. Indeed, since Josephus' account is so full and vivid, it provides, together with the purely legendary and unhistoric story of the Slaughter of the Innocents, the popular picture of the king, and has caused his real ability to be often overlooked. The story can be briefly told.

In his palace dwelt his several wives—he had had ten in all—each with her children; his sons and daughters with their mates and children; his brother Pheroras who for several years contented himself with receiving the

[15] Josephus, *Antt.* 15,10,3. Pheroras became thus tetrarch of Perea.

revenue from his tetrarchy and took up his residence there only towards the end of his life when his brother's palace was closed to him; his jealous and trouble-making sister Salome, now with one husband, now another; numerous eunuchs, courtiers, and other servants. Among them moved Herod, exultant in having his relations with him, but suspicious and wishing to have no secrets kept from him. It has been well said: "He heard everything, but saw nothing. When he entered his palace, his eyes grew dim." In such a setting only tragedy could result.

His marriage to Mariamne has often been acclaimed as a most politic move. Perhaps it was, but its consequences were dire, for he was thus brought into the most intimate and galling relationship with a family which would have none of him. The earlier chapter of the story—his passionate and clumsy love for his beautiful queen; the constant plotting of her completely malignant and vicious mother; the pathetic end of her aged grandfather; and the murder of her younger brother—has been told. It had seemed, when the sons of Babas had been harried out, that the contest between the dying house and its ruthless supplanter was over. But this was far from the case.

By Mariamne he had had five children. Of these a son died at an early date, the two daughters play no part in the story; in the veins of the two sons, Alexander and Aristobulus, flowed true Hasmonean blood—the pride and arrogance of an Antigonus, the stupidity of a Hyrcanus. Their father sent them to Rome immature boys to be educated under the personal direction of Asinius Pollio. They returned some years later (18 or 17 B.C.) stalwart men. Their arrival spelt disaster. Whatever public sentiment had been years before when Antigonus and his forbears had ruled, those years had taken on a roseate hue. The good old days may often have been very bad old days—and in this case they were—but in the light of present difficulties past disasters fade. At once they caught the fancy of the populace. Salome regarded them, as she had her imperious sister-in-law, with bitter hatred, and at once sought to undermine them with their father. This task was made the easier both by the favour they had aroused in the popular eye and by their own unguarded resentment at their mother's fate. The situation was intensified through the marriage of Aristobulus to Salome's own daughter Berenice. His brother married Glaphyra, daughter of the crafty and powerful Archelaus of Cappadocia.

Salome, aided by her brother Pheroras, played her cards well. Injudicious words of the two princes, dutifully reported by Berenice to her mother, were repeated to Herod, together with the charge that the youths were conspiring to enlist Archelaus' aid in accusing Herod before Augustus. To check their ambition Herod reinstated an older son, Antipater, who together with his mother Doris had been repudiated by Herod at the time he had wedded Mariamne. This afforded Antipater, who now takes his place as the archvillain of the piece, his entering wedge. Now he was appointed chief heir, accompanied Agrippa to Rome to be presented to Augustus, and his mother took up her residence in the palace. The next year he contrived to bring matters to a head: Herod takes Alexander and Aristobulus to Rome to accuse them formally before the emperor. Augustus contrived to smooth matters down, and Antipater, hypocritically masking his rage, congratulated his two half-brothers for being appointed co-heirs with himself. Next Pheroras fell into disgrace. Twice he had refused to divorce his beloved wife in order to marry a daughter of the king. To add to this, he was accused of having told Alexander (falsely) that Herod had been intimate with Glaphyra. Alexander, in wrath, appropriated to his own passions Herod's favourite eunuchs, and furthermore spread the most scandalous stories of doings in the royal court, lending an air of probability by involving himself in the story—he had, he said, yielded to Salome's insistent lustful advances. Then all hell broke lose. Eventually, however, Archelaus straightened the matter out by pretending rage at his worthless son-in-law and threatening to take his daughter home. At this, Herod rallied to his son's defence, as Archelaus had hoped, and the wily Cappadocian returned home satisfied.

Soon, as if these heartrending quarrels with his sons and brother were not enough, he became involved in further difficulties in which Salome played an important, if innocent, part and which might well have cost him his favour with Augustus if not his crown. It chanced that the energetic young Sylleus, prime minister of the Arabian king Obodas, visited Herod's court, and chancing to see Salome, at that moment a widow, fell passionately in love with her, although she was old enough to be his mother. Salome, to quote for a moment Josephus, "because she was at this time less in favour with her brother, looked upon Sylleus with some passion and was very earnest to be married to him." If the whole affair had not had such serious consequences, it would have been ludicrous. Herod, learning of the romance through the titterings of the court women, had his brother observe their actions at table. And "by the signals which came from their heads and eyes" he was straightway convinced "that they were both evidently in love." At this interesting juncture the bashful Sylleus hastily departed, but returned a few weeks later to make formal request for Salome's hand. Herod, persuaded by Salome, was willing, provided Sylleus would submit to circumcision and become a Jew. This Sylleus refused, and returning home in anger involved Herod in serious trouble with Augustus. The circumstances were as follows.

In Trachonitis there had been for years considerable restiveness towards Herod. During Herod's absence in Rome a rumour was spread that he was dead; instantly a revolt broke out. This was checked by Herod's officers, but the ringleaders fled to Arabia. On his return Herod took stern measures to punish the trouble-makers. Their relatives were executed, but the culprits themselves, now augmented to about a thousand, were beyond his reach, but were constantly raiding his frontier. Herod appealed to Saturninus, governor of Syria, for permission to force the Arabians to surrender the trouble-makers and to pay the six hundred talents which Sylleus owed him. Upon receiving this permission he proceeded to enforce his rights. In spite of Arabian opposition he was successful, summarily executed the robbers, settled three thousand Idumeans in Trachonitis to keep the peace, and returned to Jerusalem.

News of this affair came to Sylleus, who was now in Rome. At once he proceeded to use it to Herod's disadvantage. He completely garbled the story to Augustus, representing Herod as a reckless disturber of the peace. This touched Augustus on a sore point. It was the one unforgivable sin. In anger he wrote Herod that while heretofore he had considered him a friend, he should now treat him as a subject. The Arabians, egged on by Sylleus, began to invade the Perea, while the inhabitants of Trachonitis rose against the Idumean garrison. Herod, in disgrace with Augustus, was afraid to move. To be sure, Aretas, who had succeeded Obodas as king in Arabia, wrote Augustus that Sylleus was a dishonest and licentious servant, had actually murdered his erstwhile master Obodas, and was plotting to gain the kingdom for himself. Still Augustus refused to believe the stories. In this crisis Nicolas of Damascus set out for Rome. He finally convinced Augustus of Sylleus' duplicity and proved that the latter had completely distorted the facts; that Herod had been guilty of no recklessness, but had been entirely justified in what he had done, had been authorized by Saturninus, and had been most moderate. Augustus was convinced. Sylleus was sent home to repay his debt to Herod and then to be executed. Augustus was on the point of dispossessing Aretas of Arabia—he had incurred his anger for not having waited for Roman confirmation—and transferring it to Herod to make amends for his unjust suspicion, when a letter was received from Herod asking permission to execute his sons, Alexander and Aristobulus. Eurykles, a scoundrelly member of Herod's band of literati, had acted as a continual plotter and had engineered the whole scheme. Herod was convinced, and upon the advice of Salome decided to act. This letter cost Herod Arabia, for, although Augustus granted permission to Herod to act as he saw fit, he felt it unwise "to add another government to him, now he was old, and in an ill state with relation to his sons."[16] Upon Augustus' advice Herod called a council, composed half of Romans, half of Jews. The evidence was heard; the majority of the judges were convinced of the guilt of the accused; the two sons were executed and three hundred supporters were stoned to death (7 B.C.).

So far Antipater had been successful. Now he started to corrupt his

[16] Josephus, *Antt.* 16,10,9.

father's friends; even Pheroras became his tool. The lynx-eyed Salome could not be fooled. Step by step she followed the plot and reported to her brother. Finally becoming suspicious, Antipater sought and received permission to go to Rome. During his absence there Salome convinced her brother of the true character of his favourite son. Finally Herod's eyes were opened. Antipater was summoned home. A little apprehensive, yet not realizing that the game was up, for Herod had not revealed his true feeling in the letter, Antipater returned. At once he sensed his danger, but it was now too late to fly. Putting on a bold face, he entered his father's presence—Varus, the new governor of Syria, sat at Herod's side—and sought to embrace him. The air was electric. Herod rose:

> Even this is an indication of a parricide, to be desirous to get me into his arms, when he is under such heinous accusations. God confound thee, thou vile wretch; do not thou touch me till thou hast cleared thyself of these crimes that are charged upon thee. I appoint thee a court where thou art to be judged: and this Varus, who is very seasonably here, to be thy judge; and get thou thy defence ready against tomorrow, for I give thee so much time to prepare suitable excuses for thyself.[17]

The next day he was convicted. Herod, now an old and broken man, stayed punishment until word should come from Augustus. Word finally came. Augustus had approved the death sentence, although he gave Herod permission instead to banish the villain, should he choose. It is reported that Augustus, always a coiner of *bon mots*, had remarked, "Better is it to be Herod's pig than son."[18] Herod was on his death bed. An insolent demonstration took place. The golden eagle over the temple was torn down. Indomitable Herod, dying though he was, rallied; the forty ring-leaders were burnt alive, the rest executed. And Antipater, just as he thought he had escaped death, for word had been brought that Herod was dead, was led out to his well-deserved execution. Five days later in Jericho Herod died in agony (4 B.C.).

The funeral was magnificent. The bier was of gold embroidered with precious stones; the body, dressed in royal purple, wearing both diadem and crown of gold and holding his sceptre, lay on a rich purple bed. His many sons and relations, heavily armed guards, five hundred servants with spices in their hands—all these conveyed the dead monarch to his last resting-place in Herodium. In all the pomp there was not a single trace of sorrow. Like Jehoram before him, he "departed without being desired."

---

[17] Josephus, *Wars* 1,31,5.
[18] Macrobius, *Saturnal.* ii,4,11. In Greek, of course a neat pun ὗν – υἱόν.

Chapter IV

TETRARCHS, PROCURATORS, AND AGRIPPA

THE death of Herod left Palestine without a king. Herod had made three wills in rapid succession. In the first, Antipater, then basking in his father's favour, had been nominated with Herod (Philip), a son of the second Mariamne, as successor. When Antipater's wickedness came to light, the will was promptly altered. Antipas, a son by Malthace, became heir to the whole kingdom. But this will, too, was speedily changed by the bewildered old man. In place of one heir, three sons of Herod were to share the kingdom: Antipas was to receive Galilee and Perea with the title tetrarch; his elder brother Archelaus Judea, Samaria, and Idumea with the title king; Philip, their half-brother and son of Cleopatra of Jerusalem, the heterogeneous district to the northeast of the Sea of Galilee which had been granted Herod piecemeal by Augustus—Gaulanitis, Trachonitis, and Paneas. His title, like Antipas', was to be tetrarch. Salome received the three important cities, Jamnia, Ashdod, and Phasaëlis. Other members of his family received grants of money; to Augustus a princely sum was left. Thus Palestine was dismembered, although a half-century later it was to be once more temporarily reunited.

Even before Archelaus could hasten to Rome for the sanction of Augustus the storm broke. At first Archelaus may have tried conciliatory measures; against his will he deposed the high priest and appointed a new one. During the Passover season, however, fresh disturbances broke out; Archelaus sent out his troops; three thousand of the rioters were killed, and the rest of the pilgrims sent home. At this juncture the new king sailed for Rome. His was a critical situation. The confusion he had left at home speedily turned into anarchy. Philip, who had remained behind, was powerless. The Roman officer, Sabinus, whom Augustus had sent temporarily to administer Herod's domain, was worse than useless. Not only was he unable to quiet the troubles, but actively fomented them by robbing the temple openly at the time of Pentecost. The holiday visitors, always ready for excitement, joined in, and Bedlam was let loose in the city. Quickly the insurrection spread. Leaders arose simultaneously in Idumea, near Jericho and Emmaus, in Galilee, and across the Jordan. Several of these—Judas, the son of that Hezekiah whom Herod had summarily executed, near Sepphoris in Galilee; a former slave of Herod named Simon in the Perea; a shepherd Athronges supported by his four militant brothers—actually sought to gain the kingdom themselves.

In this crisis, which was fast becoming dangerous, Varus, then governor of Syria, found it necessary to intervene. He had already come south at the time of Sabinus' arrival, but thinking the situation in hand had returned to Antioch. Now he hastened south with relief legions. The first blow was struck in Galilee. Sepphoris, the scene of Judas' insurrection, was burned to the ground and its populace sold into slavery. Then by forced marches through Samaria—this alone of Herod's domain had refrained from insurrection—he hastened to Judea. The rebels melted before the dreaded legions. Relentlessly Varus pursued them, thoroughly dispersed them, crucified two thousand of the ringleaders, and returned to Antioch, leaving the land numbed if not quiet. Archelaus and his brother Antipas returned to find their land in a sorry plight, many towns in ruins, the people sullen and hostile.

During this interlude of blood Augustus had considered the disposition of the territory. At least two hearings had been held. Archelaus' claims had been challenged by Antipas, who demanded the whole domain as the second will had specified. He even claimed, and he was supported by many of his other relatives, that Herod had been insane when he issued the third will. Two delegations of Jews had pleaded that Judea be annexed directly by Rome; if this were refused, they preferred Antipas to Archelaus. But the eloquence of Nicolas of Damascus, whom Archelaus had inherited together with his land, saved the day. Augustus was loath to alter Herod's will—another proof of the favour which the dead king had enjoyed in Roman eyes—and the final will was ratified practically as written: The Greek cities, Gaza, Gadara, and Hippos, were taken from Archelaus and added to the province of Syria. Archelaus must content himself with the title ethnarch. He should receive the title king if he should later prove worthy. This was never realized.

Now Palestine—like "all Gaul"—was divided into three mutually independent parts: the ethnarchy of Archelaus, roughly half of the former kingdom, including Samaria, Judea, and Idumea with the exception of the cities above mentioned; the tetrarchy of Antipas, comprising Galilee and Perea with a tribute roughly one-third of what his brother received; and the tetrarchy of Philip, the remaining territory—Batanea, Auranitis, Trachonitis—with a still smaller tribute.

Archelaus, of whom we know little—Josephus' sources obviously ran dry for this period—at once commenced to rebuild his limited domain. We learn, curiously enough, only of the activity in and about Jericho. In this city the palace which had been demolished during the days of the rebellion was restored; twelve miles to the north appeared a new city, Archelaïs; a valuable palm grove near by received a new water supply. In addition to manipulating the office of high priest—during his short reign he appointed two—he completely scandalized Jewish scruples by marrying Glaphyra, the widow of his ill-fated half-brother Alexander. Not only had Glaphyra borne three children to Alexander, but had separated from her second husband, King Juba of Libya.[1] Thus from every angle the union was outrageous in Jewish eyes, although quite innocent from the standpoint of sophisticated Rome. He even alienated the Samaritans who had been staunch supporters of Herod and had remained completely aloof from the hostile demonstration of 4 B.C. Finally in the tenth year of his rule Jews and Samaritans alike appeared in Rome to bring formal accusations of gross mismanagement against him (6 A.D.). This was the one offence Augustus would not condone. Archelaus was summoned peremptorily to Rome, convicted of the charge, and banished without ceremony to Vienna, a city on the Rhone. His territory became a Roman province with a governor, called a procurator, directly responsible to the emperor. This situation continued through the ministry of Jesus. But, before we consider the steps taken to transform Judea into a Roman province, we may turn for the moment to see how the other two brothers fared in their domains.

At the same time that Archelaus had returned to Jerusalem as ethnarch his two brothers, Antipas and Philip, had been confirmed in their rule. Though Archelaus was removed after nine years of incompetence—during the boyhood of Jesus—and his domain was turned into an imperial province under procurators of whom Pontius Pilate was the fifth, both Antipas and Philip were more successful. Philip remained in office till his death in 34 A.D.; Antipas five years longer (39 A.D.), then, as a consequence of the ambition of his wife and the greed of his brother-in-law, to fall into the bad graces of Caligula and to be banished. Both of them were thus ruling throughout Jesus' life and ministry, while it was in Antipas' territory that almost all his life was spent.

Antipas was the shrewdest and ablest of Herod's sons. Of him we know little except for gossipy bits from Josephus and occasional comments in our gospels, as "that fox," which Jesus is said to have employed.[2] He was never a favourite with Augustus, as his father had been, although no charges were ever brought against him. Disappointed at the beginning of his term of office at receiving but a small part of the kingdom when he had expected the whole domain, he may well have hoped to receive the territory of Archelaus at the time of the latter's disgrace. But no such fortune was his. With the accession of Tiberius, however, everything changed. Through the twenty-three years of this emperor's reign Antipas basked in royal favour. Apparently he occupied the position of spy to keep the morbidly suspicious emperor informed of affairs in the East. It has been not improbably conjectured that

---

[1] Josephus' (*Wars* 2,7,4) statement that Juba was dead is quite in error, as Schürer, *op. cit.,* Div. I, Vol. II, p. 40, n. 7, demonstrates.

[2] Luke 13:32.

it was this function which brought him into Pilate's bad graces;[3] certainly his relations with Vitellius, legate of Syria, were often strained.

He inherited his father's fondness for magnificence and building. Some ten years after his appointment he rebuilt the city of Sepphoris which had been razed by Varus, and made it his capital. Sepphoris was but an hour's walk across the hills from Nazareth. That Jesus was one of the workmen who helped in restoring it to be "the ornament of all Galilee" is surely quite within the reach of probability. Across the Jordan in the Perea he rebuilt the fortress town Betharamphtha and named it Livias, later changed to Julias, both names in honour of the wife of Augustus. A few years later (26-27 A.D.) he built the magnificent city of Tiberias near the hot springs of Emmaus on the heights overlooking the west shore of the Sea of Galilee. The fact that this city was built on the site of an old burying-ground made it unpopular for the stricter Jews. This was not so serious as it would have been in Judea, for the population in both Galilee and Perea was hybrid. Many were compelled to settle there; gifts and largesses were granted others to ease their consciences. Thus with its mixed population it became a definite Hellenistic centre. Its organization was definitely Greek with a council of six hundred headed by an archon and committee of ten. Along with its palace and synagogue was a stadium. Its streets were colonnaded, while the whole was surrounded by a wall. Although not so large as Sepphoris, which it now supplanted as capital of the whole tetrarchy, it is said to have been even more magnificent. Today it remains the only town of the many which then girdled the lovely lake.

Although a pagan at heart, he sought successfully not to affront his Jewish subjects. Like Herod before him, he put no image on his coins. Apparently he joined with the Jews in a successful protest against Pilate's attempt to set up the votive shields in Jerusalem. The fact that he remained in office over forty years speaks well for his tact and ability.

His disastrous downfall was due to the cardinal weakness of all the Herods—entanglements with women. Early in his career he had married the daughter of Aretas, king of the Nabateans. This was a wise political move, for the Nabateans had always been restive as they saw territory they felt their own in Jewish hands. Now some years later while on a trip to Rome he had lodged en route with his half-brother Herod—called Philip, probably through confusion with Philip the tetrarch, by gospel writers[4] but not by Josephus—who had been appointed by Herod to be Antipater's eventual successor in the first will, but who had later incurred his father's suspicions and had lived as a private citizen. During this visit Antipas fell in love with his sister-in-law Herodias. On his return home she soon came to him with her daughter Salome. Antipas' first wife, getting wind of her hus-

---

[3] Luke 23:12.
[4] Mark 6.17; Matt. 14:3; Luke 3:19 (inferior Mss.).

band's unfaithfulness, contrived to go to her father Aretas. Now the latter's only tie with Antipas was broken, and he became openly hostile, but apparently had to bide his time for revenge. In 36 A.D. actual hostilities broke out. Antipas was signally defeated and appealed to his patron, Tiberius. The latter, incensed at Aretas' high-handed measures, sent Vitellius, still legate of Syria, against the disturbers of the peace, with orders to bring back Aretas dead or alive. Vitellius, as already remarked, had no love for his colleague, but could not disobey the imperial order. While the campaign was under way, word came of Tiberius' death. At once Vitellius left Antipas in the lurch and returned to Syria, ostensibly to await orders from the new emperor.

Antipas' star was setting. Not only was he obliged to see his enemy, Aretas, who was well in his grasp, escape, but he had lost his powerful friend, Tiberius. He soon found that in the new emperor Gaius (Caligula) 37-41 A.D. there had once more arisen a new king who knew not Joseph. The young wastrel brother of Herodias, Agrippa, whom Antipas at his wife's request had once had to aid, had long been a boon companion of the new emperor. Soon he contrived to bring Antipas into disfavour at Rome. He, Agrippa, had received the tetrarchy of Philip, now dead, and with it the title king. This piqued the ambitious Herodias. Finally she prevailed upon her husband to request the same title for himself. Antipas was reluctant, for he rightly feared Gaius. Finally he yielded and started for Rome. Agrippa craftily contrived to have Antipas accused of plotting with Rome's enemy, Sejanus, and of having a large arsenal stored up. The latter charge Antipas could not deny. His disgrace was immediate. Shorn of his power, he was summarily banished and his territory entrusted to the unscrupulous Agrippa. Thus ended the long rule of Antipas. The only bright spot in his sudden downfall was the loyalty of Herodias, who had involved him in the fatal mess. Scorning imperial clemency for herself, she followed her husband into exile with the words:

> Thou, indeed, O emperor! actest after a magnificent manner, and as becomes thyself, in what thou offerest me; but the kindness which I have for my husband hinders me from partaking of the favour of thy gift, for it is not just that I, who have been made a partner in his prosperity, should forsake him in his misfortunes.[5]

We can defer until later the question of John the Baptist's part in Antipas' misfortune. What is now of moment is to remember that during Jesus' ministry Antipas was high in Roman favour at the head of the tetrarchy of Galilee and Perea.

Of the last of Herod's three heirs we know next to nothing. By his father's will he had received the territory to the east and north of the Sea of Galilee. It was far from being a promising inheritance. Naturally turbulent, one of

[5] Josephus, *Antt.* 18,7,2.

the reasons Augustus had given it to Herod was to ensure its peace. Herod had had to employ strong measures to bring it into line. In Batanea he had settled a Jewish colony from Babylon as a garrison; in Trachonitis some three thousand Idumeans to keep the peace. For the most part its inhabitants were Arabs and Syrians. Philip, however, proved an excellent ruler. He appears to have been just, peace-loving, and with his people's interests at heart. Until his death he kept the peace, and, better yet, the goodwill of his turbulent subjects who had hitherto been such a menace to the *pax Romana*. Of him Josephus writes:

> He had shown himself a person of moderation and quietness in the conduct of his life and government; he constantly lived in that country which was subject to him; he used to make his progress with a few chosen friends; his tribunal also, on which he sat in judgment, followed him in his progress; and when any one met him who wanted his assistance, he made no delay, but had his tribunal set down immediately, wheresoever he happened to be, and sat down upon it, and heard his complaint: he there ordered the guilty that were convicted to be punished, and absolved those that had been accused unjustly.[6]

Well outside Jewish influence, his was openly a gentile court. Images were used on his coins, but without disturbing his subjects. Like all the Herods, he was fond of building and on the site of Panium, his capital, erected the beautiful city of Cæsarea Philippi which had the rights of asylum. On the northeast shore of the Sea of Galilee, where the Jordan flows in, he transformed the village of Bethsaida—apparently not to be identified with the Bethsaida of the gospels—into a flourishing city which he named Julias, after the profligate daughter of Augustus. Since Julia was banished by her father in 2 B.C., this building took place early in Philip's reign.

The one other item preserved to us is concerned with his family life. A bachelor for many years, he finally married Salome, the daughter of Herodias[7] by her former marriage, and thus allied himself even more closely with his half-brother Antipas, with whom he seems to have been on friendly terms. At his death in 34 A.D. his territory was first annexed to the province of Syria, and then three years later was transferred by the new emperor Gaius (Caligula) to his boon companion, Agrippa, under whom for a short time all Palestine was once more to be united.

In 6 A.D., while Antipas was tetrarch of Galilee and Perea and Philip remained secure in his domain, Archelaus had come to grief. Angered at the evident proof of mismanagement, Augustus had banished him and, ignoring Antipas' wistful hopes, had decided to place the confiscated territory under direct Roman rule as a province. Quirinius, who at this time chanced to be

---

[6] *Antt.* 18,4,6.
[7] Apparently to be identified with the dancer who asked for John the Baptist's head according to the gospel story (Mark 6:22; Matt. 14:6).

governor of Syria, was entrusted with the preparatory measures. Here we may briefly consider the types of provinces Rome had.

As we have already seen, Octavian—soon to be known as Augustus—following the defeat of his erstwhile ally, Antony, had speedily become the chief figure in Roman politics. Quickly he had gathered the various threads into his own hand and by the senatorial decrees of 27 and 23 B.C. had become the undisputed master of the situation. Control of the military and absolute authority over all frontier provinces which required troops had been achieved in a masterful manner. The remaining provinces, which constituted no especial problem nor danger, he graciously allowed the Senate to control.[8]

Augustus' provinces, known as the "provinces of Cæsar," fell into two classes: (1) the more important and wealthy districts received as governors men of senatorial rank, to be sure, but whose entire responsibility was to the emperor; their title was *legati pro prætore*; (2) minor provinces which required troops to keep order, either because of their frontier location or the restlessness of their inhabitants, on the other hand, received as governors members of the equestrian class—an order which Augustus had shortly restored. These governors, who like their brothers, the proprætors, were responsible solely to the emperor, were known as *procuratores*. Egypt, too, was directly in Augustus' hand, but its administration was different. Nominally Augustus was king of Egypt. His local representative was accordingly a viceroy. This officer was also a knight, for no senator might ever set foot in Egypt. This precaution was taken to prevent any senatorial *coup de main*, for Egypt was of vital importance to Rome, being, as it was, the great granary of the empire.

The remaining provinces were known as the "provinces of the people" and were responsible to the Senate. Annually they each received as governor an officer with the title *proconsul*. The proconsul might or might not have actually held the consulship in Rome; in the case that he had, five years must elapse before his provincial incumbency began. In contrast to the imperial governors (*legati pro prætore* and *procuratores*) whose term of office depended on the pleasure of the emperor, the office of proconsul was limited strictly to one year with no possibility of reappointment. With these general facts in mind we can pick up the threads of the story.

At the same time that Coponius was sent as first procurator to Judea, Quirinius, the new proprætor of Syria, was sent to Jerusalem to enroll the inhabitants as provincials and to assess the taxes. To achieve these ends a census was necessary. To Quirinius' surprise, opposition met him. Together

[8] In this connection it will be well to reread pp. 51-53; Duckworth's essay, "The Roman Provincial System" in Jackson and Lake, *The Beginnings of Christianity,* Vol. I, pp. 171-217, provides a full and authoritative account of the whole matter.

with an age-long reluctance to any "numbering," as intense as it was irra-
tional, was the feeling that since the land belonged to God all taxes there-
from were his peculiar property and that a personal (poll) tax was a fresh
badge of servitude. The real opposition, however much the leaders may have
stressed a religious note, was surely a patriotic unwillingness to lose the last
vestige of the independence which they had fought so hard to achieve. Judas
of Galilee (called by Josephus, "a Gaulonite of a city whose name was
Gamala")[9] and who probably, although this has been disputed, is to be
identified with Judas the son of the Hezekiah whom Herod had many years
before executed,[10] sought to raise an insurrection in Galilee. Though Galilee
was not included in the census or taxation, the feeling of Jewish solidarity
had not been affected by the dismemberment of Herod's kingdom. The revolt of Judas was short-lived; he was soon defeated and killed, and Judea
was now definitely under Roman rule.

A word of caution may not be out of place here. It is often said that this
revolt of Judas' was the start of the Zealot party which from that time on
was constantly fomenting opposition to Rome and which ended by plunging
the nation into its final bloody destruction. Far from this being the start of
the movement, it would appear to have been but one additional step in the
opposition that blazed out first many years before in Galilee as a protest
against Rome's hireling Antipater and his son Herod. Josephus, with his
desire to minimize Jewish opposition to Rome, had stigmatized Hezekiah
as a robber and brigand. It is most probable that Hezekiah and his followers
had considered themselves patriots of the first water. Again, the term Zealot
for this home-rule party, while almost universally employed, is most uncertain. Josephus contents himself with calling them "the fourth philosophy,"
i.e., the fourth group or sect in Judaism, whom he thus distinguishes from
the other three: Pharisees, Sadducees, and Essenes. His first explicit use of
the term "Zealot" is of one group of these disgruntled patriots who many
years later (66 A.D.) under the leadership of John of Gischala started a reign
of terror. Nor is the revolt of Judas, or for that matter any of the subsequent
disturbances of "the fourth philosophy," safely to be dubbed "Messianic."
The first leader in the history of Judaism who seems to have called himself
definitely a Messiah was Bar Cochba in the days of Hadrian (*ca.* 132 A.D.).[11]
No greater danger confronts a student of Christian beginnings than that of
using technical phrases in a loose and inexact sense, popular though the
practice be.

Although the new province of Judea (comprising the three districts Judea,
Samaria, and Idumea) was nominally quite distinct from Syria, in special

[9] *Antt.* 18,1,1.
[10] See p. 42.
[11] For the moment we can reserve the question as to whether Jesus of Nazareth made such a
claim. With this possible exception the above statement holds.

emergencies the procurator appears to have been required to consult his northern colleague. The latter apparently had authority to interfere at his own discretion if he feared the situation was becoming unmanageable. At any rate, several such occasions are mentioned by Josephus.[12] That the Syrian legate could himself call a procurator to account is doubtful; that he could relieve him from office, send him to Rome for trial, and assume temporary command is proved by the action of Vitellius, who in 36 A.D. sent Marcellus to relieve Pilate whom he ordered to Rome.

Except for this power of intervention, the procurator, who was directly responsible to none save the emperor, was supreme in his province. In him were vested full military, judicial, and financial authority. In contrast, to an important province such as Syria with a standing army of several legions,[13] Judea had only auxiliary troops, raised from the country itself. Since Jews were exempted from military service from the time of Julius Cæsar, these troops appear to have been largely recruited from the district around Sebaste, and were popularly known as the Sebastians. Garrisons were maintained in strategic points through the province; in Jerusalem a cohort was garrisoned in the Antonia, just to the north of the temple.

The procurator lived in Cæsarea and contented himself with seeing that the machinery of government ran smoothly. He would go up to Jerusalem with an additional guard at the times of the various feasts to make certain that the festival throngs did not become over-boisterous. On other occasions Jerusalem was quite free from his presence. Judea was divided into some eleven toparchies, each with its local Sanhedrin. Before these local courts the great majority of cases were tried. Those of sufficient importance to warrant it were referred to the great Sanhedrin in Jerusalem which had gained a new lease of life and importance with the new system of administration which entrusted it with most matters of government. It has usually been assumed, not alone from the express statement in John 18:31 but from the descriptions of the trial of Jesus as given in the Synoptists, that the sentence of death was forbidden the Sanhedrin; that this sentence the procurator alone might pass. But this, while perhaps not improbable, is by no means sure and has often been flatly denied.[14] Further questions as to its composition and province may be reserved until a later page.

The picture, often painted, of Judea being ground down by harsh governors is hardly historic. Rome was a remarkably cautious and long-suffering mistress. Her governors were always instructed to allow the provinces as much freedom from irksome control as was possible. The Jews were accorded especial privileges. Their religious prejudices were scrupulously guarded. Roman guards aided the temple police in keeping the sacred pre-

---

[12] *Antt.* 18,8,2-9 (cf. *Wars* 2,10,1-5); *Antt.* 20,1,1; *Wars* 2,14,3; 2,16,1; 2,18,9-11.

[13] Three in the days of Augustus; four in the days of Tiberius.

[14] See Juster, *Les juifs dans l'empire romain*, Vol. II, pp. 132-142.

cincts inviolate. No attempt to force emperor worship upon Judea was ever made, save perhaps by the mad Caligula—and that attempt was speedily given up after its dismal failure. A simple superscription, without the head of the emperor, appeared on the coins. To be sure, the governors had the authority—and exercised it—to appoint and depose high priests. This, though a scandal, was nothing new, for Herod and Archelaus had both done it. Until 36 A.D. the robes of the high priest were kept in the Antonia under the authority of the governor, and were formally handed over to him at such times as he needed them. Later this restriction was removed. The abuses of taxation which are familiar to all readers of Cicero's blistering arraignment, *Against Verres,* were no longer practised. Rome carefully audited the financial sheets of her provinces. The governor received a fixed salary. The taxes, amounting perhaps to six hundred talents, were for the most part spent in bettering the province itself—roads, harbours, and public buildings. The balance went to the imperial treasury. No longer were the taxes farmed out, but were collected by salaried government officers. The procurator was of course the head of the financial organization. He apparently worked in conjunction with the local Sanhedrins in the actual collection.

The most real source of grievance in an otherwise excellent arrangement was the matter of the customs (internal revenue). These, in contrast to the direct taxes, were still farmed out. That is, bids were made for the right to collect the duties in the various districts. To the highest bidder went the privilege. All the money collected by this individual, known as a publican,[15] over the bid was his; should he fail to collect the full amount, he must make it good from his own pocket. It need hardly be said that this latter circumstance rarely occurred. The position of publican and his subordinates was open to abuse of power, especially if the governor winked at excesses. For the most part there seems to have been a fixed tariff for each sort of duty and an attempt to prevent extortion and graft. None the less, since the duties were so numerous—the list is a truly formidable one—and could be collected so often on the same consignment on even a short journey, they constituted a sore point. The collector was naturally cordially hated. Was he not a servant of Rome engaged in a legal theft of what belonged to Jehovah? For a Jew to be engaged in such a nefarious trade—and not a few Jews succumbed to the temptation of a lucrative position—was doubly obnoxious. Both the rabbinical literature and the gospels heap contempt upon them. In the former they are usually designated "robbers"; in the latter they are regularly associated with sinners and harlots.

Thus the actual government was pretty much in the hands of the native aristocracy, of which the high priest was the head. Both at the time of the death of Herod and later at the deposition of Archelaus there had been a

---

[15] The individuals referred to as "publicans" in the gospels are improperly so styled. They were his underlings.

definite request that the territory be appended to Syria. This request had been prompted by the double hope of getting rid of the house of Herod and of obtaining actual self-government under the Roman ægis. Though this request had been refused and a governor was now in the field, it soon must have become clear to the unprejudiced that affairs had turned out far better than had been feared. Actually the more solid and stable element in Judea appears to have accepted the new order with resignation, if not with alacrity. But the fires of revolt were not out. They were to be kept alive by the fanatic patriots who stubbornly believed that eventually, and that right early, God himself would rally to their defence and would overthrow all opposition, even that of proud Rome herself, should they but make the initial move. In spite of the fears of the politically powerful and the disapprobation of the learned and devout, this band was destined to persist in their mad hopes which ended in a dreadful carnival of blood.

The first four procurators of Judea are hardly more than names to us. Coponius, Marcus Ambivius, Annius Rufus, and Valerius Gratus followed one another in rapid succession. The last of these, Josephus says, was in office eleven years, but of these years he records next to nothing.[16] In 26 A.D. the fifth was appointed, Pontius Pilate. Estimates of Pilate are difficult. Christian prejudice, due to his part in the execution of Jesus, finds confirmation in the story of Josephus of his several clashes with his subjects and in the bitter words which Philo quotes from the letter of Agrippa to Gaius.[17] On the other hand, it is to be observed that Tiberius kept him in office for ten years (26-36 A.D.). This is no light recommenda- tion, for Tiberius, especially in his latter years, kept a lynx-eyed watch on his provinces. And when in 36 A.D. Pilate dispersed a crowd which he well might have thought dangerous to peace and order, he was promptly sus- pended and sent to Rome by his senior colleague in Syria. Accordingly, when reading the stories of Josephus, one should remember that the latter is at pains to cull out and magnify all the outrages of the later procurators in order to try to prove his contention that a naturally friendly and grate- ful nation had been driven against its will into the fearful rebellion of the years 66-73 A.D., largely as a result of the reckless and incompetent governors whom Rome had sent. Nevertheless, since Pilate is of especial interest to us because of his minor part in the tragedy on Calvary, we may briefly mention the little that is known.

Hardly had Pilate reached Judea when the first clash came. For reasons which are by no means clear, troops were dispatched from Cæsarea to Jerusalem, ostensibly to go into winter quarters, but actually, according to Josephus, "to abolish the Jewish laws." Under cover of the night the im-

---

[16] *Antt.* 18,2,2.
[17] *Legatio ad Gaium* 38(§§299 ff.)589M.

perial standards bearing Tiberius' image were taken into the city. In the morning they were discovered and the word spread. Incensed at this deadly insult—no previous governor had attempted this—many flocked to Cæsarea to demand that the offence be removed. For five days Pilate remained obdurate; on the sixth the mob was admitted to the racecourse, only to find itself surrounded by soldiers who threatened them with death if they did not desist and return quietly home. Far from being cowed, the Jews bared their necks to the Roman swords, preferring to die than to yield. Pilate could not afford to take such a step, and ordered the offending banners withdrawn to Cæsarea.

This incident is significant. It reveals the restraint under which a governor worked. He must keep order but without unnecessary violence. Furthermore, it reveals the essentially freer atmosphere in Cæsarea; there the banners were at least tolerated, in Jerusalem they were taboo. Pilate may well have felt such distinctions too subtle for him.

A little later another difficulty occurred. Pilate started the construction of a new aqueduct to bring water to Jerusalem from a distance of some twenty-five miles. A distinct advantage for Jerusalem, and a costly one, he not unnaturally considered that the expense might be borne by the temple treasure. When, in spite of opposition, he persisted, he was confronted by a wrathful, shrieking mob and personally insulted. This he would not brook. Soldiers in civilian dress mingled with the crowd and dispersed it.

A third incident, somewhat resembling that of the banners, is mentioned in the letter of Agrippa to Gaius, already mentioned. Votive shields were set up in the palace of Herod—used by Pilate as his Jerusalem residence. Although these shields bore no images, but were simply inscribed with the name of Tiberius, an uproar resulted. Agrippa and his four sons joined their pleas to those of the Jerusalemites, but in vain. Finally a letter was sent to Tiberius. Peremptory word came to Pilate and the shields were withdrawn.

The statement in Luke 13:1, "Now there were some present at that very season who told him (i.e., Jesus) of the Galileans, whose blood Pilate had mingled with their sacrifices," indicates that Jewish restiveness provoked other disturbances in addition to those described by Josephus.[18] An outburst of fanaticism in Samaria caused his downfall. An imposter claimed to be able to reveal the sacred utensils of the temple which from the time of Moses had lain concealed. His hearers were impressed and followed him with weapons to a little town at the foot of Gerizim. From there they planned to ascend the mountain. The scheme miscarried. In the village they were surprised by Pilate's soldiers; many were slain, others imprisoned and later executed. In indignation the Samaritans complained

---

[18] Cf. also the reference to those men "who in the insurrection had committed murder," of whom Barabbas was one (Mark 15:7).

to Vitellius, the propraetor of Syria; in spite of the fact that the crowd had been heavily armed—which may well have led Pilate to be skeptical regarding the innocence of their design—Vitellius at once relieved Pilate from office and ordered him to make his defence to Tiberius. Before Pilate arrived in Rome Tiberius had died; here the luckless governor, who seems throughout his ten year service to have sought zealously to maintain order and to better his province, drops from the pages of history but not from those of legend and romance.

Marcellus, whom Vitellius had appointed procurator pro tem. until Pilate should be returned or his successor appointed, appears, if we can believe Josephus, to have been hardly more than a figurehead during his brief incumbency. Josephus does not further mention him, but contents himself with recounting the popularity of Vitellius who remitted all taxes on fruits bought and sold in Jerusalem, and did away with the custody of the vestments of the high priest. It is not improbable that even before his disgrace Pilate had suffered some diminution in authority due to the advent of Vitellius, endowed as that latter was with extraordinary power by Tiberius.[19] With the death of Tiberius Marcellus was replaced by Marullus, who remained in office during the four years of Gaius (37-41A.D.), but without exciting any comment from Josephus.

The death of Tiberius was not such a blessing as his subjects had enthusiastically believed. Tiberius' prophecy that his young grandnephew, Gaius (Caligula), would prove to be a curse both to himself and everyone else[20] was speedily justified. Tiberius' will, in which Gaius was named only co-heir with the emperor's weakling grandson, was annulled by the Senate, and the son of the beloved Germanicus was invested with the title *imperator* and the full power which Augustus and Tiberius had enjoyed. Hopes ran high at the thought of having exchanged the morbid and dread misanthrope for the gallant young Gaius, who but a few years before—he was now but twenty-five—had been the idol of his father's troops and had received the affectionate nickname *Caligula*, from the little boots his doting mother Agrippina let him wear to please them. Those hopes were destined to cruel disappointment. His opening speech to the Senate was full of the fairest promise. His aim was to be that of Augustus. Like his illustrious predecessor, he would share his responsibilities with the Senate. After a gala six months he fell dangerously ill. Unfortunately, he recovered; the remaining three and a half years of his rule were one long debauch of murder, lust, and theft, brought to an end in his own palace

[19] Cf. Tacitus, *Annal.* vi,32—"*Et cunctis quæ apud Orientem parabantur L. Vitellium præfecit.*"

[20] "'*Exitio suo omniumque Caium vivere*' et '*se natricem populo Romano, Phaëthontem orbi terrarum educare*'"—Suetonius, *Caligula* 11.

by the hand of one of his prætorian guards. That the empire continued its course in spite of its madman ruler was due partly to the fact that Augustus had welded together an organization so able that it could run itself, partly to the wise and courageous statesmen, both at home and abroad, who dared to call down the lightning on their own heads by modifying their ruler's mad demands.

One of the first acts of the new emperor, Gaius, had been to give to his boon companion, Agrippa, grandson of Herod the Great, the territory which had formerly been the tetrarchy of Philip, together with the smaller tetrarchy of Lysanias. For several years these districts had been loosely appended to the great province of Syria. With them went the title of king. The story of his whole career, as sketched by Josephus,[21] reads like a romance. With Hasmonean blood in his veins—his grandmother was Herod's favourite, Mariamne—educated in Rome; befriended by the Roman matron Antonia; constantly getting into one financial scrape after another; at one time on the verge of suicide; for a time occupying a minor position in the tetrarchy of Antipas through the good offices of the latter's wife, Herodias, Agrippa's sister; soon leaving this position and taking up with the proprætor of Syria; speedily convicted of taking bribes there and forced to leave that province; barely escaping arrest more than once for his debts, yet always contriving to borrow from some sympathetic friend—he had finally found himself in a Roman prison as a result of an incautious word to his friend Gaius, which had been tattled to Tiberius and construed by the latter as treason against himself. Since Gaius rightly considered this last misfortune of Agrippa's to be the result of the latter's loyalty to himself—how disinterested Agrippa had been is quite another matter—it is not surprising that when he had become emperor

there did not many days pass ere he sent for him to his house, and had him shaved, and made him change his raiment; after which he put a diadem upon his head, and appointed him to be king of the tetrarchy of Philip. He also gave him the tetrarchy of Lysanias, and changed his iron chain for a golden one of equal weight.[22]

How Agrippa soon contrived to gain for himself through sharp dealing the domain of his brother-in-law Antipas (39 A.D.), although the latter had once proved to be a friend in need, has already been told.[23]

Soon came the assassination of Gaius and the accession to the Roman throne of his fifty-year-old uncle Claudius (41-54 A.D.). Estimates of this new emperor are difficult. Destitute of practical experience in governing, long looked upon with ill-disguised contempt by his intimates for his irresolution of character, dominated by the imperial freedmen—chief among

[21] *Antt.* 18,6,1-11.
[22] Josephus, *Antt.* 18,6,10.
[23] P. 65.

whom was the wretched Callistus who had aided him to the throne—he soon proved as unsatisfactory to the Senate as had his predecessor. The coarseness of life in the imperial court and the outrageous insolence of the freedmen is vividly portrayed in the fragments of the *Satyricon* of Petronius known as "The Banquet of Trimalchio." On the other hand, Claudius had been an eager student of Roman history and gave himself whole-heartedly to the administration of his empire. Due perhaps partially to his desire to follow the precedents of his predecessors, especially Julius and Augustus, he adopted the wise plan of managing Judea as Augustus had done, through a local prince who understood the people and was at the same time loyal to Rome.

King Agrippa was the logical man. Claudius was already under obligation to him for his influence upon the Senate. Furthermore, Agrippa had become a popular hero in Jewish eyes and would be most useful in quieting an outraged Judea. During the anti-Jewish uprising in Alexandria Agrippa had been mobbed and thus had become a martyr; a little later he had presented a petition to Gaius in behalf of the Alexandrian Jews. Most popular of all was his effectual aid to the Palestinian Jews in dissuading Gaius from his mad insistence that a statue of himself be set up in the temple in Jerusalem. To kotow to the emperor, who was now demanding divine honours from his subjects, and to annoy the local Jews, an altar to Gaius had been set up by the heathen citizens of Jamnia. This the infuriated Jews promptly demolished. Wind of this came to Rome. Wrathfully the emperor commanded that a statue of himself be set up in the Jerusalem temple. At the same time word was sent to Petronius, the new propraetor of Syria, to proceed to Jerusalem with a strong force to see that the order was executed. To all this the latter most reluctantly complied. As he expected, deep-seated opposition broke out; in vain he counselled the Jewish leaders not to make a bad matter worse. They replied that though they would not raise arms against Rome, they would die rather than see their laws thus shamefully violated. In desperation Petronius wrote a cautious letter to Gaius requesting a delay "until the harvest was over." This did not aid matters; it simply deferred the evil day and exasperated Gaius. Finally the growing opposition led the perplexed Petronius to take the final step. He withdrew his soldiers to Antioch and wrote the emperor to advise him to rescind the obnoxious edict which he had not dared to enforce.

At this juncture Agrippa, who was in Rome and had not heard of the crisis in Palestine, learned of it. In horror he used his personal influence with Gaius and, contrary to expectation, succeeded where even Petronius had failed. The edict was withdrawn, although Gaius pettishly forbade any interference with altars or temples to himself which might be built outside of Jerusalem and sent word to Petronius to commit suicide for having ventured to disobey his command. Fortunately for Petronius, the message was delayed; four weeks before the belated messenger arrived word had come to Antioch that Gaius was dead.

Accordingly, the whole Roman province of Judea—Judea, Samaria, and Idumea—was added to the kingdom of Agrippa. Once again a Jewish king sat in the seat of David. The Jewish blood might be thin, but through the Hasmonean grandmother it was there. For three years (41-44 A.D.) he ruled over the reassembled Palestine of his grandfather Herod. He seems to have been as popular as Herod had been hated. He had come in on the flood wave of popularity; his first act was to hang up in the temple, as a sign of reverence for its sanctity, the golden chain he had three years before received. Before such piety hatred against Rome, which might well have led to a flash-in-the-pan rebellion, quickly subsided. While probably no more a Jew at heart than his illustrious predecessor, he was always meticulous to avoid shocking the religious scruples of his subjects. How well he succeeded is illustrated by the encomiums pronounced upon him by Josephus and the rabbinical writings. One example may suffice. The story is told that on the Feast of Tabernacles he read the passage Deut. 17:15, "One from among thy brethren shalt thou set king over thee; thou mayest not put a foreigner over thee, who is not thy brother." Remembering his Idumean blood, he burst into tears, thinking himself meant, only to be comforted by the shout: "Be not grieved, Agrippa! Thou art our brother, thou art our brother!"[24] His prospective son-in-law, Epiphanes of Commagene must first promise to be circumcised; an outrage upon a Jewish synagogue on the Phœnician coast was speedily stopped through his influence; Palestinian coins were free from images. Although, like a true Herod, he built lavishly, erected outside of Palestine theatres and baths at his own expense, had the games cele;rated in Cæsarea, and apparently erected statues in that latter city to his daughters,—of this activity Josephus tactfully remarks: "But Agrippa's temper was mild and equally liberal to all men. He was humane to foreigners, and made them sensible of his liberality"[25]—"he kept himself entirely pure; nor did any day pass over his head without its appointed sacrifice."[26]

Apparently he flirted with the dream of making his little kingdom independent of Rome. At any rate, Marsus, the new governor of Syria, thought the walls of Jerusalem were becoming suspiciously high and broad. His report to Claudius brought from the latter an order to stay this building.

---

[24] This tradition is found in the Mishna Sotah 7,8; Sifrè Deut. §157; Midr. Tannaim *loc. cit.* It is, however, to be observed that all the later rabbis were not so complaisant. According to a Baraita in the name of R. Nathan, "The Israelites made themselves liable to extermination when they flattered Agrippa," *i.e.*, by disregarding Deut. 17:15—G. F. Moore, *Judaism*, Vol. II, p. 190.

[25] *Antt.* 19,7,3.

[26] *Ibid.*

Shortly after, Agrippa invited five of the other vassal princes[27] to a conference at Tiberias. Unfortunately for his scheme Marsus, though uninvited, appeared, too, and promptly interfering sent the others home. Thus the two tentative attempts towards a free Jewry proved worse than useless, for it is not impossible that they were among the reasons that led Claudius' advisers to oppose the latter's plan to send Agrippa's young son to succeed his father. At any rate, when in 44 A.D. a sudden and dramatic illness[28] brought the brief rule of the popular king to a close, Rome reverted to her former policy of sending procurators to the little state. But since in Agrippa Palestine had been reunited, the jurisdiction of these later procurators, of whom Cuspius Fadus was the first, was no longer limited to the former province of Judea—that is, Samaria, Judea, and Idumea—but embraced the whole domain. The appointment of Agrippa had allayed the increasing hatred of the Jews for Rome; now that foreign governors were once more in the land they were to find their task increasingly difficult. The brief interlude had whetted the appetites of the revolutionaries; its close was easily construed a fresh degradation. Small wonder it is that as the years rolled on the air grew tenser and tenser. Each overt act on the part of the populace brought stricter supervision from the governor; this in turn provoked greater opposition. It needed no prophet to see that there could be but one outcome. Disaster was sure; the only question was when would the moment come.

With the fate of the Jewish state trembling in the balance, we can now leave the outward history of the period to review briefly some other aspects of the thought and organization of Judaism, without a knowledge of which a true understanding of early Christianity would be quite impossible.

[27] Herod of Chalcis, Sampsigeram of Emesa, Cotys of Lesser Armenia, Antiochus of Commagene, and Polemon of Pontus.

[28] Josephus, *Antt.* 19,8,2; Acts 12:21-23.

Chapter V

IN THE TIDEWAY OF GREEK THOUGHT

DURING the brief survey of Jewish history we have been chiefly concerned with Palestine; but all the Jews did not live there. In fact, those who lived in Palestine comprised but a fraction, and a small fraction at that, of all Jewry. Furthermore, many Jews who resided in Palestine were actually as much in the dispersion as their brethren in Alexandria or Antioch. The seacoast towns, except Joppa and Jamnia, were prevailingly gentile; the tetrarchy of Philip almost completely so. To be sure, Galilee and part of the Perea were nominally Jewish, but the population was far from pure. When Judas the Maccabee had made his stand against Syria, one of his first moves had been to send Simon into Galilee to round up the Jews there and to settle them near Jerusalem; he himself had performed a similar service across the Jordan. In the very heart of Antipas' domain was a league of ten independent Greek cities. This confederation had taken place when Pompey had freed them from the domination unto which they had been brought by Alexander Jannæus. The largest of them, Scythopolis, was on the west side of the Jordan. The other nine—Hippos, Gadara, Pella, Philadelphia, Gerasa, Dion, Canatha, Raphana, and Damascus[1]—lay in Batanea and the Perea. To speak of the Decapolis as a political unit is surely incorrect. It was simply a league of cities, united by trade bonds, free from Antipas and each apparently loosely under the oversight of the governor of the province of Syria. One needs but recall that even Tiberias, the capital city of Antipas, was built on the site of a graveyard and the great herds of swine who played an important part in the tale of the Gerasene demoniac[2] to find fresh light cast upon the words attributed to Jesus, "Go not into any way of the gentiles, and enter not into any city of the Samaritans: but go rather to the lost sheep of the house of Israel."[3]

Attempts at numbering ancient populations are of necessity largely guesses; consequently the number of Jews at the time of the Christian beginnings has been variously computed. Perhaps four to four and a half million, or roughly seven percent of the total population of the Roman world, is a fair guess. In line with the early and fairly probable statements[4] that there

[1] Pliny, *Hist. Nat.* v,16(18). The exact status of Damascus has been often discussed and is not clear.
[2] Mark 5:1-20.
[3] Matt. 10:5 f.
[4] Cf. Philo, *In Flaccum* 6(§43)523M.

were a million Jews in Egypt alone, rather more in Syria, probably at least ten thousand in Rome at the time of Tiberius, this figure does not seem excessive. Of this total probably not more than seven hundred thousand were to be found in Palestine.

After the northern kingdom had fallen (722 B.C.), about the only part of Palestine of which the inhabitants could claim to be true Israelites were the highlands of Judah and Benjamin. The various conquests of Tiglath-Pileser, Sargon, and Sennacherib and the more systematic deportations of Nebuchadnezzar while not depopulating Palestine, as has sometimes been assumed, removed the flower of Jewry and may be seen as one of the important factors leading to that invisible empire upon which in reality the sun never sets, for, as Agrippa wrote Gaius, Jerusalem was the capital not only of Judea, but of most of the countries of the earth. Subsequent years saw fresh deportations of Jews outside their traditional borders, as those of Artaxerxes Ochus (340 B.C.) on the shores of the Caspian Sea, or of Pompey (63 B.C.) to Rome. These enforced migrations may well be the reasons why Jewish writers regularly regarded the dispersion as a great misfortune—which it distinctly was not, at least for Judaism—a punishment from God for Israel's sins, which would in the golden future be withdrawn when the time of chastening should be over. This familiar view finds expression in one of the Psalms of Solomon:

> They were cast away among every nation, from out of the inheritance which the Lord gave them: that Israel might be dispersed according to the word of God; that thou mightest be justified, O God, in thy righteousness by reason of our transgressions.[5]

Later rabbis, as Eleazar (third century), might make virtue of necessity and see the dispersion of Israel among the nations as God's way of making proselytes.

But deportations were not the only causes of the dispersion. Voluntary migrations to Egypt were also taking place as the overthrow of Jerusalem before Babylonia became imminent. Jeremiah's fulminations,

> Thus saith Jehovah of hosts, the God of Israel, If ye indeed set your faces to enter into Egypt, and go to sojourn there; then it shall come to pass, that the sword, which ye fear, shall overtake you there in the land of Egypt; and the famine, whereof ye are afraid, shall follow hard after you there in Egypt; and there ye shall die,[6]

were disregarded; many turned to the south, and, tragedy of tragedies, forced the prophet to go with them. Colonies of Jews appeared in Migdol,

[5] Psalms of Solomon 9:2 f.
[6] Jer. 42:15 f.

Tahpanhes, Memphis, and Pathros.[7] In Syene and Elephantine were flourishing colonies with a sanctuary and apparently sacrifice to Jehovah. Even
after the Persians destroyed the Egyptian sanctuaries this one seems to
have remained until finally it was destroyed by Egyptians enraged against
Persia. Thus many years before Alexander the road from Palestine to
Egypt was open and was trod by many Jews.

Throughout the Persian period Jewish colonization went on apace. By
the fourth century there were thousands of Jews in Egypt, Mesopotamia,
Persia, and Media, in addition to scattered groups near the Caspian. Due
to the religious toleration shown by Persia, the connecting links with the
homeland were unbroken. Then came Alexander the Great, and the Jews
began to go west. His conquests turned what had been barred and dangerous tracks into safe and open roads for trade, and many Jews hastened
to make the most of them.

Of the doings of the emigrant Jews we know little, for they left few
permanent memorials. Strabo's remark as quoted by Josephus,[8] "Now these
Jews are already gotten into all cities; and it is hard to find a place in the
habitable earth that hath not admitted this tribe of men, and is not possessed by them," was anticipated by the Sibyllist who sang in the middle
of the second century B.C.,

> All the earth is full of thee,
> Aye, and even all the sea.[9]

While the catalogue of those who were present at Jerusalem for the Feast
of Pentecost[10] raises many critical problems which may be reserved for a
later page, it evidences the far-flung front of Jewry. Josephus' oft-repeated
story[11] of the exploits of the two brothers, Asineus and Anileus, in the
city of Nahardea on the Euphrates is not without value to the student as
an indication of the numbers of Jews who lived quite content away from
Palestine, as well as of their twofold devotion to their ancestral customs
and to brigandage and of the not unnatural disfavour with which they
were regarded by their neighbours. Another story of Josephus[12]—that of
Helena and Izates of Adiabene—which is equally worth the reading, shows
their zeal for making proselytes and the not infrequent success—especially
among the women—even in the highest circles. Juster[13] refers to a community of Jews in Media at the town of Gazaca so ignorant that they had

[7] Jer. 44:1.
[8] *Antt.* 14,7,2.
[9] *Orac. Sibyll.* iii,271.
[10] Acts 2:9-11.
[11] *Antt.* 18,9,1-9.
[12] *Antt.* 20,2,1-5.
[13] *Les Juifs dans l'empire romain*, Vol. 1, p. 203, n. 2. This very important work, while
scarcely adapted for continuous reading, provides an immense amount of information.

never even heard of the Halakah[14] and who found the stories of the Flood and of Job, as recounted to them by Akiba, fascinatingly new.

While actual evidence for Jews in Arabia, as listed by Juster, is scanty and very late, there can be little question that they were there at an early date. Josephus mentions them in his preface to the *Wars*,[15] while "Arabians" were present at Jerusalem according to the catalogue of Acts mentioned above. It will be remembered that Paul went thither immediately after his conversion.[16]

Syria and Asia Minor contained vastly more Jews than did Palestine itself. The intimate, if not always pleasant, connexion between Palestine and the Seleucid empire to the north resulted in large migrations northward. As already mentioned, the title "citizen of Antioch" was one which many Jews had coveted and obtained at an early date. From an early date Ephesus had been a great Jewish centre; in Antioch of Pisidia and in Iconium Paul is said to have frequented the Jewish synagogues, as was also the case when he had crossed over into Europe. In the great mercantile cities of Corinth and Thessalonica and in Athens itself synagogues were to be found. Had we the full story of the uprising of Jews in Cyprus against Trajan, it would probably be as dramatic as the account of the awful struggle a generation earlier in Palestine.

In Alexandria we have the clearest picture of the changes that came into Judaism as a result of residence in an alien but friendly environment. As mentioned in a preceding page, at least a million Jews dwelt complacently in this second Athens and the country to the south. The city itself had been built by Alexander as a step in his program of linking east and west. At his death it had passed into the hands of the Ptolemies. They had proved excellent rulers, and achieved their dreams of making their capital city the chief centre of the intellectual and religious, as well as of the economic, world. The famed museum with its chapels, halls, and libraries has been aptly called the prototype of our college foundations. Such names as Euclid, Apollonius, Eratosthenes, and Ptolemæus give it a fame that can never die. The library was one of the wonders of the world; at the death of Ptolemy Philadelphus numbering 100,000 rolls it was increased by each successive emperor till it reached the stupendous total of 700,000. Then in 47 B.C. during the siege of the city by Julius Cæsar it was burnt—Gibbon says totally. Reëstablished, it once more achieved fame, only to be destroyed by the fanatical caliph Omar in 640 A.D. Incidents such as these turn the historian sick at heart. What a wealth of knowledge of the past would have been ours had it not been for such wanton outrages.

[14] The rules for observing the written law. Readers who share this ignorance may consult p. 106 below.
[15] §2.
[16] Gal. 1:17.

In this truly cosmopolitan city with its temple to Serapis, the cult to Isis replete with imposing and noble ritual, the Jew dwelt an honoured citizen. Not alone in the specifically Jewish quarters to the east of the island Pharos, but throughout the city, his synagogues were to be found. One of them is described in lavish terms in an ancient quotation in one of the tracts of the Talmud as so huge as to be able to contain twice as many as had left Egypt under Moses, and that it was found necessary to indicate to the waiting congregation the proper time for the "Amens" by waving flags.

Here in this oasis to the south, free for the most part from persecution, the Jewish citizens readily assimilated the alien culture and philosophy of the Greeks. Alexandrian Judaism, which made its direct contribution to life and thought through the literature it produced, is of prime importance to us not alone because it throws into clearer relief by contrast the peculiarities of Palestinian or, as it has been called, "normative" Judaism, but because of its influence upon Christianity through the great Alexandrian teachers of the second and third centuries—Pantænus, Clement, and Origen.

Although outside of Alexandria Greek culture never made any very real impress upon the Egyptians, in the city it came to its greatest bloom. From the days of Alexander Greek soon became not only the language of culture, but of business. Inhabitants of the city simply could not live without it. It was in Alexandria that its effect upon Judaism was soonest noticed. Although the Jews of the dispersion retained their religious loyalty and ceremonial observances, and though Jerusalem remained, as Agrippa wrote, "the mother city, not of a single country, but of most of the countries of the world," to which pilgrimages were ever being made, it was impossible for Jews who had spent their lifetime in business in Greek cities to retain Semitic speech. Just as Aramaic had superseded Hebrew, after Alexander Greek became increasingly necessary. In Alexandria it was a sheer necessity, not a luxury. Its adoption was a tribute which the Jews gladly paid to the great gentile community which sheltered them. The Greek was not the scholastic Greek of the museum nor the artificial imitation of it which is seen in those who aped the Attic diction. Rather it was the street patois, a strange conglomerate of many alien elements.

Soon a problem arose. Judaism was primarily a religion of a book. That book was the Torah. And the Torah was written in Hebrew, now an almost unknown tongue to the rank and file in Alexandria. If Judaism was here to survive, a translation was necessary. This need was soon met, and successive years saw the sacred Scriptures appearing in a Greek dress. The so-called *Letter of Aristeas* gives a romantic account of the origin of the translation, known to us today as the Septuagint. Aristeas, a courtier in the service of Ptolemy Philadelphus, in his letter to his brother Philocrates relates a trip he had recently made to Jerusalem. The reason for the trip was as follows: One day the chief librarian in Alexandria had told the king, who was interested in Jewish antiquities, that they needed a translation of the Jewish laws. Philadelphus agreed and sent a deputation to the high priest Eleazar asking for men to perform the task. To this request the high priest gladly acceded, and sent accredited scholars—six from each of the twelve tribes—bearing a copy of the Hebrew Scriptures embossed in gold on fine skins. After the king had tested them with hard questions at a banquet, the work of translation began on the island of Pharos. Each day they compared what they had written and thus produced their text. In seventy-two days the work was finished as if the very period had been prearranged. The work was enthusiastically received by the Jews; when read to the king, he expressed his approval and reverence.

The letter is pseudonymous and legendary, obviously the work of a Jew who, desirous of magnifying the importance of his race, puts this panegyric upon Jewish law and wisdom into the mouth of a gentile noble. Both Philo and Josephus are familiar with it, and the latter points out that it was only the Pentateuch that was thus translated:

For he [*sc.* Ptolemy Philadelphus] did not obtain all our writings at that time; but those who were sent to Alexandria as interpreters gave him only the books of the law, while there was a vast number of other matters in our sacred books.[17]

Early Christian writers who quoted and added to the letter did not always observe this limitation, and the whole Greek Old Testament came to be known as the Septuagint. Jerome, to be sure, was better informed and remarked, "All Jewish scholars assert that only the five books of Moses were translated by the seventy." Epiphanius, whose claims to sanctity do not rest on either his accuracy or truthfulness, apportions the thirty-six books of Scripture among an equal number of pairs of scholars! Thus stories grow.

Thus the legend casts very little light on the origin of the version. Perhaps the Pentateuch may have been translated early in the third century, but it was almost certainly done, not to enrich the royal library but for the use of Jews whose knowledge of their ancestral tongue had lapsed. The remaining books were apparently translated sporadically as the years went by. The prologue to the Wisdom of Jesus ben Sirach (Ecclesiasticus) indicates that all the Prophets and some of the Hagiographa had been translated by 132 B.C. By the dawn of the Christian era probably almost all of the remaining writings had appeared in Greek dress. The importance of this version can scarcely be exaggerated. Without it it is hard to see how Judaism could have survived among the masses of the dispersion. Nor was its influence limited to Judaism. The early Christians adopted it as their sacred Scripture and exercised such proprietary rights that the second century of our era saw three successive Greek versions—those of Aquila, Symmachus,

[17] Preface to *Antt.* §3.

and Theodotion—produced by an outraged Jewry, nominally to provide more accurate translations; actually because the Septuagint had become essentially a Christian book.

Precisely because Greek had entirely supplanted Hebrew and even Aramaic as the language of thousands of Jews, and because even in Palestine Hellenism had made such advances, a brief excursus here may not be out of place.

That Greek was being spoken in cities such as Cæsarea, Sebaste, Tiberias, Sepphoris, and those of the Decapolis is of course certain. Undoubtedly it was also understood by many Jews in Jerusalem. It should not, however, be taken for granted that it had replaced Aramaic or was even on a parity with it in the smaller towns and villages of Palestine or the East. In spite of many modern loose statements the bilingual nature of Palestine should not be unduly stressed. It is utterly impossible to argue from analogy or to get a cross section of the whole land, since the usage was apparently totally different in different places.

This is made strikingly clear by a detail in the fascinating *Life of Porphyry* by Mark the Deacon. Porphyry was bishop of Gaza (*ca.* 395-420 A.D.), a city which from its very beginning had been non-Jewish. He was very much disturbed by the presence of the heathen temple of Marnas in his diocese. Finally he betook himself to Constantinople and by a series of clever tricks which revealed that at least one son of the light was as wise as those of the world obtained imperial sanction for the demolition of the obnoxious Marneion. On his return to Gaza he still found his task uncompleted, for the devotees of Marnas had fortified their temple. While pondering as to the best means of procedure, a seven-year-old child stepped forward and through divine inspiration gave them instruction in Aramaic. Then to the vast amazement of the listeners he repeated it in Greek. Then Mark says, "And calling his mother the bishop asked her whether she or her son knew the Greek tongue: but she affirmed with oaths that neither she nor her son knew Greek."[18] This incident, occurring about four hundred years after the ministry of Jesus, and in a Greek city, indicates that the Greek tongue was but little known to the lower classes of Palestine at any time.

To cite the presence of Greek inscriptions[19] and the presumption that in the cities Greek was known among the educated classes is as futile as to try to prove that Americans know Latin from the fact that college diplomas are penned in that tongue and that Catholic priests are supposed to be able to converse in it. Occasional Greek words and terms may have worked their

[18] *Vita Porphyris* 68. This very important document is available in English translation and will prove a mine of useful information to the student of Christian beginnings.

[19] The Hasmoneans had coined their money with both Greek and Hebrew inscriptions. From the time of Herod it was limited to Greek.

way into the Aramaic speech, but because a man today uses such words or phrases as *rendez vous, café, restaurant, hors de combat, menu,* and *table d'hôte* does not constitute evidence that he speaks or understands French. When Paul wished to speak to people in Jerusalem he spoke in Aramaic.[20] Similarly, when Titus repeatedly called the Jews to surrender, he "sent Josephus to speak to them in their own language."[21]

Among the better educated classes, on the other hand, it was probably pretty well known. As we have seen, Hellenistic districts surrounded Palestine; even in the interior there were cities like Scythopolis and Sebaste. Before the Maccabean revolt Palestine had been in the hands of rulers whose culture was Greek. Many of the high priests had been on the side of Greek civilization. Some of the Hasmoneans had promoted it. Herod and the Romans had been definite protagonists; the former had surrounded himself with Greek literati; one of them, Nicolas of Damascus, was his chief adviser. Festivals and Greek games, mercenary soldiers, whom Josephus says Herod had employed, the throngs of Greek-speaking Jewish pilgrims who came to the feasts—all these must have made it easy for the Jerusalemites to have picked up a smattering of the language. Galilee was nominally Jewish, though probably largely by the path of conversion, but the cities had large numbers of Greeks, as is indicated by Josephus' remark:

But Jesus and his party slew all the Greeks that were inhabitants of Tiberias, and as many others as were their enemies before the war began.[22]

Finally, it may be remembered that in the Mishna[23] it is said that at the time of Titus fathers were forbidden to allow their sons to learn Greek. This has usually been interpreted to mean that formerly this had been practised.

We may accordingly conclude that the educated and richer classes in the cities did know Greek—in greater or less degrees—but that the uneducated peasants in the hill countries, among whom were Jesus and his early disciples, did not for many years. And this conclusion is all the securer from the hint in the *Life of Porphyry* that even in the Hellenistic city of Gaza the lower classes had failed to learn the tongue.

The Septuagint may well be called the flower of Alexandrian Judaism; in addition to this were other works which may be briefly mentioned. Any detailed examination would lead us far afield. While Judaism in Palestine was summoning defenders to throw off the galling yoke of enforced hellenization from Syria in the Maccabean revolt, the Jews in Alexandria were concerned with a very different problem. Their attempt was to commend their faith to the gentiles, if not to win converts, at least to create a favourable

[20] Acts 21:40; 22:2.
[21] *Wars* 5,9,2; cf. 6,2,1; 6,6,2.
[22] *Life* 12 (end). This Jesus was the son of Sapphias, one of the rebels in the great war.
[23] M. Sotah 9,14.

and respectful disposition toward Judaism and the law. Accordingly, in contrast to the pugnacious Daniel or gloating Esther the Hellenistic literature is largely apologetic, an attempt to put the best foot forward. Of course in religion apologetics is always combined with polemics. God's herald must always war against the emissaries of Satan. Thus in these writings is regularly contained a bitterly sarcastic attack on the animal worship of Egypt. Of the few monuments of Alexandrian Judaism five may be listed: (1) Wisdom of Solomon; (2) IV Maccabees; (3) Letter of Aristeas; (4) parts of the so-called Sibylline Oracles; (5) Philo.

In all this literature is the attempt to approve Judaism to students of Greek philosophy and to prove that all that is worth while and sound in the latter is contained—was, in fact, anticipated—in the former. Epicureanism was to every Jew an abomination on account of its reputed atheism and emphasis on pleasure as the *summum bonum* of life. His hatred of it was only surpassed by his ignorance of what it actually was. Academic Skepticism as taught by Carneades and Cicero was completely beyond his horizon. Its emphasis upon "suspension of judgment" illustrated by the saying of Sextus Empiricus, "Nothing of itself is either good or ill,"[24] ran counter to everything in his religion. Popular Stoicism, on the other hand, with its theistic turn, its popular monotheism, corresponding hostility to polytheism, and belief in divine retribution, was highly acceptable. Thus in all these writings the classic tetrad of virtues, which from the days of Plato had been the law and the prophets to all Greek ethical thought regardless of school and which Stoicism had appropriated as its own (prudence or wisdom, fortitude, temperance, and justice), plays an important rôle. In the Wisdom of Solomon wisdom is recognized as the root of all the virtues and is practically identified with the "Spirit of God"; her fruits, however, are the classic four.[25] Similarly IV Maccabees evidences Stoic influence:

> For reasoning does not rule over its own affections, but over such as are contrary to justice, and manliness (*i.e.,* courage), and temperance, and prudence; and yet over these, so as to withstand, without destroying them.[26]

> And the forms of wisdom are prudence, and justice, and manliness, and temperance.[27]

Philo finds (allegorically) in the four streams that encompassed Eden an indication of these four cardinal virtues.

The Wisdom of Solomon, written sometime after the Septuagint and before the Christian era, is in regulation manner attributed to Solomon, who is made to prize wisdom above all else. The book is in a way a polemic

[24] xi,140, p. 716.
[25] Wisdom of Solomon 8:7.
[26] IV Macc. 1:6.
[27] *Ibid.* 1:18.

against irreligion in general and against Skeptics and Epicureans in particular. Wisdom is the best thing in the world. Wisdom is religion. True religion is revealed religion as God has given it to the Jews in Scripture. Consequently, the height of folly is irreligion, particularly the denial of divine providence and retributions, and, almost as bad, false religion with its worship of many gods and idols, which finds its culmination in the animal worship of the Egyptians, which every pious Jew, be he ever so irenic, delighted to ridicule. The writing is valuable not alone for itself, but for the light it casts upon its author—probably representative of many of his time. His knowledge of Greek philosophy was but rough-and-ready, acquired, so to speak, "in the air," not as the result of the study of books. That he was of Alexandrian origin is almost certain from his spite toward the worship of animals and his tone in the chapter on the exodus from Egypt and the plagues. Here we have a Jew who thought in Greek; there is no slightest evidence that he knew Hebrew or Aramaic. The Septuagint was his Bible.

Little need here be said of IV Maccabees. Its contrast with the Wisdom of Solomon, however, is instructive. The author, while but a dilettante in Greek philosophy, is very proud of his knowledge and writes in a bombastic and pseudo-literary style, attempting to phrase the most ordinary and commonplace truths with profundity and rhetoric. His thesis is simply: One can live a pious life if he follows the demands of pious reason. This he seeks to prove "with the greatest force from the fortitude of Eleazar, and seven brethren, and their mother, who suffered death in defence of virtue."[28] Then follows a gross and gruesome epitome of those tales of torture from II Maccabees. That the author came from Alexandria is not clear; he is a good illustration, however, of the Hellenistic Jew who sought to ape Greek ways but without the knowledge or ability of a Philo.

Of the Sibylline Oracles only the barest mention is possible. Suffice it to say, from an early time written records of supposed oracles from the Sibyl—later she came to have numerous sisters!—were known and held in the highest reverence. Apparently it was in Alexandria in the second pre-Christian century that Jewish ingenuity turned this effective type of writing to its own advantage. Just as some nameless Jew adopted the clever device of making the courtier Aristeas speak in reverential terms of Judaism and its law, so now the ancient Sibyl is cast in that rôle. Few works of antiquity bristle with more literary and historical problems, for these writings were edited and rearranged not alone by many Jews, but also by later Christians again and again.

In Philo we meet the greatest mind Hellenistic Judaism produced. To what extent he influenced his fellow religionists is uncertain; the influence he exerted upon Christian theology through the famous Alexandrian school

[28] IV Macc. 1:7,8.

cannot be over-emphasized.[29] In contrast to the layman author of the Wisdom of Solomon and the superficial producer of IV Maccabees, in Philo we meet a man thoroughly trained in Greek philosophy but at the same time a fervent Jew whose chief interest is religion. In this latter respect he is head and shoulders above Josephus, who lost what little interest he may originally have had in religion for its own sake as a result of the disaster which his nation had suffered at the hands of those who had a zeal, but not according to knowledge.

For Philo, Greek philosophy and biblical revelation were identical in scope and content. He thus, perhaps in a unique degree, stood as the bridge between Judaism and Hellenism over which Christian theology was to cross. His contributions were many and important. Two may be selected for brief comment. The first of these is his conception of the Logos. God, as pure Being, was transcendent, yet he exercised effective oversight over the phenomenal world. This was effected through the Logos, that is, active divine intelligence, the creative word and revealer of the absolute God. This conception of the Logos—actually almost a secondary god—was a veritable amalgam of the Platonic-Stoic Reason and the Jewish Wisdom and creative word of God. Christianity came later to see in Jesus the embodiment of this divine preëxistent Logos. For Philo, in addition to the Logos were subordinate and partial manifestations of divine reason or logoi. Over this dizzy and swaying bridge between pure Being and the world of phenomena the thinking of millions of his spiritual descendants has sought to pass.

Though his teaching of the Logos has often been hailed as his greatest contribution, his use of allegory as the philosopher's stone which would turn biblical stories into sound philosophical principles has had perhaps even greater effect upon subsequent generations. From the days of Anaxagoras (460 B.C.) the antics of the gods on Olympus had been interpreted in an allegorical sense, for a growing sense of ethical responsibility, quickened by the gibes of the philosophers, had forced the issue. If Homer—the Bible of the Greeks—was not thus to be interpreted, either he was impious or the gods were grossly immoral. Thus the robust story of the loves of Ares and Aphrodite, with the outraged husband Hephæstus standing in the background, was to be seen as a picture of iron subdued by fire and restored to its original hardness by water. When Odysseus filled his ears with wax to drown the songs of the Sirens, we have an allegory of the righteous filling their senses and powers of mind with divine actions and words, so that passions and pleasures which tempt all men on the sea of life might knock at their doors in vain. Of course, according to Homer, Odysseus did no such thing at all. Cornutus, to whom we are indebted for this gem of interpretation, evidences the two requirements for the successful allegorist: *viz.*, (1) indifference to

[29] W. Fairweather, *Jesus and the Greeks*, pp. 161-216, is well worth reading at this juncture.

historical details, with a readiness to suppress or alter them whenever necessary; (2) a complete lack of even a rudimentary sense of humour.

Orthodox Judaism had long seen the values in this type of interpretation.
In the Old Testament lay hidden senses and teachings, implicit but not explicit. These were to be recovered at all costs. Sentences, individual words
(especially when spelled in an unusual manner), and at a later time even
vowel points were of the profoundest value in making the text teach something entirely different from its real meaning.[30] Trivial points thus bore
great weight. Rabbi Akiba claimed to have saved the Song of Songs by this
means of interpretation. Certainly later Christians did so. Solomon in these
exquisite but erotic poems typified Christ; the Shunamite maiden, the Christian church. Thus Christ could sing of the charms of the Church without
the somewhat minute anatomical descriptions of the poems offending.

In Philo allegorical interpretation was reduced to a system. Although pro-
fessing—and believing—to retain the literal sense of the narratives as carrying
in themselves historical facts as well as moral insights, he nevertheless made
the allegorical more prominent, and never scrupled to turn the story upside
down to gain the allegorical significance. Jacob, for example, took a stone
for his pillow at Bethel. What this lover of virtue actually did was to select
one of the incorporeal intelligences of which the sacred region was full and
to apply it to his own mind as to the head of a united body, and, using the
pretext as if he were going to sleep, placed the whole of his life as the lightest
possible burden upon it.[31]

At times Philo willingly altered the text if he felt that it represented
God in an unworthy or impossible sense. How, for example, could Adam
actually *hide* from God? Nor did he hesitate to say flatly that some of the
statements of the Pentateuch—curiously he rarely quoted either the Prophets
or the Writings—could have nothing but an allegorical meaning. How then
were we to understand references to "talking serpents" and "trees of life"?
In fact, in his writing, especially in the *Allegories of the Sacred Laws*, the
modern reader is surprised to see how frankly, if prolixly, Philo recognizes
some of the narratives, as the six-day creation of the world or the forming of
Eve from Adam's rib, as purely mythical.

I have given more space to this type of pseudo-exposition than it deserves,
because of the use made of it by early Christian writers. For Paul the precept,
"Thou shalt not muzzle the ox when he treadeth out the corn," was written
to allow Christian missionaries to be supported by the people to whom they
ministered.

Is it for the oxen that God careth, or saith he it assuredly for our sake? Yea, for
our sake it was written: because he that ploweth ought to plow in hope, and he

---

[30] See further pp. 104-106.
[31] *de Somniis* 21(§§127 ff.)640M.

that thresheth, to thresh in hope of partaking. If we sowed unto you spiritual things, is it a great matter if we shall reap your carnal things?[32]

When the children of Israel drank from the rock, they "drank of a spiritual rock that followed them: and the rock was Christ."[33] Of the story of Hagar and Sarah he explicitly says:

Which things contain an allegory: for these women are two covenants; one from Mount Sinai, bearing children unto bondage, which is Hagar.[34]

Early Christians found it very valuable as a means of discovering traces of Christ in the Old Testament. The author of the so-called Epistle of Barnabas was peculiarly expert in this sort of thing. When Moses spoke to Joshua— since Barnabas wrote in Greek the latter, of course, was Jesus—and told him that the people should listen to him alone, he did so because the Father was revealing everything concerning his Son Jesus.[35] The classic instance, however, occurs a few pages earlier in the same writing. It is worthy of being quoted in full:

Learn fully then, children of love, concerning all things, for Abraham, who first circumcised, did so looking forward in the spirit to Jesus, and had received the doctrine of the three letters. For it says, "And Abraham circumcised from his household eighteen men and three hundred."[36] What then was the knowledge given to him? Notice that he first mentions the eighteen, and after a pause the three hundred. The eighteen is I and H—you have Jesus[37]—and because the cross was destined to have grace in the T[38] he says "and three hundred." So he indicates Jesus in the two letters and the cross in the other. He knows this who placed the gift of his teaching in our hearts. No one has heard a more excellent lesson from me, but I know that you are worthy.[39]

Similarly Justin Martyr interprets "The government shall be upon his shoulders" to mean "Christ will be hung on the cross." This type of interpretation is, of course, a relic of an earlier, pre-scientific day. No serious student pays any heed to it today, although its exponents still exist. They are usually far less clever than their earlier forbears, for English is not nearly so productive of these subtleties as were Hebrew and Greek.

No survey of the dispersion of Israel would be complete without a brief

---

[33] I Cor. 9:9-11.

[33] I Cor. 10:4.

[34] Gal. 4:24.

[35] Barn. 12:8.

[36] Greek expresses numerals by the letters of the alphabet. I (iota) is 10; H (eta) 8; T (tau) 300. Thus 318 would normally be expressed TIH. Barnabas' ingenuity is piqued because instead he read IHT, i.e., 18 and 300.

[37] IH are the first two letters of Jesus when spelled in Greek characters (ΙΗΣΟΥΣ).

[38] From the resemblance of the Greek letter tau (T) to the cross.

[39] Barn. 9:7-9.

mention of Rome, even though the story has often been told. Before the capture of Jerusalem by Pompey it is improbable that there was any Jewish colony on the Tiber. At least that may be inferred from the oft-quoted remark of the later Roman historian, Valerius Maximus:

> He [he is speaking of the prætor Hispalus] compelled the Jews, who had endeavored to corrupt Roman morals by the worship of Jupiter Sabazius, *to return to their homes.*[40]

This took place in the year 139 B.C. The italicized words suggest the transient nature of their visit, and (so Schürer) may refer to the embassy which Simon is said to have sent. If this hypothesis is correct, the reference to "Jupiter Sabazius" would seem to be a confusion between the Phrygian deity so called and Jehovah Sabaoth, and would suggest that some of the members of the embassy were rash enough to try a little missionary work.

On his triumphal return to Rome in 62 B.C. Pompey carried many Jews and settled them on the left bank of the Tiber. There they seemed to have enjoyed many privileges and exemptions. The Roman poets—notably Juvenal—allude to their presence with no great enthusiasm. Suetonius comments on their sincere and noisy grief at the death of Cæsar, whom, as we have already noticed, they had come to feel their benefactor. Augustus did not alter his predecessor's policy, but in 19 A.D. an event occurred which showed that after all they were only tolerated. Fulvia, a Roman matron who had become proselyte, made a donation to four Jews who had pretended it was to be sent to Jerusalem. Her husband, getting wind of it, protested to Tiberius, who ordered four thousand to Sardinia to aid in ridding that island of outlaws; the remainder appear to have been banished.[41] According to Philo, Tiberius allowed them to return, while Josephus asserts that Claudius began his reign with two edicts of toleration for the Jews. A few years later the Roman Jews were expelled as brawlers, or at least suffered a drastic curtailment of their privileges. The brief word of Suetonius, *Judæos impulsore Chresto assidue tumultuantes Roma expulit,* while far from clear, may imply that the "tumult" was between Jews and Christians, and that the historian, writing nearly a century later, thought that the "Chrestus" was himself personally present as ringleader. If so, this would indicate Christians in Rome by 49-50 A.D., as is inherently probable.

Enough has been said to justify the statements of both Strabo and the Sibyl as to the ubiquity of the sons of Abraham in the days of the Christian beginnings.

A subsequent chapter on the nature and emphases of Judaism will indicate how it was that this religion contained in itself the means of cementing into

---

[40] *Idem Judæos, qui sabazi Jovis cultu Romanos inficere mores conati erant, repetere domos suas coegit*—i,3,2.

[41] Tacitus and Suetonius as well as Josephus attest this edict.

one unit its sons and daughters wherever they might chance to reside. One or two other points may be noticed here in concluding this rapid survey of the far-flung front of Jewry.

At first sight, the student might be inclined to feel that the reforms of Josiah with the centralizing of worship and the prohibition of sacrifice outside of Jerusalem might have proved the doom of Israel when the city fell, and its inhabitants went to the four corners of the earth. That this was not the case is but another proof of Jewish ingenuity in constantly changing and adapting, yet with the calm conviction that it was continuing to stand where the patriarchs had stood.

In theory Judaism was a religion of sacrifice; the temple in Jerusalem was the sole place where sacrifices could be offered. Accordingly a surrogate for the temple became imperative if Judaism were to survive. This was found in the synagogue. In the days of the New Testament synagogues were to be found not alone in Palestine and Egypt, but in all the lands of the dispersion. They had become the rallying-points of Judaism. Here twice each week in addition to the Sabbath services Jews met for study of the Scripture and for prayer. The temple remained the symbol of Judaism; the synagogue exerted the real power. Whatever its actual origin had been, by the Christian era it had become hoary with age and dignity and was popularly believed to go back to Moses; its prayers to the "men of the Great Synagogue."[42]

In the synagogue service selections from the law, that is, the Pentateuch, were read. Ultimately the Pentateuch was divided systematically into lections that it might be read through in a stated period—three years, or later, following the Babylonian practice, in one year. In Palestine and Babylonia the sections would be read in Hebrew, the reading stopping frequently to allow the now unintelligible Hebrew to be translated into Aramaic. For centuries these translations continued to be rough-and-ready paraphrases; later they were reduced to writing and are known as Targums. The skill of the translator must have been taxed if the standard set by Rabbi Judah was often followed:

He who translates a verse with strict literalness is a falsifier, and he who makes addition to it is a blasphemer.[43]

Outside Palestine and Babylonia the sections were read from the Greek Bible.

Following the section from the law came one from the prophets and historical books. Eventually a cycle of lections, parallel to those from the Pentateuch, was adopted; apparently this was comparatively late. Then followed the sermon which was based on the daily lesson, or used it as a convenient point of departure. There was no fixed ministry. Any qualified man might

[42] For further discussion of this tendency to read back, see below, pp. 105 ff.
[43] See G. F. Moore, *Judaism*, Vol. I, p. 304.

be invited to read, translate, or speak. Scholars who were either members of the particular congregation or present as visitors might be invited; they had no especial rights. This is illustrated frequently in the New Testament. On one occasion Jesus is represented as being invited to read; after reading the lesson which chanced (appropriately) to be from the scroll of Isaiah he handed it back to the attendant, sat down, and expounded it.[44] Similarly in the synagogue in Pisidian Antioch it was said to Paul and Barnabas by the rulers of the synagogue, after the law and the prophets had been read: "Brethren, if ye have any word of exhortation for the people, say on."[45] Of the ancient liturgy two parts are still in use: the Shema and the Shemoneh Esreh. The former, consisting of three short paragraphs from the Pentateuch[46] beginning with the words, "Hear, O Israel, the Lord our God is one Lord," was apparently taken over by the synagogue from the temple service, and thus at least antedates 70 A.D. The latter, while somewhat more recent, is still very ancient (70-100 A.D.). The title means *eighteen* (benedictions); at an early date an additional prayer against apostates—in the modern texts the word "slanderers" has been substituted—was inserted as the twelfth, thus bringing the total to nineteen.

Yet, while the synagogues, which were to be found in every Jewish community at home and abroad, provided the means of worship in lieu of the distant temple, their chief function, as all the early Jewish writers reveal, was instruction. They were, as Philo calls them, houses of instruction. Judaism was, as we shall see, a religion where knowledge was imperative. God had revealed his will to men; they in turn must know it to do it. Thus Josephus remarks:

> Our legislator . . . demonstrated the law to be the best and the most necessary instruction of all others, permitting the people to leave off their other employments, and to assemble together for the hearing of the law, and learning it exactly, and this not once or twice, or oftener, but every week.[47]

Thus study of the law, even though many of its requirements could not be carried out away from Jerusalem, was not only at once the duty and privilege of every Jew wherever he might find himself; it was also one of the most powerful factors in keeping ever before his eye the fact that he was one of the children of Zion. It was the sacred responsibility of parents to teach their children God's law. The very fact of dwelling in an alien land amid surroundings that tended to make law observance difficult must often have tended to make this responsibility the more keenly felt.

Regarding the existence of schools, apart from the synagogue, the evidence

[44] Luke 4:16-21.
[45] Acts 13:15.
[46] Deut. 6:4-9; 11:13-21; Numb. 15:37-41.
[47] *c. Apion.* ii,18.

is not clear. In the Talmud is an interesting tradition, although it is palpably late:

> Verily, let it be remembered to that man for good, R. Joshua ben Gamaliel[48] is his name, for had he not been, the law would have been forgotten in Israel. At first every one that had a father received from him instruction in the law, but he that had no father learned not the law. . . . Thereafter teachers for the children were appointed in Jerusalem. . . . But even this measure sufficed not, for he that had a father was brought by him to school, and was taught there, but he that had no father was not brought there. In consequence of this it was ordained that teachers should be appointed in every district. To them the children were sent when they were sixteen or seventeen years of age. When a teacher became angry with a scholar, the latter stamped his feet and ran away. In this condition education remained until the time of Joshua ben Gamaliel, who acclaimed that in every province and every town there should be teachers appointed, to whom children should be brought at the age of six or seven years.

On the other hand, in praise of the merits of Simon ben Shetach, the brother of Queen Alexandra under whom the Pharisees had had halcyon days, it is recounted in the Palestinian Talmud that he made statutes, of which the second was: The children shall attend the elementary school.

Thus exact statement regarding the prevalence of schools, even in Palestine, during the days of Jesus would be rash. They were probably to be found in Jerusalem and in the larger cities, at home and abroad; that they existed in the remoter country villages, while possible, is by no means certain. When they did exist, they appear to have been of two grades: elementary and more advanced. In the former, the children learned to read the Hebrew Bible and received elementary instruction in its meaning. In the latter, the law was systematically studied following the weekly cycle of the synagogue lections and the unwritten law[49] was memorized. But even where these schools were not available the Scribes sought whole-heartedly to acquaint the masses with the content and implications of the law. Occasional sporadic esoteric sects, like the Essenes, there may have been who jealously guarded their secrets; such, however, was not the temper of Judaism. "Seek and ye shall find" was a lesson Jesus had learned in the synagogue.

Furthermore, there seem to have been very few attempts on the part of the local governments—at least during the days of Roman control—to destroy the sense of solidarity among the Jewish colonists; and those few attempts signally failed. Contributions to the temple in Jerusalem were constantly being sent. A Flaccus in Asia might confiscate such money,[50] but this was exceptional. Augustus had permitted this remitting of gifts and treated the appropriation of such sums by the local authorities as sacrilege. In addition

[48] High priest ca. 63-65 A.D.
[49] See below pp. 106 ff.
[50] See Cicero, pro Flacco 28.

to these occasional gifts every Jewish male over eighteen years of age contributed annually his half-shekel (two drachma) tax for the support of the
temple.[51] This appears to have been one of the few taxes in the history of the
world that was cheerfully paid.

Considerable latitude was allowed the local Jewish congregations in the
Roman world in the exercise of jurisdiction over their own members, at least
in civil matters; that this jurisdiction was extended to criminal matters *outside of Palestine*, while often maintained, especially in the light of the book
of Acts,[52] is by no means certain. On the other hand, Paul's own words, "Of
the Jews five times received I forty stripes save one . . . once was I stoned,"[53]
indicate that such authority was at times exercised, whether lawfully or not.
Exemption from military service, because of its demands for Sabbath service,
was the order of the day. To use the later phrase coined by Tertullian, Judaism was a *religio licita*.[54] Emperor worship at first might have seemed to
endanger the status of the Jew, for he alone remained aloof and refused to
subscribe to their claims of divinity. Most of the emperors recognized that
this was not constructive disloyalty or treason and winked at it as but another
of the silly and barbarian prejudices of this curious people. Josephus pains
takingly makes the exact reason for the refusal clear:

But then our legislator hath forbidden us to make images, not by way of de-
nunciation beforehand, that the Roman authority was not to be honoured, but as
despising a thing that was neither necessary nor useful for either God or man; and
he forbade them, as we shall prove hereafter, to make their images for any part
of the animal creation. Yet hath our legislator nowhere forbidden us to pay
honour to worthy men, provided they be of another kind, and inferior to those
we pay to God: with which honours we willingly testify our respect to our emperors and to the people of Rome; we also offer perpetual sacrifices for them; nor
do we only offer them every day at the common expense of all the Jews, but although we offer no other such sacrifices out of our common expenses, no, not for
our own children, yet do we this as a peculiar honour to the emperors, and to
them alone, while we do the same to no other person whomsoever.[55]

This refusal to be as other men of necessity drew the bonds of union between Jew and Jew the more tight, and tended to insulate him from outside
influence, although at the expense of gaining the title, later borne by Christians as well, "haters of the human race."[56] Philo laments that Jews alone
were exempted from the universal religious toleration of the empire.[57] To an

[51] Cf. Matt. 17:24-27.
[52] Acts 9:2; 22:19; 26:11 f. For the critical difficulties underlying this account see pp. 409 f., 414.
[53] II Cor. 11:24,25.
[54] *Apologet.* 21.
[55] *c. Apion.* ii,26 (end).
[56] Cf. Tacitus, *Hist.* v, 5—*Apud ipsos fides obstinata, misericordia in promptu, sed adversus omnes alios hostile odium.*
[57] *Legatio ad Gaium* 16(§117)562M.

extent his words were true, but simply because the Jew himself alone was intolerant.

Yet, none the less, there was a steady stream of gentile converts—prose-lytes—to Judaism. The very fact that the Jew claimed loudly that he and only he was right threw a glamour then—as such similar claims do today. Many were inclined to take him at his own valuation. In spite of the somewhat jaundiced word, attributed to Jesus,

> Woe unto you Scribes and Pharisees, hypocrites! for ye compass sea and land to make one proselyte; and when he is become so, ye make him twofold more a son of hell than yourselves,[58]

Judaism does not appear to me to have ever been a religion actively engaged in making converts—today we call such an attitude evangelistic—in the sense that early Christianity was. With a feeling of complacency, as it thought of its own long history and especial favour in the eyes of God, there never was a manifest tendency to cheapen all this or try to swell its numbers. Hillel might say, "Love the creatures, and bring them nigh to the Torah," but the emphasis seems to have been one of passive readiness—whosoever would might come; the door stood open—rather than of any general attempt to go into the highways and hedges to constrain men to come in. In the third century R. Eleazar could declare that the reason Israel was scattered among the nations was to make proselytes; that Abraham himself was the type of proselyte and a great maker of them. But the temper of Judaism is seen in the word:

> A man may wish to become a priest or a Levite, but he cannot, because his father was not one; but if he wishes to become righteous he can do so, even if he be a heathen, for righteousness is not a matter of descent.

That is, teachers were willing and glad to make proselytes of those who were willing to pay the price. They must in every case follow the ceremonial laws, including the Sabbath, festival, and food legislation and, above all, must submit to the painful rite of circumcision and the ceremonial bath. The gentile who met these demands became a Jew, entitled to all the privileges and subject to all the requirements of the born Jew. He and he alone may be spoken of as a proselyte. The terms, "half proselyte" and "proselyte of the gate," are unknown to early Judaism and have no place in any serious discus-sion. To be sure, there were many gentiles who were not ready to burn all their bridges behind them and to become Jews, but who were ready to re-nounce idolatrous practices and who frequented the synagogue. They were welcomed—or at least tolerated—but had no status whatsoever in Judaism. They were regularly expected to observe the so-called Noachian laws pro-hibiting: (1) idolatry; (2) blasphemy; (3) cursing judges, *i.e.*, enjoining

[58] Matt. 23:15.

obedience to the Jewish courts; (4) murder; (5) *araiyot, i.e.,* prohibition of various sexual offences; (6) theft; (7) eating flesh cut from the living animal, *i.e.,* the prohibition of flesh with the life blood in it. These were believed to have been binding upon all decent men from the earliest beginning. It was incredible that there could have been a time when they were not in force. Thus, said Judaism, the first six of these laws had been communicated to Adam; they had been repeated to Noah and the seventh added when he was permitted to eat the flesh of animals.

The lofty, if uncompromising, monotheism of Judaism in contrast to the down-at-the-heel polytheism of the Græco-Roman world which had to a measure been discredited through the preceding centuries; the central place that ethics played in the Jewish law; a sort of grudging admiration for the race which seemed to flourish the more it was persecuted; the fact that religions from the East were becoming popular—one might almost say, the fad—in the Roman world—all this justified Josephus' boast,

Many of [the Grecians] have come over to our laws, and some of them have continued in their observation, although others of them had not courage enough to persevere, and so departed from them again.[59]

If we can believe him, nearly all the women of Damascus were "addicted to the Jewish religion."[60] Nero's empress Poppæa is said to have been distinctly friendly to Judaism. All sorts of legends have gathered around the head of the emperor Antoninus Pius, who, it is claimed, will lead the procession of proselytes in the Age to Come because he had become circumcised. The oft-repeated story of Queen Helena and her son Izates, king of Adiabene,[61] while replete with all the gossipy details so dear to Josephus—especially when his historic sources for a period were running low—reveals that occasionally even reigning princes took the full step to Judaism. The biting words of Juvenal pictures the younger generation in Rome going beyond their fathers and becoming proselytes:

Some, who have had a father who reveres the Sabbath, worship nothing but the clouds and divinity of the heaven, and can detect no difference between eating swine's flesh, from which their fathers abstained, and that of man. Finally they take to circumcision. Although accustomed to flout the laws of Rome, they learn to practise and revere the Jewish law and all that Moses committed to his secret tome: not to show the way to any not worshipping by the same rite nor to conduct any save the circumcised to the desired fountain. For all this was the father to blame for whom every seventh day was one of idleness and kept apart from all the concerns of life.[62]

Before the eye of every Jew, wherever he might reside, hovered the hope

[59] *c. Apion.* ii,11.
[60] *Wars* 2,20,2.
[61] *Antt.* 20,2,1-4,3.
[62] *Sat.* 14,96-106,

of seeing the holy city at least once before he died. All that was tangible in his religion was embodied in Zion, "whither the tribes go up." Each festival season saw thousands on the roads to and from. Returning, they brought tales of the glories of the temple, of the actual sacrifices there conducted—to the foreign Jew simply rules to be memorized and idealized—of the chanting priests and the fragrant smoke of incense. All this tended to wipe away the intervening miles. This too was his city, his temple. In the future—when he did not know—God would sound his call. The time of punishment and absence would be over. Until then he would wait in hope.

Chapter VI

THE GENIUS OF JUDAISM

MUCH has already been said in the preceding pages of Jewish beliefs and practices. A more detailed and exact statement is here in order. Although, as we shall see in the following chapters, by no means all Jews saw eye to eye, there were certain fundamental concepts held in common by all. These we must now examine.

With the religious life in Israel before the exile we need not concern ourselves. It was not till the promulgation of the Deuteronomic code (*ca.* 621 B.C.) that we can speak of Judaism as such. It was then that the Jew, as we know him, came into existence, with his feeling of uniqueness and corresponding separateness from the non-Jew, to result in the great chasm between Jew and gentile. This feeling of separateness increased until he believed that it had always been in force. Even before the legislation from Mt. Sinai which had given it definite expression, recognition of it had been vouchsafed to Abraham, who had received in his own body a visible sign of his immediate relationship to Jehovah and consequent separation from all not similarly privileged. Since as a people he stood apart from the rest of the world, he must of necessity be more closely joined to his fellows. The result of this was unity and strength, but bought at the expense of popularity, since gentiles in every age have not unnaturally looked askance at this quintessence of clannishness.

Judaism was a revealed religion and took itself seriously as such. Failure to grasp this central fact has led to all sorts of misconceptions about the Jewish law and its fancied burden to Israel. God was the centre of the Jew's life and thought. He it was who had revealed a religion through the fathers and Moses which was destined to become the universal religion of mankind. God had revealed his whole will; everything that men were to do he had revealed to them. Moral conduct, the way men were to worship him and regard him, even their attitudes of mind and will—all these things had been revealed and were man's for the learning. The law—the Jew called it Torah—was thus God's great gift to his children.

Accordingly, the Jew strove with all his might to learn God's will and to do it. Keeping the law was synonymous with morality and religion. And he sought to keep it with no ulterior motive: He did it because he loved God and wished to do his will. Had he been asked why he did it, he might have answered that God's long-deferred promise of a future golden age was dependent upon the conformity of his people to his will as he had revealed it and as they knew it; that if Israel would keep the law but a single day the golden age would dawn. But such an answer, which would simply have reflected the central place the law occupied in his thinking, would have been to a large extent an explanation, not a reason. He sought to do what was right because it was right—and because he desired to do it. God's will had become his.

Say not, I will study the Torah with the purpose of being called Sage or Rabbi, to acquire fortune or to be rewarded for it in the world to come; but do it for the sake of thy love to God, though the glory will come in the end.[1]

Accordingly, keeping of Torah was no hardship. Much nonsense has been written about the burden of the law. We are apt to approach the matter from our own experience with legislatures and Congress which grind out endless absurd and contradictory enactments, which if they were kept would indeed be a burden. Thus for us law is too apt to be regarded as the result of the ingenuity of interested politicians. Such a notion would have been incomprehensible to ancient Judaism. God, not venial men, was its author; his motives were entirely pure and beneficent. Such a difference of attitude makes all the difference in the world. Thus the pious Jew sought to know and to keep the law, not because he *ought* or *must*, but because he *wanted to*. Many were the Jews at the beginning of our era who could have echoed the words of the Psalmist with the fullest sincerity; "Oh, how I love thy law,"[2] or have agreed that for the righteous man "His delight is in the law of the Lord, and on his law doth he meditate day and night";[3] while for him, "The law of thy mouth is better unto me than thousands of gold and silver."[4] To hear that law-keeping was a wearisome burden, a noose around his neck, would have amazed him. The answer was ready to hand: "And I shall walk at liberty; for I have sought thy precepts."[5] Far from being burdened "whosoever receiveth upon him the yoke of Torah, they remove from him the yoke of royalty and the yoke of worldly care."[6] It was rather the gentile who was hedged about with dreads and fears:

The son who serves his father serves him with joy, saying, "Even if I do not entirely succeed (in carrying out his commandments), yet, as a loving father, he will not be angry with me: while the gentile slave is always afraid lest he may commit some fault, and therefore serves God in a condition of anxiety and confusion.[7]

[1] Sifrè 79 b—quoted by Schechter, *Some Aspects of Rabbinic Theology*, p. 68.
[2] Psalm 119:97.
[3] Psalm 1:2; cf. Psalms 19:7; 40:8.
[4] Psalm 119:72.
[5] Psalm 119:45.
[6] Abot 3,6.
[7] Tanḥuma Noah 19.

God had revealed the law; but conversely the law also revealed God, and the true Jew sought as the *summum bonum* of life to be as near like God as possible. This Philo states expressly:

My good man, the best of all prayers, and the end, and proper object of happiness, is to attain to a likeness of God.[8]

This was possible since every man was created in the image of God. Thus the adage, "Ye shall be holy; for I Jehovah your God am Holy,"[9] was the heart of the law. He was to walk in God's ways. As God was kind to the widow, and orphans, and strangers, so must he be.

The notion that for the Jew at the beginning of the Christian era God had become remote, that as the King of the universe he was likened to an Eastern despot, completely inaccessible, to be feared, not worshipped, while still widely held, is entirely mistaken. An examination of the titles with which God was addressed and of the petitions of early Jewish prayers would be sufficient to destroy this misunderstanding.

O our Father, merciful Father, ever compassionate, have mercy upon us. . . . Thou hast chosen us from all peoples and tongues, and hast brought us near unto thy great name forever in faithfulness, to thank thee and proclaim thy unity in love; blessed art thou, O God, who hast chosen thy people Israel, in love. . . . Forgive us our Father, for we have sinned; pardon us our King, for we have transgressed . . . blessed art thou, our God, who art gracious and dost abundantly forgive.[10]

God might be supramundane; he was not extramundane. R. Johanan phrased it aptly: "Wherever you find the almighty power of God, you will find in the context his lowly deeds."[11]

In the later apocalypses angels came to play a prominent part, but they did not lessen the confidence that no intermediary was necessary between man and God. The priest might offer the sacrifice, angels might serve as God's messengers to men, but every Israelite had direct access to him. An occasional reference to the pleading of an intercessor—as Abraham for Sodom[12] or the angel of Jehovah for Jerusalem in ruins[13]—occurs. None the less the confidence of orthodox Judaism is found in the word of R. Judan:

If a man has a patron, when a time of trouble comes upon him, he does not at once enter into his patron's presence, but comes and stands at the door of his house and calls one of the servants or a member of his family, who brings word

[8] *de Decalogo* 15(§73)193M.
[9] Lev. 19:2.
[10] For this catena of passages I am indebted to S. Schechter, *Some Aspects of Rabbinic Theology*, p. 22.
[11] See Moore, *Judaism*, Vol. I, pp. 440 ff.
[12] Gen. 18:22-33.
[13] Zech. 1:12.

to him, "So-and-so is standing at the entrance in your court." Perhaps the patron will let him in, perhaps he will make him wait. Not so is God. If trouble comes upon a man, let him not cry to Michael or to Gabriel; but let him cry unto me, and I will answer him forthwith, as the Scripture says, "Whosoever shall call on the name of the Lord shall be delivered."[14]

Not only was the "humility of God" clearly expressed in Psalm 18:35(36) —though rendered in our English versions by such mistranslations as "gentleness" or "condescension" through the mistaken feeling of reluctance of the Christian translators to posit such a virtue for God[15]—but the rabbis had no hesitation in heaping human qualities and acts upon God. Thus he was best man at the wedding of Adam and Eve; he teaches Torah to Israel and keeps school now in heaven for those who died in their infancy; he prays himself and thus teaches Israel how to pray; he visited Abraham when the latter was sick and mourned with Isaac at his father's death. Not the ascription of the humbler qualities to God, but the exaltation and deification of man aroused the ire of the rabbis. So God could say to Moses:

Though I made thee a God to Pharaoh, thou must not become overbearing (and think thyself God); *I* am the Lord.[16]

In this connection it may be said that all this does not reveal merely a later phase of Judaism. After the second century of the present era conditions were by no means of a nature to make any great advances in Judaism probable; nor is there any evidence that such a change took place. Continuity, and that with very little change, is the most striking impression. It is often said that Rabbinical Judaism took its stand in the great schools, as in that of Hillel. It is far more probable that the phenomenon was much older, going back to the days of the restoration, and that the real revival took place, due to the efforts of those men who were styled the "Men of the Great Synagogue." They laid the tracks on which later Judaism continued to run.

Accordingly, it is reasonably certain that the phrase, "Our Father who art in heaven," which occurs in the Gospel of Matthew was not, as has often been popularly supposed, an indication of a radical about face from the conception of God held by orthodox Judaism, but was one of the many legacies of the Synagogue to the Church. Nor is it to be argued that while for Judaism God may have been the Father of the nation, it remained for Christianity to personalize the relationship, to make him the Father of the individual. There seems to be absolutely no warrant for such a notion, however deeply entrenched it may be in popular belief. It may not be out of place to observe that while the Christian gospels represent Judaism as

---

[14] Quoted by Moore, *Judaism*, Vol. I, p. 439.
[15] Enslin, *The Ethics of Paul*, p. 257.
[16] *Idem*, p. 258.

often scandalized by Jesus' actions—especially his laxness with regard to the laws of the Sabbath—the prayer he is said to have taught his disciple, "Our Father who art in heaven," did not appear to arouse a ripple of protest. Had not even Solomon remarked: "Thou hast chosen me to be a king of thy people, and a judge of thy sons and daughters;"[17] had he not condemned the wicked for their protest against the just man for making his boast that God was his father?[18]

Since the Jew believed that in the law God had revealed his entire will for man, sin was not a matter of error of judgment or of missing the mark. It was an unfilial act of defiance to a loving, gracious father; in short, rebellion against God. The father said, "Son, go work today in the vineyard"; the son replied, "I will not."[19] In such a situation only one course of action was possible: The son must repent and go into the vineyard; the prodigal must come back from the far country and seek the father's forgiveness. This Isaiah phrases explicitly in his famous word, "Cease to do evil; learn to do well."[20] Repentance was a cardinal point in Jewish thinking. He knew he could never hope to achieve perfect law observance, though he sought to hitch his wagon to the star. God was not unreasonable. "He knoweth our frame; he remembereth that we are dust."[21] Before the earth was created, while the law was still only in the mind of God, there abode coëval with it the possibility of repentance. This vivid phrasing of the later rabbis simply gave expression to the confidence Israel long had had.[22]

God was preëminently a God of justice. "The first question a man is asked at the Last Judgment is whether he has dealt fairly with his neighbour." God never shows partiality or favouritism, never accepts bribes; neither must his people. The ideal man is

He that walketh righteously, and speaketh uprightly; he that despiseth the gain of oppressions, that shaketh his hands from taking a bribe, that stoppeth his ears from hearing of blood, and shutteth his eyes from looking upon evil.[23]

Nor is regret at past misdeeds sufficient. Like Zacchæus, he must make restitution before he can hope to gain divine forgiveness.

Another emphasis of Judaism was upon moral purity with a corresponding emphasis upon a sane and wholesome family life. God was a God of purity. None of the amours or other scandalous action of the gods of the Babylonian and Greek pantheons were ascribed to him. Sexual purity was thus a fundamental requirement for Israel. Adultery was forbidden in the

[17] Wisdom of Solomon 9:7.
[18] *Idem* 2:16. The student who is still skeptical will do well to read Moore, *Judaism,* Vol. II, pp. 201-211.
[19] Matt. 21:28-32.
[20] Isa. 1:16 f.
[21] Psalm 103:14.
[22] For further discussion of sin and repentance, see below, p. 159.
[23] Isa. 33:15.

decalogue; incest and the other perversions were forbidden in Leviticus 18. Marriage was ordained and blessed by God. Had he not chosen precisely this figure to illustrate his bond to Israel? The average Jewish boy was married by his eighteenth year; celibacy was both abnormal and rare. The lament of the Psalmist, "Behold I was brought forth in iniquity; and in sin did my mother conceive me,"[24] was never intended or understood as implying anything reprehensible or defiling in the marriage relation. It was simply the prayer of the contrite sinner, aware that from his very beginning he had erred from the Father's path.

Nor was asceticism ever a characteristic of Judaism. Occasional ascetics and groups of ascetics there may have been; but they were exceptional and exerted very little, if any, influence. The tone of Jewish thinking in this regard is well illustrated by the sayings:

He who subjects himself to needless self-castigation and fastings or even denies himself the enjoyment of wine is a sinner.

Are not the things prohibited you in the law enough for you, that you want to prohibit yourself other things?

These were lofty and noble conceptions. Naturally all did not reach the standard set for them then any more than all do now. None the less these were ideals toward which the pious reached. Such was the heritage of the Church from the Synagogue; such the environs that helped to produce a Jesus and a Paul.

Its Literature

A lasting memorial to the central place occupied by the law and its significance as the perfect and complete revelation of God's will for the world is found in the huge literature of interpretation which the law produced. It is only as one understands this phenomenon, commonly dubbed "the rabbinic literature,"—and unfortunately for most students Jew and gentile alike, this knowledge is at second hand and accordingly imperfect and inexact—that he can hope to look through the eyes of the Jew at the time when Christianity made its appearance and gained its growth.

Normative Judaism is a straight line development from the Old Testament and is due, as has already been pointed out, to the fact that the religion took itself seriously as a revealed religion. All the peculiarities of the rabbinic literature—and they are many!—are due to this. God had revealed his whole will for the whole life of man; this revelation, however, was not explicit, but implicit. The Scripture is not at all points clearly intelligible: parts *seem* to be conflicting, but really are not. In short, there was no such thing as a development in God's revelation. All had come

[24] Psalm 51:5.

from Sinai; it could not and did not contradict itself. Since all was implicit—written, so to speak, in invisible ink—a premium was laid on ingenuity. No slightest detail could be overlooked. For example: In Lev. 25:36 it is said, "That thy brother may live with thee." On the significance of these words Akiba and Ben Paturi are said to have had a heated discussion, as to how these words applied to two men thirsting in the desert and with water sufficient for only one. Said the one: "They are to share the limited supply, for the Scripture says 'that *thy brother may live* with thee.'" Said the other, "No, there would not be enough for both; the man is to keep the limited supply for himself, for the Scripture directs that the man himself is to live: 'that thy brother may live *with thee.*'"

Or again, every variant in spelling, every case of unusual word order, might be pregnant with meaning. Thus the school of Akiba found an explanation of the prohibition of the use of the tetragrammaton in the so-called defective spelling of the Hebrew word לעלם in Exod. 3:15. The ordinary way to spell it was לעולם. Now God knew how to spell. Hence there must be a reason for the difference here. It was not to be pronounced לְעֹלָם (lᵉōlām) "for ever," but לְעַלֵּם (lᵉʿallēm) "to conceal." Akiba was so proficient in this atomistic interpretation and so skilled in finding meat in the most unlikely places that, according to the later rabbis, Moses is said to have been amazed as he sat in a back seat in Akiba's classroom to have heard the learned exegete find matter in his law that he himself had never dreamed of.

All this was no mere casuistic exercise, as has sometimes been said; it was the natural consequence of Judaism's confidence that from the very beginning God had foreseen all the circumstances of life that would ever arise and had been at pains to anticipate them. Whatever was now under his blessing had always been dear to him. God had told all to Moses—all that even later writers as in Esther should say. Many of the prescriptions and proscriptions in the later developed law—even the Passover meal!— were practised in Abraham's household. The law had been created before the creation of the world and was privately communicated to occasional especially eminent figures, but it was not promulgated. It had been revealed to Moses at Sinai, but had been in part forgotten and needed to be recovered exegetically. The custodians of this "unwritten law" were the learned; in it their learning consisted.

Failure to grasp this fundamental thread, namely, that for Judaism there was not—could not be—such a conception as the modern "progressive revelation," not only renders the rabbinic writings totally unintelligible, but throws much of the Old Testament into hopeless confusion. A few illustrations will suffice. From the days of Solomon the temple stood as the outward symbol of the presence of Jehovah. Here was his house. As the years went by it became inconceivable that there could ever have been a time when he had not dwelt with his people. But the time of the building of the first temple was too firmly etched in the memory of man to make possible an error here; there had been no earlier temple. Hence apparently arose the notion of the tabernacle—a movable temple, so to speak—which the children of Israel could bear about with them through the wilderness wandering.

Similarly the office of high priest, as we have seen, apparently emerged during the exile, when a king no longer overshadowed. But there could be nothing new for Judaism; hence we find Aaron in the robes of the high priest many centuries before. Or again, the synagogue, peculiarly an institution of the exile, was read back to the time of Moses. The Noachian laws were known in part to Adam; were completed for Noah.

Perhaps the most striking example is found in the matter of the eighth-century prophets. To us, they seem to have heralded a right-about-face. This should not obscure the fact that not only for later Judaism but for the prophets themselves theirs was no such rôle. They were simply calling Israel back to the paths of true religion which God had long before revealed, in which they had at first walked, but from which they had strayed away.

As has been well said, all rabbinic literature is but an expansion of the Shema. It was the reduction to writing of the unwritten law which had previously been passed on from teacher to pupil, and which—in spite of the frequently quoted ideal that a student should be like a plastered cistern which never lost a drop but which never itself added to its content—had grown so mightily that eventually a rescript of it became a sheer necessity. This reduction took two forms: Midrash and Mishna.

The former were running commentaries on the Scripture. The material—and this applies not only to the Midrash but also to the Mishna and its later interpretations, the Talmuds—was of two kinds: Halakah and Haggadah. The former was the legal matter—the term means literally "rule to go by"—and consisted of a minute discussion of the law, often in hyper-critical fashion; it was usually stated very succinctly and without quoting the actual words under discussion. Haggadah, on the contrary, was the exposition of those portions of Scripture not primarily connected with the law itself; it was largely concerned with the practical—didactic and sermonic—values to be found in the Scriptures, and expounded and developed the sacred history and literature in an edifying and often entertaining vein. Nor was the importance of this material lightly viewed. The Halakah might be the substance, the "kidney-fat of wheat," but the Haggadah was the "blood of the grape," which attracted a man's heart like wine. And in the Sifrè it is explicitly said:

If you would learn to know Him at whose word the world came into being, learn Haggadah, for by this means you will come to know the Holy One and cleave to his ways.[25]

The oldest three Midrashim were those on the Pentateuch: the Mekilta on Exodus; the Sifra on Leviticus; and the Sifrè on Numbers and Deuteronomy. While occasional bits of Haggadah were contained in these, they were primarily halakic. In addition to these halakic Midrashim—often called "Tannaite"[26]—were other later Midrashim in which Haggadah largely predominated. The chief of these were the Rabboth, that is, haggadic Midrashim on the Pentateuch and Megilloth.[27] Of these homiletic Midrashim the one on Genesis,[28] called Bereshit Rabbah (from the Hebrew name for Genesis), is the most revered because of both age and subject material. It is a running verse-by-verse commentary on Genesis, omitting only such non-edifying material as the genealogies or repetitions. A book like Leviticus obviously did not yield itself readily to such treatment; accordingly, the haggadic Midrash on this book (known as the Wayyikra Rabbah) is a series of sermons on selected passages, and abounds in popular proverbs and sayings, usually in Aramaic.

The other form in which the oral law was codified was known as Mishna. Here the material was not arranged in the form of running commentaries, but was classified systematically on the basis of an ordered list of subjects called "orders," which in turn were subdivided into treatises and chapters. Tradition ascribes this method of classification to Akiba. These orders, six in number, are:

(1) Seeds (Zeraim). Here are found the laws about agriculture, sabbatical years, and the like. To this order is prefixed the Berakot, a book of prayers and blessings.

(2) Festivals (Moed). Here was included, as the name suggests, the legislation for the Sabbath and the various festivals and fasts.

(3) Women (Nashim) with the rules for betrothal, marriage, divorce; status of widows; the levirate, adultery, and the like.

(4) Injuries (Nezikim) or, as it would be called today, torts and delicts, *i.e.,* civil and criminal law. To this is appended the famous Pirke Abot, sayings of the Fathers, which is purely haggadic and is contained in the Jewish Prayer Book.

(5) Holy Things (Kodashim): laws about sacrifice, excommunication, the furniture and equipment of the temple, and the like.

(6) Uncleannesses (Toharot). Here, as the name suggests, was systemized the legislation regarding the ritual and purificatory baths for women after

[25] Quoted by Moore, *Judaism*, Vol. I, p. 161, to whom I am here, as elsewhere, deeply indebted.
[26] For the meaning and reason for this word, see p. 109.
[27] The "five rolls"—Song of Songs, Ruth, Ecclesiastes, Esther, and Lamentations.
[28] There is no halakic Midrash on Genesis.

menstruation, childbirth; after intercourse or after contact with a corpse; leprosy, and the like.

During the second Christian century this type of codification was cultivated, and several such collections were made. But, when early in the third century one of these, that of Judah the Patriarch, gained preëminence, the designation Mishna gradually became restricted to this particular collection. Individual sayings from the parallel works are preserved in the Talmuds and are known as Baraitas, that is, traditions extraneous to the official Mishna, which latter, gaining almost canonical rank, served for further development of the law. The Mishna, written, of course, in Hebrew, is not to be conceived as coming from the pen of Judah. It is perhaps fair to call him the editor. Some 150 authorities are cited and quoted.

One somewhat similar work may be briefly mentioned, the Tosefta. Its arrangement in six orders is the same as the Mishna, while much of the material is the same. Although the name Tosefta ("Supplement") indicates the views of later Judaism about the relationship of the two works, it is actually not so much a supplement as an amplification. The most conspicuous difference between the otherwise largely parallel works is that the Tosefta frequently cites the biblical passages which serve as the authority for the detailed legislation; this the Mishna almost never does. Furthermore, it contains rather more Haggadah than does the Mishna.

The Mishna was the result of the effort to explain and interpret the law. Now that it had become canonical, it soon became necessary to explain and interpret the Mishna. Since the Mishna cited 150 scholars, there were many contradictions; these must be explained away, and other obscurities or ambiguities clarified. The result was the two Talmuds, one proceeding from Palestine, and properly known as the Palestinian Talmud—although it is often incorrectly called the Jerusalem Talmud—and dating from the middle of the fifth century; the other, the Babylonian Talmud, or in practice *the* Talmud, about half a century later and nearly four times as large. Owing to the closing of the rabbinical school in Tiberias the Palestinian Talmud was never finished, nor did it receive the thorough editing of its fellow from the east.

The Talmuds might be roughly called "Mishnas on the Mishna." Paragraph by paragraph—often sentence by sentence—the Mishna is quoted verbatim, the quotation being followed by the discussion and interpretation, in which especial emphasis was laid on clearing up difficulties and seeming contradictions. Thus the Talmuds consist of alternate sections—Mishna and interpretations. These interpretations, that is, the *new* material, are known as Gemara. It consists largely of the comments of later scholars— the Amoraim—but in addition has occasional Baraitas from the other Mishnas, as well as material from the Tosefta[29] and from the earlier

_____
[29] The Tosefta never had a Talmud.

Midrashim. Together the two Talmuds cover nearly all the Mishna, although the Pirke Abot has no Talmud (Gemara). The bulk of the Gemara is in Aramaic, although the Baraitas are in Hebrew, as of course are the cited blocks of Mishna. Although of necessity Halakah bulks large in the Talmud, it is by no means the only kind of material. On the contrary, the (Babylonian) Talmud contains much edifying and entertaining matter, romantic literature having to do with Alexander the Great, such stories as how Hadrian—always a favourite character in Jewish legend—went down to the bottom of the sea in a diving-bell.

In the preceding pages mention of Tannaim and Amoraim has been made. A brief word of explanation may be useful. According to the traditional view, the canon of the Old Testament closed with the work of Ezra. He was followed by the *Sopherim* (literally, "men of the book") or "Men of the Great Synagogue"; they continued to the Maccabean times and were followed by the famous *Pairs*, that is, two colleagues, more or less friendly rivals, who carried on the tradition in successive generations until the end of the Herodian age, culminating in Hillel and Shammai, the founders of the two great rival schools. The Pairs were in turn followed by the *Tannaim* (teachers) (10-220 A.D.), *i.e.,* to the end of the codification of the Mishna; they by the *Amoraim* (speakers or interpreters) in the years 220-500 A.D., *i.e.,* in the period of the growth and development of the Gemara. Judaism is very careful to preserve these distinctions. Accordingly, such Halakic Midrashim as the Mekilta, Sifra, and Sifrè are called Tannaite Midrashim, since they were produced by the Tannaim, as were also the Mishnas and Tosefta. The Gemara, aside from earlier quotations from the Tannaim, was, of course, the work of the Amoraim.

The nature of these sources explain why they are so difficult to operate with. In the first place stand the technical difficulties. They contain a chaotic mass of material in which legal matter, theology, philosophy, science, anecdotes, and legend hobnob together. Written partly in Hebrew, partly in Aramaic, in an unpointed text, innocent of punctuation save at the end of paragraphs, they are, to quote one who knows them well, "concise to a degree that Thucydides might have envied, and Tacitus striven in vain to imitate."[30] They are not equipped with indices nor other apparatus—nor can they be. One must know where the desired material is or hunt for it. Furthermore, if ever the words of warning, "A little knowledge is a dangerous thing," have point, it is here. The compend of hundreds of scholars, some as early as the second century, others as late as the sixth century, it is necessary to pick and choose, if they are to be of value in revealing the nature of Judaism in the days of the rise of Christianity.

Not alone are they not calculated to answer many of the questions put to them—outlook and interests change through the centuries—but they have

[30] Herford, *Christianity in Talmud and Midrash*, p. 21.

been altered through the years as a result both of copying and of censorship. The first Christian act was to burn them; when this extreme was not resorted to they were rigidly censored to remove all objectional references to Christianity. During the days of the Inquisition this censorship was particularly rife. Perverted Jews—since they turned against their nation to save their own skins, this term is justifiable—enrolled as Dominicans, ferreted out all objectional references. Sometimes they would delete whole blocks, leaving blank spaces; at other times the wording was changed. One device was to print "Sadducee" in place of "heretic" when the latter term might reasonably be supposed to mean Christian. Were one to seek to discover from an uncritical text the tenets of the Sadducees, a curious picture would thus emerge.

When critically used by experts they reveal a Judaism totally different from that pictured by either the ardent apologist or the unsympathetic enemy. The main streams of Judaism flowing down from the earliest sources are here to be seen, but, muddied by the waters from lesser tributaries, only when an expert is at the wheel can they be navigated in safety.

Chapter VII

THE MAKE-UP OF JUDAISM

THE glibness with which we speak of Pharisees, Sadducees, and Zealots, not to mention Scribes, Boëthusians, Herodians, and Therapeutæ, tends to give the impression that we know a great deal more about the make-up of Judaism in the first century than is actually the fact, and that we are so exactly informed as to the peculiarities of each group that, were we to be transported back miraculously to Jerusalem and have the population pass in slow review before us, we could unerringly tag each one, at least after getting into casual conversation with him. Many modern writers have uncanny ability in this direction. From half a line—and that not always of certain text—they can tell whether its author was a Pharisee or Sadducee or Zealot.

All this tends to obscure the fact that actually we know amazingly little about the various sects. In fact, we do not have sufficient information to justify us in calling them sects. Were there different associations to which men belonged? Did a man *become* a Pharisee or Sadducee? Contemporary sources provide no answer to these questions. As we have seen, the rabbinic writings are totally silent;[1] all attempts at identification of sects fail. The fourth century Christian writer Epiphanius in his *Panarion (Refutation of All Heresies)* lists seven sects, and for good measure classes the Samaritans as standing halfway between Jew and gentile and containing four different varieties, of whom the Essenes were the first! Epiphanias' reputation for complete untrustworthiness, and for dependence upon personal likes and dislikes instead of facts as a basis for his statements, has led most historians to discount what he here has to say.[2]

Philo has left us a short eulogistic account of an otherwise unknown group of ascetics, and made passing reference to the Essenes; Josephus provides us with most of our all too scanty information regarding the four "sects" into which he divided Jewry—Pharisees, Sadducees, Essenes, and

---

[1] Here, as in other phases of what we are pleased to call a "dispassionate and scientific investigation of the past," there is an obvious fallacy. We say: "We will let the ancient writers speak for themselves; they shall answer our questions as they themselves will." But we naïvely forget that most of the questions upon which we wish light never occurred to them at all, and that by this inquisitorial device we effectively distort our sources and prevent them from emphasizing the things that seem to *them* significant. A particularly vivid illustration of this attitude is seen in such a work as *In His Steps—What Would Jesus Do?* but there are many others which do not wish to remain in the field of homiletics.

[2] See Jackson and Lake, *The Beginnings of Christianity,* Vol. I, pp. 84 f.

Fourth Philosophy. A manuscript discovered in Egypt at the end of the last century reveals another movement, apparently within the ranks of Judaism, although this has been occasionally challenged, while other names appear in passing reference in the pages of the gospels and elsewhere.

The Pharisees and Sadducees

Of the Jews in the days of Jesus the Pharisees were by all odds the most important. Much labor has been expended upon the derivation of the name. What its origin was we do not know. That it was originally applied by opponents as a nickname is perhaps probable, though by no means certain. Furthermore, the name apparently came to be understood in the sense of "Separatist," although the exact significance is not clear. Some have seen in it those who separated themselves from Judas the Maccabee at the advent of Alcimus.[3] For those who hold this view the later Pharisees were the successors of the Asideans (Ḥasidim). For others the separation was from sin, and referred to their ceremonial purity and diligence in striving to keep the law. Others understand it in the sense of exegetes: those who separated or distinguished the meaning of the law. In the last analysis we could only guess; even if we knew the derivation and significance of the name, we would know no more of the group itself.

Furthermore, their origin is unknown. Perhaps it is to be seen in the Haberim or "associates" who pledged themselves in the time of Hyrcanus to the scrupulous keeping of the laws, especially those having to do with matters of uncleanness, and to the setting apart of the tithes.[4] Such groups are mentioned in the Mishna and may have had their roots here. Under John Hyrcanus the Pharisees make their first definite appearance, although mention is made of them, along with the Sadducees and Essenes, by Josephus in the days of Jonathan.[5] The story of their gradual dissatisfaction with the political aspirations of the ruling house, of the break with Hyrcanus and his successors, and of their rise to the position of unquestioned leadership in things religious during the days of toleration under Alexandra has already been told and need not be repeated.[6] Although (with rare exceptions) they had no hankering for civil power but held aloof, they had become the spiritual mentors for Israel with an influence over the people that their rivals, the Sadducees, could not hope to equal, even though the latter had far greater wealth and political power. So Josephus can say of them:

Whatsoever they do about divine worship, prayers, and sacrifices, they (*i.e.,* the people) perform them according to their direction.[7]

[3] See pp. 16 f., 19.
[4] So Herford, *The Pharisees,* pp. 30-35.
[5] *Antt.* 13,5,9.
[6] Pp. 28 f., 33 f.
[7] *Antt.* 18,1,3.

An anecdote, in itself of no consequence, illustrates the truth of Josephus' words. According to the teaching of the Sadducees the incense was to be lighted outside the holy place and carried burning within; according to the Pharisees, on the contrary, it must be lighted inside. Once a young priest—a Sadducee—performed this function in the manner approved by the Sadducees. Later his father admonished him: "Though we are Sadducees, we must do as the Pharisees teach, for they have the people behind them."

Suffice it to say that in the days of Jesus and during the rise of the early church they constituted the backbone of Judaism. Firmly entrenched in their religious leadership, revered by the masses, with the synagogues virtually in their control, they alone of the groups known to us survived the dreadful years of revolt against Rome. With the fall of the temple in 70 A.D. the Sadducees leave the field of history; the collapse of the rebellion of Bar Cochba saw the utter downfall of the Home Rule Party. But the Pharisees remained. Herford is well within the facts when he writes:

The Pharisees were the only guides and teachers who had a word for the people; and they, and none others, saved from the ruins of the Jewish nation all that could be saved, and spoke to the stricken hearts of their countrymen the words of comfort and hope. The Judaism which has come down through the centuries is essentially Pharisaism.[8]

Josephus' description of the views of the Pharisees is in the form of a favourable comparison with those of the Sadducees and Essenes. The Essenes were complete fatalists: "All things are best ascribed to God."[9] The Sadducees, on the contrary, insisted "that to act what is good, or what is evil, is at men's own choice."[10] Between these extremes stood the Pharisees: "It hath pleased God to make a temperament, whereby what he wills is done, but so that the will of men can act virtuously or viciously."[11]

Another characteristic of the Pharisees was their beliefs about life after death.

They also believe that souls have an immortal vigor in them, and that under the earth there will be rewards or punishments, according as they have lived virtuously or viciously in this life; and the latter are to be detained in an everlasting prison, but that the former shall have power to revive and live again.[12]

These words are obscure and have been interpreted in different ways. It seems quite unnecessary to understand them as implying the transmigration of souls or any other non-Jewish notion. Apparently what Josephus means is that the Pharisees believed in the resurrection of the dead. His obscurity of

[8] Herford, *The Pharisees*, p. 52.
[9] *Antt.* 18,1,5.
[10] *Wars*, 2,8,14.
[11] *Antt.* 18,1,3.
[12] *Ibid.*

utterance is due to his attempt to couch this belief in language which should be intelligible to his Greek readers, to whom resurrection of the body seemed as absurd as immortality of the soul certain.

Belief in the resurrection of the body had been a fundamental part of Jewish thinking at least from the second pre-Christian century. Once the view had become orthodox, Judaism quite forgot that it was new and soon was easily convinced that it had been taught in the Scriptures from the beginning. The Sadducees denied this, not on theological grounds, but because it was an innovation: What was good enough for Moses was good enough for them. Against them the Pharisees quoted Scripture to support their views. Although the notion was of course not a part of these passages, the Scribes were able to read it in. Thus from the words, "Ye shall give Jehovah's heave-offering to Aaron the priest,"[13] R. Johanan deduced that Aaron was still living and hence concluded: "Here is also the resurrection of the dead signified." Many other equally unlikely passages were cited in proof. For example, R. Simai, after referring to Exod. 6:4, cites with approval Gamaliel's dictum that the Pentateuch, Prophets, and Hagiographa all contain proof that the Blessed One will raise the dead. To this the Mishna agrees:

He has no part in the world to come who denies that the resurrection can be proved from the Pentateuch.

In the Synoptic gospels we find Jesus arguing in precisely this fashion with the Sadducees, while the Pharisees listen in approval.[14] To ridicule the notion of resurrection, the Sadducees propound the hypothetical case of a woman who in turn buried seven less lusty husbands. Who would be entitled to claim her as spouse in the resurrection? Jesus answers in regulation manner. Does not the Scripture say that God said to Moses, I *am* [not, I *was*] the God of Abraham, Isaac, and Jacob? It is inconceivable that God is the God of dead people; hence they are living and the resurrection proved. Furthermore, the other stricture of Jesus, "For when they shall rise from the dead, they neither marry, nor are given in marriage; but are as angels in heaven,"[15] is paralleled by the saying of Rab (a third-century teacher):

Rab used to say, "In the world to come there is no eating or drinking or marrying or envy or hate; but the pious rest with crowns upon their heads, and are satisfied with the glory of God."[16]

Although the Talmud passage is late, there seems no good reason to question the antiquity of the view expressed, or to assume that it was borrowed

[13] Numb. 18:28.
[14] Mark 12:18-28; Matt. 22:23-34; Luke 20:27-40.
[15] Mark 12:25 and parallels.
[16] Berakot 17a.

from Christianity. Again, the book of Acts asserts that the Pharisees and Sadducees were also divided on the question of angels.[17]

But the distinguishing characteristic of the Pharisee was his acceptance of and reverence for tradition as supplementing the written law. This Josephus phrases explicitly:

What I would now explain is this, that the Pharisees have delivered to the people a great many observances by succession from their fathers, which are not written in the law of Moses; and for that reason it is that the Sadducees reject them, and say that we are to esteem those observances to be obligatory which are in the written word, but are not to observe what are derived from the traditions of our forefathers. And concerning these things it is that great disputes and differences have arisen among them, while the Sadducees are able to persuade none but the rich, and have not the populace obsequious to them, but the Pharisees have the multitude on their side.[18]

In a word, they were, as he writes in another place, "a certain sect of the Jews that appear more religious than others, and seem to interpret the laws more accurately."[19] Not differences of belief regarding the resurrection or angels, but acceptance or denial of the validity of the oral tradition as a supplement and authoritative interpretation of the law—this was the point of dispute between the Pharisees and Sadducees. The Sadducees maintained that the law (by this was meant the whole written Scripture, not the Pentateuch alone, as is often erroneously stated through confusing them on this point with the Samaritans) was binding, but did not "regard the observation of anything besides what the law enjoins them."[20] It is absurd to see in them, as they are often pictured, simply a political group, bloated millionaires indifferent to things religious. They were Jews, and from their point most loyal Jews. Actually the point of cleavage between Pharisee, Sadducee, and Essene appears to me to lie in their capacity for change. The bulk of the law came from the past when life was simple and uncomplicated. The years had brought their changes; the old law just would not fit. This the Sadducee simply denied; by closing his eyes to the changes he saw no need for alteration. The Essenes, on the contrary, recognized the changes, and sought to turn life back to the simpler days. By retiring from civilization they cut the Gordian knot. The Pharisees sought by their interpretations to make the law fit the new environs, believing as they did that God had provided for every circumstance that could arise. In this they had no idea that they were introducing new notes, although of course they were; they were simply rediscovering old truth. Stand-patters, as the Sadducees were, they none the less had, willy-nilly, to interpret the law, and regularly their interpretations

[17] Acts 23:8.
[18] *Antt.* 13,10,6
[19] *Wars* 1,5,2.
[20] *Antt.* 18,1,4.

were more austere than those of their rivals, but they never considered these interpretations sacred in the same sense that the Pharisees did theirs.

Failure to observe this difference in point of view not only has resulted in a distorted view of the differences between the groups, but in a total misunderstanding of the aim of the Pharisees. The law might say: "Remember the Sabbath day to keep it holy." This, however, was not enough. It was necessary to amplify and explain just what was work and what was not. Many and wonderful were the interpretations which were made. Here lies the origin of the popular notion that the chief joy of the Pharisee was devising new and difficult twists to put in the law. He is thus often pictured as singing:

> Count that day lost, whose low descending sun
> Finds no new "must" that simply can't be done.

All this is simply not historic. These fine-spun distinctions were not dictated by the desire to make the law burdensome, but to facilitate its fulfilment under changed conditions. One example will suffice. Food might not be carried outside of your house on the Sabbath. At once it became necessary to know what "outside of your house" meant. Commonly, houses were built in blocks about a common court. Provided no Sadducee lived in such a unit, all the houses could be considered one. Hence "outside the house" would signify "into the street," but not "into the courtyard." Thus food might be carried from one house to the other without transgressing the law.

Furthermore, the Sabbath legislation was calculated to make the Sabbath a peculiarly delightful day—our "blue Sundays" are no bequest from the Synagogue. To be sure, food might not be cooked on the Sabbath, but the Jews did not relish cold victuals on the Sabbath any more than we do. Accordingly, a clever anticipation of the fireless cooker was devised whereby the stomachs of men might rejoice and the law of God be unflouted. On the Sabbath a peculiarly good dinner was demanded. If necessary, a family should go light for several days to have the wherewithal for a proper meal.

Nor was fasting a requirement as is often supposed. The canting hypocrite portrayed in the gospel[21] with his smug, "I fast twice in the week; I give tithes of all that I get," has tended to give a quite erroneous view here. Fasting on Monday and Thursday was often practised, but was entirely voluntary and an act of uncommon piety. How many people practised it is not clear. Certain classes of people—students, for example—were flatly forbidden to fast. The general assertion that the fast was imposed upon all by the Pharisee or was considered a *sine qua non* of piety appears quite unjustified by the evidence. In the matter of setting apart the tithes the situation appears much the same. Those who banded themselves into associations to separate their tithes (the Haberim) had done it of their own will and accord.

[21] Luke 18:9-14.

Again, it should be pointed out that much of the discussion that seems to us casuistry and hair-splitting was to facilitate the keeping of the law by making it next to impossible to commit what we might call "the deadly sins."[22] Terrible penalties were imposed, but the legislation was so hedged about that in many cases the crime was almost impossible; in others, the conviction. The penalty for blasphemy was death, but blasphemy was not committed by uttering the sacred name or even by using it as an oath. It consisted in "cursing God by the name of God"—"God damn God!"—which it will be admitted would not often occur. Adultery, to be sure, was punishable by stoning to death, but to gain a conviction two eye-witnesses were required. Here, too, convictions were probably infrequent. These instances might be multiplied. Their opponents might charge them with transgressing the commandment of God because of their traditions, or with "teaching as their doctrines the precepts of men."[23] Such criticisms are easy; perhaps they were deserved. None the less, we should not blind ourselves to the fact that the story of the centuries has been a repeated demonstration that it is only through the precepts of men that the laws of God become effective.

Of the Sadducees little more need be said. In the time of Jesus they were a power to be reckoned with, although they were not numerous and were probably rarely to be met with outside Jerusalem. They are rarely mentioned in the gospels, nor is this surprising, since by the time of the composition of the gospels they had passed out of existence. The same obscurity veils the name Sadducee that does Pharisee. It may have been derived from Zadok, who succeeded Abiathar as priest in the days of Solomon. In the time we are concerned with, the Sadducees—whatever their actual origin—were roughly the priestly party in contrast to the popular party of the Pharisees. While the evidence at our disposal would scarcely justify the assumption that all the priests were Sadducees, it is to be observed that in two passages in the book of Acts[24] the chief priests and Sadducees are linked together. In the latter passage it is expressly said: "But the high priest rose up, and all they that were with him (which is the sect of the Sadducees)." The Boëthusians, from whom several high priests were appointed, appear to have been a Sadducaic family, taking their name from Boëthus, who in 26 B.C. had been appointed high priest by Herod, whose anxiety to marry the beautiful daughter Mariamne, was matched by his insistence that she be of distinguished lineage.

Although the synagogue, thanks to the efforts of the Pharisees, had supplanted the temple as the real centre of Judaism, the temple continued to exert tremendous influence, and the priestly ring was wealthy and powerful.

[22] A concept unknown to Judaism.
[23] Cf. Matt. 15:3,9.
[24] Acts 4:1 ff; 5:17.

Apparently the Sadducees were also in the majority in the Sanhedrin, and may safely be said to have controlled what political power Rome had left the little nation.

Reference has already been made to their denial of resurrection, not on the grounds of theology, but because it was an innovation. Similarly their disbelief in angels is hardly to be adduced as evidence that they were rationalists. Rather, the exuberant angelology and demonology which had been inherited from Persia along with resurrection apparently appeared a new-fangled innovation—and a vulgar one at that.

The contrast between the rigid conservatism of the Sadducees and the greater adaptability to change on the part of the Pharisees has given rise to a theory that appears to me worthy of more attention than has hitherto been paid to it. This difference of attitude, in the judgment of Finkelstein,[25] arose from their different environs. Originally the Sadducees were the country group. Here they were removed from contact with new ideas. Some of them eventually became wealthy, in short, became the great landholders. Although in later years—as in the days we are considering—they may have come to live in Jerusalem, they continued in their track; wealth, responsibility, and traditions all conspired to make them view with suspicion all innovations. The Pharisees, on the contrary, were originally an urban group. Thus exposed to new ideas and influences, they developed along lines quite impossible for the others. Gradually by their newly acquired eschatological teachings and more democratic ideas they won to themselves the mass of the Judean farmers, leaving for the Sadducees only the comparatively few wealthy families in the nation. Whether this thesis will eventually prove itself or not, it tends to emphasize the difference of attitude between the two groups and gives a not impossible explanation of it. The one caution to be borne in mind, not alone with regard to this particular explanation, but in all attempts to understand the Sadducees, is that however much their wealth and political power may have tended to make them a veritable aristocracy, which sought to entrench itself against popular attack, yet in their own eyes, as well in those of Josephus and the rest of Judaism, they were a religious party characterized by beliefs which were to be rigidly and austerely held.

The Scribes

In the New Testament is occasionally found the phrase "Scribes and Pharisees." Were these, then, two separate classes: a sect of Pharisees, and distinct from them a group of Scribes who were not Pharisees?

The origin of the Scribes was in the far past. Back in the days of Ezra the emphasis upon the law and its interpretation had called into existence

[25] "The Pharisees: their Origin and their Philosophy"—*Harvard Theological Review*, Vol. XXII, No. 3 (July, 1929), pp. 185-261.

a group of men called *Sopherim*. These men, as has been pointed out in a previous page, came to occupy an exalted place in later thinking. They were the Great Synagogue. The very title *Sopherim* was not used of their later successors, who were called *Hakamim*. They may well have made copies of the Scripture and may have counted its letters, but they were first and foremost "Men of the Book." Theirs was the duty to teach and expound it. In a word, they were scholars, not stenographers. Whereas the priests had formerly been the ones to whom Israel had gone for advice, now the scholars had gradually come to occupy this position. What the law *said* was not enough; What did it *mean*? How did it apply in this case, how in that? Such, as we have already seen, was the start of the oral traditional law. Since it was not written down for nearly five hundred years, it had to be passed on from one generation of scholars to the next. Naturally such a responsibility brought respect and distinction.

In the New Testament the Scribes, also called "lawyers" and "teachers of the law,"[26] were the professional teachers and learned men. Although not regarded with the same awe as their shadowy predecessors, their unique knowledge of the will and dictates of God made them men of great importance and well adapted for the positions of judges. Their verdict on the law, when ratified by the Sanhedrin—to which body some of the Scribes apparently belonged—itself became law.

Now as to party. That there was no party of Scribes appears certain, although undoubtedly a sort of informal freemasonry among colleagues existed, parallel to that found today among professional theologians. By the time we are considering the majority of the Scribes were probably of the Pharisaic persuasion—once Mark calls them "scribes of the Pharisees"[27]—but by no means all of the Pharisees were scholars. The majority of the Pharisees were not technically learned men; any of the ame ha-ares[28] might become members of the "brotherhood" by taking the pledges in the presence of three. The Scribes, on the contrary, were the learned—the Ph.D.'s of their time.[29]

In the time we are considering, Judea was the centre of their activity and

---

[26] In the Synoptic gospels Rabbi is frequently used of Jesus. This is not to be understood as a title, as later was the case. If used at all during these years, it was simply a complimentary term of respect. Neither Hillel nor Shammai has the title in Jewish sources. Later in the school of Jamnia (see below, p. 131) it was applied to Johanan ben Zakkai and those after him as a title "for what we might call a diplomaed Doctor of the Law" (Moore).

[27] Mark 2:16; cf. "Some of the scribes of the Pharisees' part" (Acts 23:9).

[28] For the significance of this term see below, pp. 126-128.

[29] "The Scribes . . . were a learned class whose vocation was the study and exposition of the law. In the first instance biblical scholars, as the name suggests, they became authorities also in the unwritten branch of the law, in the development of which they had the leading part. The Pharisees were a party whose endeavor it was to live in strict accordance with the law thus interpreted and amplified, and to bring the people to a similar conformity. Most of the Scribes were of this party, but the bulk of the Pharisees were not scholars."—Moore, *Judaism*, Vol. I, p. 66.

remained so even after the destruction of Jerusalem. Years later, after the war against Hadrian (134 A.D.), the schools of Galilee gained the ascendancy, but at the time of the ministry of Jesus there was no notable teacher or school there. Consequently the Scribes (and probably the Pharisees as well) had less influence there than we have often been led to suppose. The bulk of the Galilean population was made up of the descendants of converts; now, nearly two centuries after the Maccabean revolt, the populace was strongly Jewish, but fanatically and unlearnedly so. It was not until well along in the second century A.D. that there was there an educated Judaism. On the other hand, outside of Palestine, as at Nisibis, occasional learned schools were to be found a century earlier, which remained great centres of Jewish learning, as the Babylonian Talmud proves. Thus when we speak of Palestinian Judaism—in contrast to the Alexandrian or Hellenistic Judaism—it must not be thought to mean that Palestine had a monopoly; it is simply that Palestine was prominent in the field and that we know most about it.

Three scholars who exerted great influence a little before and during the advent of Christianity were Hillel, Shammai, and Johanan ben Zakkai. The first two have already been mentioned as constituting the last great "Pair," and establishing the two famous rival schools of interpretation. Hillel, to whom is ascribed the Golden Rule—"What is hateful to thee, do not to another"—represented the less conservative and kinder aspect of Judaism. This is perhaps to be attributed to his earlier environs—he came from Babylonia. His chief emphasis was that discussion of the law must ever take cognizance of actual conditions, instead of concerning itself with pure theory. Shammai, his great rival, reflects the more unbending rigorous side of Judaism. Johanan ben Zakkai, who founded the great school at Jamnia which served to preserve Judaism in the days of reconstruction after the fall of Jerusalem and to lay the track on which later rabbinical practice was to run, is probably responsible for the ultimate triumph of the views of the school of Hillel. In typically Jewish fashion the controversy was healed: A voice from heaven was heard at Jamnia saying, "The teachings of both schools are words of the living God, but in practice the Halakah of the school of Hillel is to be followed."[30]

The Ascetic Groups

No survey, however brief, of the make-up of Judaism would be complete without mention of the ascetic groups occasionally there to be found. Three of these sects or orders are known to us, although far less is actually known of them than the voluminous discussions would imply. Of these three the Essenes are described by Josephus as comprising one of the four "philosophical" sects of Judaism (the others being Pharisees, Sadducees, and "Fourth Philosophy"). From Philo also we have received brief mention of them. For

[30] Moore, *Judaism*, Vol. I, p. 85.

knowledge of the second order, the Therapeutæ, we are dependent upon Philo alone. A manuscript discovered at the end of the last century in Cairo describes the third, usually known as the "Covenanters of Damascus." All three of these groups—at least it is true of the first two—were radical departures from orthodox Judaism and apparently exerted very little influence. They were not numerous; the Essenes comprised but four thousand; the number of the other two is not known. The disproportionate space which Josephus gives to his description is not to be explained as due to their importance; rather it evidences his fondness for discussing the bizarre and for revealing his own familiarity with the unusual. Philo's detailed and not unfriendly mention of the Therapeutæ may well have been due, at least in part, to the occasional weariness that comes to every man enmeshed in a complicated economic order and the consequent wistful longing for the simple life.

Asceticism was alien to the genius of Judaism, and not unnaturally so, since asceticism is peculiarly individualistic and dualistic: the longing to rid one's soul of the defiling corruption of the body. To be sure, we meet Rechabites and Nazarites in the pages of the Old Testament. These, however, were not ascetic sects, but were simply reactionaries, men out of step with the times, who were not content, like Nestor, to extol the good old times, but insisted on reënacting them. Thus the Rechabites forbade the drinking of wine, but not on ascetic grounds. It was simply that they believed that the ideal life was the kind the Israelites had spent prior to the occupation of Canaan. This they sought to perpetuate. Vineyards were a sign of civilization and settled life—there were none for the nomads—hence the prohibition of wine.[31] Occasional figures like Elijah and Tishbite there were, but this type was not natural to Israel and its representatives few and far between. Marriage, a sane home life, thankful acceptance of the blessings with which a loving Father had endowed his children—these characterized Israel.

1. The Essenes. From all this the Essene differed radically. According to Josephus[32] the Essenes rejected pleasure as an evil, and praised continence and conquest over pleasure as a virtue. Apparently they were divided on the question of marriage. One group—Josephus would seem to mean that this was the main body—flatly rejected marriage and the procreation of children; another group, however, permitted marriage, but solely for the procreation of children. They were all woman-haters who "guard against the lascivious behavior of women, and are persuaded that none of them preserve their fidelity to one man."[33]

[31] Cf. Jer. 35:1-19.

[32] *Wars* 2,8,2-13; *Antt.* 18,1,5. Cf. also Philo, *On the Virtuous being also free* 12(§§75-87) 457 f.M.; Fragments preserved in Eusebius, *Præparatio* viii,8 and 13. These two passages from Philo are available in Yonge's English translation, Vol. III, pp. 523 ff. and Vol. IV, pp. 219-222.

[33] *Wars* 2,8,2.

They constituted an order to which members were admitted only after passing through various degrees and tests. Vows of secrecy were demanded. Numerous lustrations were practised; women were excluded from their fellowship. According to Pliny[34] they lived apart in communities on the west shore of the Dead Sea; Josephus, however, remarks: "They have no certain city, but many of them dwell in every city."[35] With regard to legal purity they far out-Phariseed the Pharisee. Their life was organized on a communistic basis; private property was unknown. Despising riches, they lived simply, worked hard, wore the simplest of white garments, abstained from the use of oil, ate together, often in silence, had secret teachings in which the names of angels appear to have played a part.

Those who desired admission to their number must live for a year as did they, but outside the fellowship. Full membership could not be achieved until after a three-year probation, and then only after tremendous vows not to communicate their doctrines to any save in the way and manner in which they had received them. The strictest of discipline was practised. Those convicted of sin were expelled from the fellowship. This, in theory at least, meant starvation, for by his oaths the guilty man could not eat food prepared by unclean hands. So Josephus tersely: "He was forced to eat grass, and famish his body with hunger till he perish."

In contrast to the Pharisees and Sadducees they were absolute determinists, were such scrupulous Sabbath observers that they refrained from the most intimate bodily functions on that day, and, as good ascetics should, held that the body was corruptible and perishable, but that the soul was immortal and would live for ever. In this respect they appear to have been in complete disaccord with orthodox Judaism. It might be conceivable that Josephus has over-emphasized this aspect to make it intelligible to Greek readers. Since, however, he compares this opinion to that held by the Greeks, he apparently is distinguishing them here from other Jews. Furthermore, his description of them "putting up certain prayers, which they have received from their forefathers, as if they made supplication for its [the sun's] rising" and of their extraordinary care that in performing the intimate details of their toilet "they may not affront the divine rays of light" has led many students to see in this group sun-worshippers. Accordingly the most contradictory views of the origin and affiliations of this strange group have been given.[36] Was it a movement emanating entirely from Judaism, was it coloured or influenced from without Jewry, or was it an essentially heathen movement masquerading in Jewish garb? Characteristics now Greek, now Buddhist, now Persian have all been pointed out by scholars to prove the hypothesis approving it-

[34] See passage quoted p. 123.
[35] *Wars* 2,8,4.
[36] For the *hic jacet* see Schürer, *op. cit.*, Div. II, Vol. II, pp. 205-218. See also "The Essenes" printed at the end of J. B. Lightfoot's *Saint Paul's Epistles to the Colossians and Philemon*, pp. 347-417.

self to the particular investigator. Since the group was essentially a secret society, guarding its secrets so vigorously, and since our knowledge is entirely at second hand, all such speculation appears to me at best uncertain. Were I to venture a guess, it would be that the movement was the consequence of an attempt to push back the years and to regain those days when the law was workable without interpretation; but that while thus essentially a movement from Judaism it had acquired certain new elements—partially borrowed from without, partially the development from within. Perhaps, however, it was but the reflection of the wave of weariness and disillusionment which was sweeping over the ancient world, and which, then as now, found expression in occasional praise of the simpler secluded life in contrast to the effete and cloying world of society. That this little movement attracted some notice in the Roman world and had become the nucleus about which legend was growing is revealed by Pliny's somewhat fulsome, if ill-informed, description:

Lying west of Asphaltites [the Dead Sea], and sufficiently distant to escape its noxious exhalations, are the Esseni, a people that live apart from the world, and marvellous beyond all others throughout the whole earth, for they have no women among them; to sexual desire they are strangers; of money they have none; the palm trees are their only companions. Day after day their numbers are fully recruited by multitudes of strangers that resort to them, driven thither to adopt their usages by the tempests of fortune and wearied by the miseries of life. Thus it is, through thousands of ages—incredible to relate—this people eternally prolongs its existence, without a single birth taking place there; so fruitful a source of population to them is that weariness of life which is felt by others.[37]

2. The Therapeutæ. Somewhat similar to the Essenes were the Therapeutæ, if the writing, *Concerning the Contemplative Life,* is actually from the pen of Philo.[38] Although their centre was near Alexandria, this was not the only place they were to be found. In contrast to the Essenes who spent their days in toil, the Therapeutæ devoted their time to contemplation, "studying . . . the laws and sacred oracles of God enunciated by the holy prophets, and hymns, and psalms, and all kinds of other things by reason of which knowledge and piety are increased and brought to perfection."[39] The interval between morning and evening prayers was given over to meditation and the theoretic practice of virtue. The Scriptures were interpreted allegorically; hymns and melodies were composed.

Furthermore, while the Essenes constituted a cœnobite order, the Therapeutæ lived in separate huts or cells, assembling only on the Sabbath and on each fiftieth day, which constituted their special festival, and was called

[37] *Nat. Hist.* v,15(17).
[38] Formerly this was denied; see Schürer, *op. cit.,* Div. II, Vol. III, pp. 357 f.
[39] *de Vit. Contempl.* 3(§25)475M.

the *Pannuchis* ("all night festival"). Unlike the Essenes, women were admitted to the order, apparently on equal terms, but, as is said to be true in heaven, there was no marrying nor giving in marriage. In the common sanctuary was a wall extending part way to the roof. On one side sat the men, on the other the women. Here the law was expounded. On the *Pannuchis* a common meal was held. To it they came "joyful, but with exceeding gravity" and dressed in white. After this meal—it was of the simplest sort: bread and salt mixed with hyssop—they sang and danced, first in two choirs, then gradually uniting in a "spiritual Bacchanal" in which the free love of God was the only drink. Apparently desiring to emphasize the decorum that prevailed, Philo was at pains to remark:

> And the women also share in this feast, the greater part of whom, although old, are virgins in respect of their purity (not indeed through necessity, as some of the priestesses among the Greeks are, who have been compelled to preserve their chastity more than they would have done of their own accord), but out of an admiration for and love of wisdom.

The fate of this strange order, like its origin, is unknown to us. Indeed, were it not for this little essay, perhaps written by Philo as a quiet object lesson to the smart set of Egypt's capital, we would never have heard of these pre-Christian monks of Lake Mareotis.

3. The Covenanters of Damascus. The chance discovery of eight leaves of an ancient Hebrew manuscript among those found in 1896 by Schechter in the Genizah of an old synagogue at Fostat (near Cairo) reveals the existence of another—apparently Jewish—group hitherto unknown. Its origin is best set forth in the words of the manuscript:

> At the end of the devastation of the land arose men who removed the boundary and led Israel astray; and the land was laid waste because they spoke rebelliously against the commandments of God by Moses and also against his holy Anointed, and prophesied falsehood to turn Israel back from following God. But God remembered the covenant with the forefathers, and he raised up from Aaron discerning men and from Israel wise men, and he heard them, and they dug the well. "The well, princes dug it, nobles of the people delved it, with the legislator" (Numb. 21:18). The well is the law, and they who dug it are the captivity of Israel who went forth from the land of Judah and sojourned in the land of Damascus, all of whom God called princes because they sought him. . . . The legislator is the interpreter of the law, as Isaiah said, "bringing forth a tool from his work" (Isa. 54:16), and the nobles of the people are those who came to delve the well with the statutes which the legislator decreed that men should walk in them in the complete end of wickedness; and besides these they shall not obtain any (statutes) until the teacher of righteousness shall arise in the last times.[40]

From this it would seem that a number of Jews, including some priests and

---

[40] *Fragments of a Zadokite Work* 8:1-10.

Levites, had withdrawn from Judea and had settled in the neighbourhood of Damascus, binding themselves by a new covenant to live in strict accord with the law as enunciated by their legislator.

Although they were not ascetics—in the sense that the Essenes or Therapeutæ were—they had broken loose from society, disgusted by its laxities, and were ultrastrict in their habits. They have been aptly styled "come-outers from Judaism." They styled themselves "Israelites from the land of Judah"; their expected future Teacher was to come from Aaron and Israel, that is, from the tribe of Levi, not Judah. The Essenes sent offerings to the temple, although that these included sacrifices is not clear. Not so these "Covenanters"; the temple in Jerusalem was by them utterly rejected. In its stead they had their own sanctuary with sacrificial worship.

Polygamy, by no means unknown in Palestine, and marriage between uncle and niece were inveighed against; far more stringent Sabbath observance than in Palestinian orthodoxy was required. Particularly severe was the dietary legislation. For example: fish must be split and blooded while alive; grasshoppers and locusts must be boiled or cooked alive; honey in the honeycomb was forbidden. Failure to meet these requirements was severely punished. In addition to the penalties of Mosaic legislation was the dread "Separation from the Purity," that is, expulsion from their "camps."

This group appears to me to have attempted to solve the problems confronting all Jewry: an immovable law in a changing society. The Pharisee sought to adapt and modify the law to make it workable. It was precisely this that these Covenanters refused to do. Rather, leaving the more complicated society behind, they sought once more to reproduce in their "camps" the wilderness experiences of Israel. If the cause of their departure from "the land of Judah" was the activity of those men who were thus "removing the boundary" and "leading Israel astray"—that is, the Scribes—what wonder that the disgruntled in their protest reached extremes which would make the most rigid Pharisee appear a gross latitudinarian?[41] If this hypothesis be sound, the origin of all three of these groups—Essenes, Therapeutæ, Covenanters—would be seen to be due to the same cause, the attempt to go back to the good old days and to live in such a manner that the law unamended would once more exactly fit. The Pharisees, as we have seen, adapted the opposite method of modifying the law to fit the new environs, although they would have been scandalized if they had realized it. Theoretically either course of action was possible; practically, of course, there could be no question. "The moving finger writes, and having writ moves on." Between these two extremes stood the Sadducee. He stubbornly refused to see the problem; by shutting his eyes it conveniently vanished. When his temple crashed about

---

[41] In this last paragraph I do not mean that the Covenanters and the Pharisees were necessarily contemporaries. Although this appears to me highly probable, we know far too little about the date of the "exodus" of the one and the origin of the other to speak with confidence.

him in 70 A.D., he never emerged from the wreckage. Nor were these three outlooks on life unique to Judaism. Every age has seen them, and in every age the answer has been the same.

The Fourth Philosophy

To his brief survey of the "three sects of philosophy peculiar to Judaism"—Pharisees, Sadducees, and Essenes—Josephus appends a paragraph about "the fourth sect of Jewish philosophy" of which "Judas the Galilean was the author." Little need here be said of this group. I have already sought to show that this group—it would be less confusing to call them the Home Rule Party—was no new emergence in the days of Judas of Galilee, but was simply a movement of Jewish patriots irked by outside control.[42] Starting at least as far back as Hezekiah's[43] opposition to Roman control in the person of Herod and his father Antipater, this movement had continued through the years, seeking to foment rebellion. Its motto, "The sword and not sparingly; no king but Jehovah," well illustrates its temper. How much influence it exerted until shortly before the final outbreak against Rome in 66 A.D. is hard to say. It is probably fair to say that during such troublous months as those in which Gaius sought to set up his statue in the temple it gained new leases of life. But on the whole it apparently was regarded by the Pharisees as a dangerous and absurd evidence of fanaticism. When God saw fit to intervene, he would do it directly without the need of human aid. To the Sadducees and others in positions of wealth and leadership, realizing as they did how easy it would be to upset the ship of state, it was an unmitigated outrage and danger. To what extent it had leavened the thinking of the masses it is impossible to say.

The Ame Ha-ares

This phrase, literally the "people of the land," is often used to designate the common people, or, as they are euphemistically referred to today, the "masses." The singular, am ha-ares, was sometimes employed with various significance to mean "layman," much as the Greek used ἰδιώτης; commonly, however, it was used to distinguish the uneducated from the learned.

Judaism was primarily a religion in which knowledge was required, for, as has been shown in a previous chapter, to fulfil the law required a very exact and comprehensive knowledge of what the law contained and implied. Such a knowledge was naturally beyond the reach of the average man who had neither time nor inclination for the necessary detailed study. The result was that while the rich and politically powerful may be spoken of as constituting the aristocracy, in a larger sense the true aristocracy was that of knowledge, not of wealth or birth. Akiba had been an am ha-ares, but by

---

[42] At this time it would be well to reread pp. 41 f., 68, 71-77.
[43] Its roots may well have gone back to the days of the captivity.

his steadfast devotion to learning had become a prominent scholar; Aquila, the translator of the Old Testament into Greek for Jewish orthodoxy, was a proselyte. On the other hand, even the high priest himself, if he were not a learned man—and priests then as now usually were not—might be excluded from the society of the learned and regarded by them with contempt. Just as an am ha-ares might become a member of the Haberim by binding himself by oath to abstain from ceremonial defilement and to strive to conform thus to the law's demands—if he had formerly been a flagrant violator of the proprieties and decencies of life, a period of probation was usually insisted upon—and by years of study might become a student, eventually even a teacher as had Akiba; so, on the other hand, a member of the Haberim could forfeit his standing by engaging in certain occupations, or a student by abandoning his studies could sink to the level of the am ha-ares.

Thus between these groups—educated and ignorant—stood a deep gulf. Many statements are preserved expressing the hostility felt by each for the other, and reminding the student of mediæval history of the clashes between "town and gown." "Cursed is the man who lies with any beast" was not too delicately applied to the marriage of a scholar with a woman from the rank of the uneducated, for "they are loathsome and their women are unclean."

Rabbi Eleazar said, "It is lawful to stab an am ha-ares on a Day of Atonement that falls on a Sabbath" [that is, a day of superlative holiness]. Said his disciples, "You mean to slaughter him?" "No," said Eleazar, "slaughtering requires a benediction; stabbing does not."[44]

A similar hatred expressing itself often in picturesque exaggeration was felt by the uneducated.

Rabbi Akiba said, "When I was an am ha-ares, I used to say, 'I wish I had one of those scholars, and I would bite him like an ass.'" His disciples said, "You mean like a dog." He replied, "An ass's bite breaks the bone; a dog's does not."

Just as the word Pharisee has become synonymous with self-righteous hypocrite, so a romantic aura of piety has been cast about the masses. They were the truly godly of the land, the last vestige of genuine religion in a Judaism which had become sterile and arid. They were the righteous remnant of which the prophets had spoken. While the arrogant scholar and hypocritical Pharisee turned a deaf ear to Jesus, "the common people heard him gladly." This view, while widely held, is unfortunately destitute of evidence. That many a godly man or woman was styled am ha-ares in a designation so sweeping that both high priest and outcast received it is likely. Many of those designated "sinners" may have been far from bad men; so styled sim-

---

[44] For this quotation and the following one, as well as for other material in this section, I am indebted to the note of the late Professor Moore in Jackson and Lake's *Beginnings of Christianity*, Vol. I, p. 443.

ply because they did not or could not practise all the minutiæ of the law. Jesus and his disciples were undoubtedly regarded as ame ha-ares for their latitudinarianism touching the laws of ceremonial cleanness and the Sabbath. Indeed, the attitude of Jesus, an unlettered commoner, in venturing to declare what was the will of God and to criticize those who had made the Divine Will and Revelation a lifetime's study undoubtedly aroused the most intense and not unnatural antipathy from the outraged recipients of his attack. None the less, after all exceptions have been made, to argue that it was in this group that the real piety of Israel was preserved is as silly as maintaining today that the only true devotion to God is to be found among the great unchurched.

Chapter VIII

THE ORGANIZATION OF JUDAISM

In contradistinction to the make-up of Judaism, a convenient designation of the various groups or sects differing among themselves both as to thought and practice, we may speak of the organization of Judaism. Three institutions may be mentioned: the Sanhedrin, the temple with its priestly hierarchy, and the synagogue. The last of these has already been described; a brief word about the other two will not be out of place.

The Sanhedrin

Although in the days of the Christian beginnings Judea, Samaria, and Idumea no longer enjoyed independence but comprised the Roman province of Judea, governed by a Roman procurator in whom all authority was centred, a very considerable authority, both legislative and judicial, was delegated to the supreme court of Jerusalem, known as the Sanhedrin. It remained not alone the symbol of the days of lost independence, but also a very real power in Jewish life until the destruction of the temple in 70 A.D.

Of its early history we know very little. Later rabbinical exegesis sought to connect it genetically with the council of seventy elders who were said to have aided Moses in his deliberations.[1] This is of course pure fiction, and simply reveals again the rabbinic view that, as in heaven, so on earth, "as it was in the beginning, is now, and ever shall be." Romantic identification of the later body with this traditional group may well account for the number of members. Elders of Israel are mentioned frequently in the Old Testament; nothing, however, indicates that they formed any such autonomous body as the later Sanhedrin. The earliest reference to such a body is in the letter from Antiochus the Great to Ptolemy which Josephus quotes in full.[2] In this letter direction is given that the Senate ($\gamma\epsilon\rho o\nu\sigma\acute{\iota}\alpha$), priests, scribes of the temple, and sacred singers are to be freed from all taxes. The presumption is that this Senate—apparently an aristocratic council headed by the high priest—does not antedate the Greek period and is a direct result of the influence of the hellenizing policy of Egypt and Syria. With the break between the later Hasmoneans and the Pharisees, the latters' rivals, the Sadducees, who now comprised the priestly aristocracy, became the supporters of the throne and apparently formed the majority of the Senate, although

[1] Numb. 11:16.
[2] *Antt.* 12,3,3.

some recognition seems to have been given to the older priestly dynasty which
had now been superseded by the Hasmonean. Alexandra, as has been already indicated,[3] wisely granted this body more independent authority than
it had exercised during the previous reigns and in addition to the nobles and
priests who had formerly constituted its membership gave some recognition
to the Scribes, who had gained great strength through the support not
alone of the Pharisees, but of the people as a whole. Hyrcanus had annulled
their ordinances at the time of his break with them; now they seem to
have been able to force Alexandra to turn the tables. From now on they
exerted no little power in the council, although (probably) holding but a
minority of seats.

The earliest reference by Josephus to this Senate (*gerousia*) by the title
Sanhedrin (συνέδριον, literally "court"), which it was later to enjoy,
is in the account of the difficulty in which Herod, as governor of Galilee,
was involved because of his zeal in chastising Hezekiah and his band.[4] In
this circumstance the nature of the body, strongly conservative and opposed
to the growing power of Antipater, the pro-Roman, is clearly to be seen.
The casual way in which the Sanhedrin is here mentioned does not suggest
that it was any new designation for the council. Perhaps Schürer is correct
in his suggestion that Josephus used the word here because of the judicial
authority it was seeking to exert over Herod, "for it is in this sense that
συνέδριον is specially used in later Greek."[5]

One of Herod's first acts, after he had become king, was to wreak his
displeasure upon this body. Josephus says explicitly, "He slew all the members of the Sanhedrin,"[6] although in a later page he says, "He . . . slew
forty-five of the principal men of Antigonus' party."[7] Apparently these two
statements are to be reconciled by not pressing the "all" of the former, but
limiting it to designate those members of the body who were hostile to him.
During his long reign the actual power of the Sanhedrin suffered eclipse;
with his death and the dismemberment of his kingdom its authority became limited to Judea proper, thus resembling the Senate (βουλή) of the
Greek cities, which controlled not alone the city proper, but also the nearby
villages and countryside which belonged loosely to such a city. Thus Josephus can say:

> The city Jerusalem is situated in the very middle; on which account some have,
> with sagacity enough, called that city the Navel of the country. . . . Judea . . .

---

[3] Pp. 33 f.

[4] *Antt.* 14,9,4. In a preceding chapter (14,5,4) he mentions the five councils (συνέδρια) which
Gabinius had created when he divided Palestine into five toparchies in the endeavour to destroy
the unity of the rebellious little land. In the *Wars* (1,8,5) he had referred to them as "conven-
tions" (σύνοδοι).

[5] Schürer, *op. cit.*, Div. II, Vol. I, p. 169.

[6] *Antt.* 14,9,4.

[7] *Antt.* 15,1,2.

was parted into eleven portions, of which the royal city Jerusalem was supreme, and presided over all the neighbouring country, as the head does over the body.[8]

In each of these eleven toparchies into which Judea was divided when it was taken from Archelaus and turned into a province was a local court of twenty-three members before whom the less important cases were heard; the Sanhedrin in Jerusalem, however, was the supreme body and, as the frequent references in the New Testament reveal, remained the dominating force in Jewish life until its overthrow in the débâcle of 66-73 A.D. At that time it was stripped of its power. In Jamnia, to be sure, the doctors of the law formed a so-called Court of Justice (*Bet Din*), which they fondly believed to be a continuation of the Sanhedrin which had existed in unbroken continuity from the time of Moses. This new body, while modelled after the earlier body, was totally different in that it was simply a court—the legislative power enjoyed by the Jerusalem Sanhedrin had been abolished— and at least at first even its judicial power was purely theoretical. Later it apparently regained some real jurisdiction over things Jewish, but even this was actually usurped, never formally granted by the now supreme Rome.

All this makes it very difficult for the student to gain any real information about the earlier body, for the Mishna tract *Sanhedrin*—our chief source of information—describes it in the light of the later *Bet Din*. Thus in this tract the Sanhedrin was a body of Scribes, headed by the supreme teachers of Israel. "The high priest might be a member of the court, but was subject to its jurisdiction." All this is surely not historical, but is simply an ingenious reading back into the past the institution then in effect.

The Sanhedrin would seem to have been made up of two factions: the priestly group with Sadducean sympathies, who held the majority of the seats, and the doctors and scholars from the Pharisees. How the vacancies were filled and for what term the members held office we are completely ignorant. Apparently it consisted of seventy-one members: seventy plus the high priest, who, in spite of the flat denial by the later Jewish tradition, was undoubtedly the president of the body.

As has been indicated, its authority was limited to the eleven toparchies of Judea proper; accordingly, Jesus, for example, was outside its jurisdiction as long as he remained in Galilee or the Perea. Nevertheless, it may well have exerted an *influence* on Jews everywhere, but only as they were willing to yield to its prestige. In Judea, however, it was the supreme native court with almost full power—both legislative and judicial—allowed it by the Roman governors. The sole limit to its power was in the matter of the death sentence. This apparently could be pronounced by the governor alone. Not all cases would come before it; but when the lower courts could not

[8] *Wars* 3,3,5.

agree or when the matter was of sufficient importance it was referred to this body. When once invoked, the decision of the supreme body was final and beyond the realm of appeal. It possessed independent authority, could order the arrest to be made by its own police, and could move against any one within its jurisdiction save Roman citizens. In the case of one of these trespassing beyond the barrier of the temple, even he might be arrested and convicted. Apparently it assembled on Tuesdays and Fridays, as did the lower courts.

Detailed information as to its procedure is given in the Mishna tract *Sanhedrin*. Here it said that the members sat in a semicircle "like half a round threshing floor that all the judges might see the others' faces." Before them stood two clerks to record the votes; in front of them sat three rows of disciples of the learned men to learn the methods of the court. Then follows a detailed account of the treatment of witnesses, the length of the trial, the lapse of time—thirty days—that was afforded the condemned to adduce new evidence before the pronouncement of the sentence, the majority required for a vote of acquittal and of condemnation.

How much of this actually reflects the proceedings of the Sanhedrin when it functioned with real authority, how much it reflects simply the theoretical procedure of the later body which, shorn of its power, could afford to draw up the most intricate rules of procedure since they could never be put into practice, is far from clear. Accordingly, it is perhaps not without value to warn that the not infrequent analyses by modern lawyers, quite destitute of any historical perspective or knowledge, of the trial of Jesus in the light of what they fondly call "the legal proceedings of the Sanhedrin" are utterly worthless in spite of their pseudo-scientific ponderousness and display.

The Temple and the Priestly Hierarchy

The priesthood of the temple had long constituted the aristocracy of the nation. Surely by the days of Ezra and Nehemiah, and probably earlier, none but those of unquestioned descent from Aaron had been allowed to officiate in the temple. Since the fourth century, perhaps even earlier, the high priest had been the recognized head of Israel. Just when the office of high priest arose is difficult to say, although this constituted no problem for traditional Judaism, confident that Aaron had graced that august office.[9] Actually the question is fictitious, since the office never arose suddenly. Rather it was a dignity which grew in the days of the second temple, due to the fact that there was now no king to overshadow. In Haggai and Zechariah (but not in Ezekiel) is clear reference to a chief priest who occupies an office distinctly different from his fellows. In the "Holiness Code" men-

---

[9] Josephus, *c. Apion.* i,7, mentions the list of "names of our high priests, from father to son, set down in our records, for the interval of two thousand years."

tion is made of the "high priest among his brethren, upon whose head the anointing oil is poured."[10]

The high-priesthood became an hereditary office, and continued as such to the days of Antiochus Epiphanes. Then the Syrian court claimed the right to appoint whom they pleased, and, banishing the rightful Onias, gave the office to the highest bidder. With the estabishment of the Hasmonean line Simon was consecrated high priest "forever until a faithful prophet should arise." From then on until Alexandra the office of high priest and king was held by the same man. This situation, unique in the history of Israel, made the incumbent absolute dictator in things both secular and religious. With the fall of the Hasmoneans and the rise of Herod the office was stripped of much of its power. Herod used it for his own advantage, appointing and deposing at his own pleasure. In this policy he was followed by the Roman authorities. The hundred years between the advent of Herod and the outbreak of the great rebellion saw no less than twenty-eight high priests,[11] of whom Herod himself made seven. Since now the office was not hereditary, it was transferred from one family to another. These families through intermarriage formed an elite inner circle. Since the tremendous wealth of the temple and unceasing revenue came into their hands, they became a very powerful group, veritably a "closed corporation." Thus the term ἀρχιερεῖς ("chief priests") came to be applied not only to the actual incumbent and the past high priests still alive, but to these allied families from which as a general rule the high priest was chosen. As has already been pointed out, they generally tended to sympathize with the Sadducees, although not all the priests were from this group. In the days with which we are chiefly concerned they were at the head of the Sanhedrin—the high priest who chanced to be in office was president—and thus of the local national government.

The priesthood was a distinct order, and was fenced about with restrictions to keep it of pure blood. The priest might marry only an undefiled virgin or a widow. She must be of Israelitish stock, for "he who is a partaker of the priesthood must propagate of a wife of the same nation."[12] The high priest was forbidden to marry a widow. He must be totally free from all bodily defects. In addition to the bodily disqualifications listed in Lev. 21:16-23 the later rabbis went into the matter with painful specificness, listing 142 different bodily defects which debarred. Apparently he must be at least twenty years of age before he could serve.[13] The consecration of a priest was attended with three distinct rites: the washing of his body with

[10] Lev. 21:10.

[11] The succession of high priests was almost kaleidoscopic, but it had not turned into an annual office, as might be implied by the words, "for he [Annas] was father-in-law to Caiaphas, who was high priest that year" (John 18:13; cf. 11:49 and 51).

[12] Josephus, c. Apion. i,7.

[13] At least the later rabbinical tradition so relates. See Schürer, op. cit., Div. II, Vol. I, p. 215.

water; the investment with the sacred garments; a series of sacrifices and ceremonies. The

> . . . precious oil upon the head,
> That ran down upon the beard,
> Even Aaron's beard;
> That came down upon the skirt of his garments;
> Like the dew of Hermon,
> That cometh down upon the mountains of Zion[14]

was restricted to the high priest, who was specifically the "anointed high priest." The actual use of oil even for the high priest was apparently discontinued at least by the time of Herod's temple; none the less, he continued to be thus designated.

The receipts of the temple—and incidentally of the priests—were very great,[15] although, if Josephus and the later rabbis are correct, it fell largely into the hands of a select few who thus became very rich at the expense of their lesser colleagues, whom they accordingly despised. This income came from three principal sources: the sacrifices, the taxes, the gifts and offerings. Of the sacrifices the priests always obtained part, for even in the case of the whole burnt offering they received the hides, a source of revenue by no means to be despised. Of the other victims the priests obtained more, ranging from the sin and trespass offerings, of which they received practically all the meat, to the peace and thank offerings, in which they got only a share. Far more important were the taxes which were independent of the sacrifices and which included the first fruits, the *terumah* or payment in kind upon all produce, the tithes, the first born of all clean animals, the equivalent redemptive value in the case of unclean animals, the five-shekel redemption of every male child who openeth the womb, as well as a portion of the proceeds from the sheep-shearing. In addition to these regular contributions, which every pious Jew felt obligated to pay, were irregular gifts and offerings incident to especial vows and the like, and finally fines collected on stolen property which could not be returned to the owner.

All of the above described income went to the priests as their personal property. The support of the temple itself was met by entirely distinct taxes and gifts, prominent among which were the half-shekel tax,[16] the gift of wood for the sacrificial fires, and all sorts of free-will offerings. Since not only the Jews actually residing in Palestine, but all Jewry, wherever dispersed, were included in these benefactions, the toll collected by the temple and its hierarchy was a huge amount.

The duties of the priests were many and varied, but since their number was so great—probably between five and six thousand—the individual priest

[14] Psalm 133:2 f.
[15] For a complete list see Schürer, *op. cit.*, Div. II, Vol. I, pp. 230-254.
[16] See p. 95.

served only a few hours during the year. In the days of Herod's temple the priests were divided into twenty-four courses, each course serving in rotation a week at a time, changing each Sabbath. On the Passover, Pentecost, and Tabernacles all twenty-four courses served simultaneously. These twenty-four courses were further divided into subdivisions, the number of which varied from five to nine. Each course and subdivision was presided over by an official. Some of the duties were performed by stated priests; others were performed by the priests of the particular course on duty, who were chosen by lot.[17] A task such as the offering of the holy incense, according to the Mishna,[18] could be performed by a priest but once in a lifetime. Since a priest was on duty but four or five weeks at most during the year, the majority of them apparently dwelt outside the city throughout Judea. It will be remembered, for example, that Mattathias, the father of the Maccabean revolt, lived in Modein. According to the evidence presented by Strack and Billerbeck[19] a very large proportion of the priests lived in Jericho. This would give point to the story of the Good Samaritan.

The high priest rarely officiated except at the times of the great feasts. Actually he was not obliged to take active part except on the Day of Atonement, although it was usual for him to do so during the preceding week, and according to Josephus on the Sabbaths and times of the new moon.[20] On the Day of Atonement he went alone behind the "veil of the temple" into the holy of holies.

The duties of the priests fell into four classes: (1) the care and custody of the temple, its furnishings, and treasure; (2) the policing of the temple, responsibility for order and decorum, keeping watch in the inner courts, the opening and closing of the great gates; (3) incidental duties such as the oversight and conduct of the music, and of the more menial duties of cleansing and repair of the building itself and its courts; (4) the conduct of the daily sacrifices.

The lesser duties, including the music, were performed by the Levites. In Deuteronomy no distinction between priests and Levites is made; by the time of Ezekiel, however, the line of demarcation was drawn. From then on they are the priests' assistants, and all distinction between the Levites and the "singers and doorkeepers" has disappeared. Like the priests they were divided into twenty-four courses and were carefully supervised.

One further official may be mentioned briefly—the *Sagan*. Although the rabbinical authorities differ as to his precise status, some making him a sort of substitute high priest, he appears to have been the prefect of the priest-

[17] Cf. Luke 1:8 ff.
[18] M. Yoma 2.
[19] Strack und Billerbeck, *Kommentar zum Neuen Testament aus Talmud und Midrasch*, Vol. II, pp. 180 f. This work is of the utmost importance to the student of the New Testament.
[20] *Wars* 5,5,7.

hood, that is, the στρατηγὸς τοῦ ἱεροῦ or captain of the temple.[21] To use a modern phrase, he was the chief of the temple police. His responsibilities and power were great. It is interesting to observe that no less a personage than Rabbi Hanina ben Teradion, a contemporary of Johanan ben Zakkai and a prominent teacher in Israel, once held this office.[22]

The daily sacrifices fell into two classes. Of the first were the public sacrifices, offered in the name of the people. The cost of these sacrifices was defrayed by the peoples' own offering—especially the half-shekel tax. Some of them occurred every day, others at the time of especial feasts and celebrations. The second class comprised the private sacrifices. They were offered in the name of the individual who sponsored and paid for them. Both of these classes were of three types: (1) the whole burnt offering; (2) the sin and trespass offerings (with all save the fat, which was burned, going to the priests); (3) the peace or thank offering (in which the sacrificer, since no sin was to be atoned for, received the bulk of the meat "as material for a jocund sacrificial feast").

Of the *regular* daily sacrifice in the name of the people (that is, of the first class) there were two. Every morning and every evening a male lamb, one year old and without blemish, was burnt on the great altar which stood in the inner court and in front of the temple proper, separated from it by the brazen laver in which the priests washed their hands and feet preparatory to entering the house.[23] With this burnt offering was a meat and drink offering of flour mixed with oil and baked into a cake and a quarter hin of wine. Immediately preceding the morning sacrifice and following the evening sacrifice (that is, at dawn and 3 P.M.), an offering of incense was burnt, not on the great altar, but on the golden altar of incense, which with the seven-branched candlestick and table of shewbread stood in the front chamber of the temple (ναός). This room, sixty feet long and high and thirty feet wide, was called the *hekal*. Behind the *hekal* and separated from it by a curtain—the veil of the temple—stood the other and smaller room, the *debir*, or holy of holies. This was entirely empty, and was entered but once a year by the high priest, who for that purpose exchanged his elaborate vestments for the simple but costly white robe of fine linen.

Together with the worship went vocal and instrumental music; at intervals two priests sounded a fanfare on their silver trumpets as a signal for the congregation to fall in prayer. Seven psalms formed a sort of sacred series, one for each day in the week, beginning with Sunday. They were the twenty-fourth, forty-eighth, eighty-second, ninety-fourth, eighty-first,

[21] Cf. Acts 4:1; 5:24,26.

[22] Moore, *Judaism*, Vol. II, pp. 114 ff., 482. This should warn that while the (Sadducaic) priests and (Pharisaic) Scribes were usually distinct exceptions occurred.

[23] The whole structure, consisting of the temple itself, its courts, walls, and porticoes, was called τὸ ἱερόν; the temple proper ὁ ναός.

ninety-third, and ninety-second. On the Passover, Feast of Tabernacles, and on each of the eight days of the Feast of Dedication the Hallel (Psalms 113-118) were recited.

But the regular daily sacrifices and those offered in the name of the nation on the feast days constituted but a tiny fraction of the total number of sacrificial victims. The jostling, sweating hosts of pilgrims who surged through the temple courts not alone on the days of especial holiness, but throughout the year, each wanting his part in the ancient custom; the many priests in attendance; the lowing and bellowing of terrified cattle in the pens and on the marble slabs; the billowing clouds of smoke and nauseous stench from burning fat and meat; the cries of the hawkers and money-changers—all this might well have seemed to an even less sensitive observer than Jesus of Nazareth a strange answer to the query of an Isaiah or a Micah.

Though the temple service continued to the fall of the city and was flocked to by thousands of pilgrims anxious to assemble to "Zion whither the tribes go up," actually it had long ceased to be the real centre of Jewish life. It remained a glamorous symbol, a visual proof of the nearness of Jehovah. Once in his lifetime a Galilean peasant might make the trip, but week in week out he attended the simple unpretentious service in his local synagogue. These were the real answer to the prophets' cry.

Chapter IX

HOPES FOR THE FUTURE

As a little state constantly endangered by her more powerful neighbours, Israel's fate was hardly commensurate with her confidence that the supreme God of the whole world was actually King in a peculiar sense of Israel alone. For Israel alone had recognized his sovereignty. At Sinai the people, when informed by Moses of Jehovah's will and laws, had with one voice cried: "All the words which Jehovah hath spoken will we do."[1] The years had told a sad story of internal discord, the rending asunder of the kingdom, the successive collapse of north and south before the powerful invader. Could this be the fate which the supreme God had decreed for his own peculiar people? There could be but one answer. Eventually the scales of the balance would right themselves. A good time was coming; it might be long delayed. God had promised; he could not forswear himself. The days of David and Solomon, when seen through the mists of the years and in contrast to the present abject state of the little land, had taken on a romantic and wholly unhistorical color. Those were the day of gold, but they gave a pattern for the future. Once more, in God's own good time, the golden age would return: freed from the oppression of ruthless and uncircumcised intruders, purged of her sins which had been the actual cause of her downfall, she would experience an era of peace and blessing which would not be transient and fleeting as the earlier good times had been. This in essence was Israel's hope for the future. During the lapse of the years it was destined to be developed, first in one direction and then another. It came to be identified with a restored kingdom with a second David on its throne. The notion of life after death, of a cataclysmic dissolution of the present earth and the birth of a new one, the garish display and eschatological nightmares of the apocalypses peopled by angels and hideous beasts, these came into the picture in the course of the years. None the less these were but developments— one might almost say excrescences. In popular speech—and too often in learned writing—all of these notions have been lumped together under the very misleading and unfortunate title, The Messianic Hope.

The first point to be observed in seeking to disentangle this curiously complex cord is that in the Old Testament the term Messiah—anointed—is not a noun. That is, it is not the title limited to one specific figure destined to appear in the future for a certain and definite purpose. Rather, it is actually

[1] Exod. 24:3,7.

more like an adjective, and as such regularly qualifies some noun expressed or implied. The normal phrase is "anointed of the Lord" and is applied to several figures. Kings, high priests, patriarchs, the nation as a whole, even Cyrus, are so designated. In the days of Herod's temple the actual practice of anointing the high priest had lapsed; none the less, he continued to bear the title "anointed high priest" just the same.

In both the canonical books of the Old Testament and in the Apocrypha the noteworthy thing is that there is no mention at all of what we are wont to speak of as "the Messiah." The earliest reference to the Messiah as a standing title is in the Synoptic gospels. The later literature contains allusions to the coming "King Messiah"; here also the phrases "days of the Messiah," and "woes of the Messiah" are to be found. But this is apparently after the dawn of the Christian era.

Accordingly, to use the term, "the Messianic hope," to describe the expectation of future blessedness to which pious Jews were looking forward in the days of Jesus is to approach the problem from the wrong end, and is open to two serious objections. First, it causes the student to assume that there was *one* expectation that every pious Jew held—a sort of carefully arranged future program or time-table. Judaism was a religion of doing rather than of believing. Obedience to the law, not orthodoxy of belief or opinion, was the requirement. In no sphere of thought is this characteristic more discernible than in the hopes for the future. Many and divergent shades of opinion are to be found. It is quite misleading to speak of *the* hope. A second objection to the usual term is that it tends to throw undue emphasis on the figure of the coming one, the Messiah. The "Messianic Age" should connote the age when the Messiah is to appear. Actually the expectation was for the *era* or *age* itself, not for the party who was to bring it in or to mark its advent. In fact, in large blocks of Jewish thinking there was no such figure. In the great prophecy of the exile[2] such is the case. Here God alone is to be King.[3] So long as Isaiah was considered one book, these later chapters were interpreted in the light of the earlier. Accordingly, the Targum interprets Isa. 42:1, "Behold, my servant whom I uphold; my chosen, in whom my soul delighteth," with the words, "Behold, my servant the Anointed (Messiah), my Chosen in whom my word (i.e., I myself) delights."[4] But we know today that that was not the meaning of the author himself nor of his contemporaries.

Accordingly, such a term as golden age is a far better designation for the hopes of Israel. It was the good time coming when all men everywhere would know and reverence God, when no man need say to his brother, "Know thou the Lord," for all would know him.

[2] Isa. 40 ff.

[3] "For this the unhappy phrase 'messianic age without a Messiah' has been invented."—Moore, *Judaism*, Vol. II, p. 327.

[4] Moore, *op. et loc. cit*.

This hope arose, or gained a fresh lease of life, after the sack of Jerusalem and destruction of the temple (586 B.C.) The temple must be rebuilt. When the temple was restored and sacrifice again was offered, all would be well. Spurred by this word from Haggai and Zechariah the temple was rebuilt, but, unfortunately, all was not well. The expected restoration, Israel's independence, did not materialize. But though many were now identifying the good time, the future golden age, with the restoration of the monarchy under the "scion of David" or David himself, this longing in its definitely national form was not universal. Even in those days many were tolerably well off under Persian rule. The memory of some of the successors of David was still too vivid to evoke unqualified enthusiasm. This attitude is highly significant. From that time on many Jews never had a very violent longing for the day to dawn. Those in comfortable circumstances—political or financial—would have little to gain and much to lose. It smacked too much of revolution. In the days of Jesus the Sadducees and their supporters illustrate well this attitude. And many of the religious leaders seem completely deaf to their warlike brothers. The experiences of the past century under the Hasmoneans were still fresh. Jannæus had occupied the throne of David. Aside from breaking the heads of the heathen—to be sure, this was one of the tasks of the coming ideal ruler (Psalm 110)—his reign had done much to cause the "scion of David" to fade into comparative inconspicuousness. When the day dawned it would probably see a completely theocratic kingdom with God, not man, enthroned. But at best this was a beautiful dream for the future, an added spur to the study of God's laws. It was best to leave the details to God. It was he that was guiding the universe. Years later, when the temple was again in ruins, when Rome's heel was galling the neck of prostrate Israel, when it was noised about that the worst blow yet was soon to fall—Jerusalem was to become a pagan city!—this indifference changed, and a whole-hearted, if utterly mad, nationalism was for the moment revealed. The Messiah would make an end of the Roman empire. But this latter outbreak was many years after Jesus' death.

But in the days of the restoration there were others who were far from satisfied, but who longed for political power—if not for themselves, at least for their nation. Nor did this hope ever die out. A popular and noisy minority constantly harped on the string of restored political supremacy. In the time of Jesus they—the Home Rule Party—were still alive, as the malicious question proposed to Jesus by his opponents makes clear.[5] None the less, although they constituted a problem to be reckoned with, by no means all the nation held those quixotic views. Later the awful fate which came upon the nation popularized the movement and swelled its numbers. But to read this later experience back to the earlier times and to assume that in Jesus' day this was the common and universally held expectation is totally unjusti-

[5] Mark 12:14 f.

fied by the evidence. There was no one view accepted by all. Many men, many minds.

The general features, however, of this peculiarly Jewish hope for the coming golden age are fairly clear. It was to be in the future, but in the present age. It would be upon this earth. It would be brought about by or be coincident with the recognition of the universal sovereignty of God. Would the heathen be converted gradually and would the golden age as a result dawn bright and fair? Would God by special fiat destroy the unbelievers? Opinions differed.[6] But all were agreed that when it dawned God would be recognized and worshipped by all. In a word, it was the good time coming, the universally recognized reign of Israel's God, on this earth but in the future. For some it would be in terms of a political restoration, perhaps with the restored Davidic king;[7] for others it would be purely theocratic; for others, pleasurably vague.

Over against this purely Jewish view is to be discerned an entirely different train of ideas, not Jewish in essence but apparently Persian, yet which none the less came to be adopted by many Jews and regarded as genuinely their own. In contrast to the golden age this other may be called the Age to Come.

The Persian concept in brief was this: There would be in the future a great cataclysm which would bring the present age to a dramatic close. The world would literally come to an end, would be consumed by fire to purify it from evil. The righteous would rise to take their places in a new and glorious world. Judgment would be held and men's fates would be settled by the great supernatural judge, Shaoshyant, God's representative.

These ideas were gradually absorbed, although they were never really thought through by Judaism. As we have seen, the notion of resurrection, which provided a convenient answer to the obvious moral injustices of life, was early taken over by Judaism and made to fit in with the older views. It became popular and came to be considered an original part of God's revelation to Israel. None the less, in spite of scribal ingenuity it remained more or less a patch on an older garment.

The book of Daniel plays an important part in the popularizing of these notions. In the apocalyptic imagery of this writing the heathen nations are represented pictorially by awesome beasts; in contrast to them stands "one like unto a son of man,"[8] who, as the author explicitly says, represents the kingdom of the holy people of the Most High.[9] In the Semitic idiom son

[6] This uncertainty is reflected by the later alternative: The Messiah, son of David, will come only in a generation that is wholly worthy or in one that is wholly guilty.

[7] By some, not David, but Hezekiah, was expected. Cf. Moore, *Judaism*, Vol. II, pp. 347 f.

[8] Dan. 7:13.

[9] Dan. 7:27.

of man (Aramaic *bar nasha*; Hebrew *ben adam*) simply means man in the sense of the Latin *homo* or Greek ἄνθρωπος.[10]

Gradually this purely colourless phrase tended to become a technical title for this supernatural figure who was destined to come to judgment, and who accordingly was totally distinct from the anointed king of the other cycle of ideas who would be of human origin and whose function was to rule over God's people.

Popular thinking is never very successful in preserving parallel notions in water-tight compartments, however much the later historian might desire it. There is a constant tendency for the two to become more or less reconciled, or for ideas of the one to become introduced into the other. Thus on the surface it would seem not improbable that eventually the (Jewish) view of the good time coming would be made to coincide with that of the Age to Come, and that in the latter the still unfulfilled prophecies would be believed to have their realization. Or if the coming Davidic king chanced to be a part of the picture—as we have seen, this was not always the case—he could be transplanted, so to speak, into the new age and, losing his function of destroying Israel's enemies in war, could gradually assume a more universal responsibility for destroying evil and acting as final judge. In a word, *son of David* and *son of man* might eventually become identified.

All this is intrinsically possible. It would be most rash to say that the equation of these two originally utterly distinct figures had never been made by Judaism before the Christian era. We know that it was done by early Christians, who came to see in Jesus the realization of both these figures and so by good mathematics—two things equal to the same thing are equal to each other—identified the anointed king with the supernatural judge to the confusion of all subsequent historians.

But because a thing is possible is not sufficient reason to assume that it was done. And we have in my judgment no clear evidence to warrant the assumption that this identification had taken place—of course, an individual here or there may have toyed with the idea—until after the Christian beginnings. From then on the two threads seem more and more intertwined and titles of the one are bestowed upon the other.

To see how in later days these two views were actually reconciled or accommodated, the one to the other, the apocalypse known as IV Ezra is instructive. Here we have a thoroughgoing attempt at harmonization: The time was near approaching when the Anointed, that is, the Davidic king of Israel, would appear, destroy all opposition, and reign for four hundred years. Then he and all mankind would die—"My son, the anointed one, will die." That marks the end of "this age." Then would come the Resur-

---

[10] Cf. the parallelism of Psalm 8:4:

> What is *man*, that thou art mindful of him?
> And the *son of man*, that thou visitest him?

rection and Final Judgment, the dawn of the New Age, that is, the "Age to Come."

Here it is to be observed that the original notion that the golden age was to be unending has been modified. It has become a period of interim, a prelude to the Last Judgment, and of limited duration, four hundred years. In the Christian apocalypse—the canonical book of Revelation—the same note is struck, but the period is a thousand years. It should also be observed that in IV Ezra it is God himself who acts as final judge.[11] In other writings his representative performs that function.

One final phrase may be mentioned, "the woes (or travail) of the Messiah." This refers to the period of anguish and horror that in the later popular belief would immediately precede his coming. It has been often interpreted of the sufferings which the Messiah himself would have to undergo. This is totally in error, for it refers explicitly to the agony of mother Zion, in travail to bring forth the Messiah. Just how early this view arose is not clear. The earliest occurrence of the exact phrase is in the generation after the destruction of Jerusalem. The notion itself may well be earlier and be a reflection of the prophetic warning of the "great and terrible day of the Lord." Paul may refer to some such belief in his warning against the dangers of marriage.[12] Apparent references to this in the Synoptic gospels (especially Mark 13:7-27 and parallels) are complicated by the fact that the gospels as we have them do not antedate 70 A.D. Omens of all kinds would herald the approach. Sun and moon would be darkened, swords and armies would be seen in the sky, blood would trickle from stones, fresh water would become salt, nations would rise against nations, families would be split asunder, elders would be insulted, babes would be torn from the arms of agonized mothers. But these dire woes—and the list I have given is not a unit, but a potpourri from several apocalypses—are for the most part late. Just when they became a definite part of the picture is not clear.

In conclusion, it appears to me most unwise to try to give a fictitious appearance of simplicity to a singularly complicated and obscure matter. It is quite rash to try to formulate *the* program and to give to it several well-defined steps—Schürer gives it eleven[13]—for in the same writings different views appear. That in the future God would take care of Israel and that his beneficent rule would be recognized by all was probably a part of every pious Jew's *confessio fidei*; but the various shades of interpretation, incident to the two distinctly different sources—Jewish and Persian—and to the development of each, with the resultant vagueness of detail, prevented any systematic or universally accepted teaching.

[11] Cf. Psalm 50, especially v. 6—"For God is judge himself."
[12] I Cor. 7:28 ff. See my *Ethics of Paul*, pp. 177 f.
[13] *Op. cit.*, Div. II, Vol. II, pp. 154-187.

PART II

THE BEGINNINGS OF THE GOSPEL STORY

PREFACE

THE claim for Christianity is often made that it is the "faith once for all delivered to the saints." To the student of history such a claim is not only false; it is positively absurd. Nor is this by any means an admission of weakness or of inadequacy. Rather it is one of the most conspicuous signs of the life and strength of this religion that to none of its tenets could the phrase *semper, ubique, et ab omnibus* be justly subscribed. Many of those in the early and formative years whom men today regard as the pillars of orthodoxy must have seemed far from the light to many of their fellow saints. What a debt every religion—and Christianity perhaps most of all— owes to its heretics, for notions dubbed heresy at bedtime often arise the next morning with a halo of orthodoxy firm upon their brows. Nor was the growth and development due alone to pioneers who dared to be different, who were ever seeking a more adequate and complete expression of their faith. As has already been emphasized, Christianity was the child of Judaism. The joys and the sorrows, the defeats and the longings, of the mother were inherited by the child. Only so can the younger religion be understood. But this, while of tremendous significance, is by no means the whole story. The new religion—even before it had come to know itself as a new religion— had been pushed out of the parent's nest. The world into which it was forced was a new and strange one. Whether it be true of individuals or not, it was certainly true of Christianity that its environment exerted a tremendous influence. Within a score of years it had become a gentile cult. It adopted new conceptions, took on a totally different character, borrowed from all with whom it came into contact, and through its extraordinary eclectic character was able to rival the older and more firmly established cults so successfully that within three hundred years the emperor Constantine, who lacked no quality more conspicuously than piety, saw emblazoned in the sky a cross and heard the congenial word that his campaign would be successful.

In a word, Christianity has never been a stagnant pool; rather it has been a rapidly flowing stream, fed, as it rushes to the sea, by many brooks and rivulets, and partaking of their qualities. As such we shall try to see it in the subsequent pages, and attempt to follow its banks back to its mountain source.

Many difficulties confront us. One is especially real. The chief source of our knowledge of the earliest beginnings is not one book, but a library by many authors, produced not at one time, but which grew many years after the start of the new religion. Contrary to many popular notions, the new religion produced its book; the book did not produce the religion. Again, these writings, which eventually came to be called the New Testament, were written for purely practical purposes: to meet specific needs felt in those days. They were not prepared to edify or to instruct subsequent generations which might desire historical insights into the past. Hence many points about which we would appreciate information are glossed over or omitted entirely. And finally, the gospels, which purport to tell us of the earliest period, were not the first, but among the last of the documents to be produced. Accordingly, we must give due regard to this lapse of time—at the very least forty years—and recognize the probability that again and again the later outlook and ideas have been reflected, at times perhaps unwittingly, yet none the less surely, in the chronicle of the earlier years.

Today we recognize that we cannot hope to reconstruct the early days of the Christian beginnings by an uncritical reading of the four gospels and book of Acts. The authors, no one of whom was himself an eyewitness of the events he recorded, had to depend upon earlier sources, written or oral, and not upon telepathy for their information. When we have reached the period in the developing history of the church in which these writings came to be produced, we shall have occasion to try to see the way the authors used the sources of knowledge at their command. Until then we must satisfy ourselves with a tentative reconstruction of the history, using the results of a century and a half's critical study without retesting or re-proving each point. Later when we consider the various books, the reasons for the assumptions will perhaps be apparent.

Chapter X

JOHN THE BAPTIST AND HIS FOLLOWERS

ALL four of our gospels begin with reference to the work of John the Baptist, who is depicted as the forerunner of Jesus, his greater successor. Of his early life we know little or nothing. According to Luke he was born of priestly stock, and, as was the case of many of the Old Testament worthies, in the extreme old age of his parents. In this same account he is represented as a relation of Jesus since his mother and Mary were related. That the story rests upon any historical foundation is most improbable. Apparently it is a consequence of the early re-writing of the story of John to bring him into conscious subordination to Jesus. In the Synoptic gospels John appears spectacularly in the wilderness of Judea and in dramatic fashion sounds a note of doom worthy of Jeremiah or Amos: "Repent of your sins; be baptized for the remission of them. If you don't, it will be the worse for you; a catastrophe is coming. Even now the axe is laid at the root of the tree. Those not bearing good fruit will be hewn down." Here is an ascetic figure, living apart from men, awing those who flocked to hear him and convicting them of guilt. In Mark, the eldest of the three accounts, Jesus is represented as being one of the group which listens, and as being baptized. There is no hint of any recognition of him by John, or that it is he who is to be the "greater one" John is so eloquently proclaiming. In Matthew, however, a new and distinctly Christian note is introduced. When Jesus comes to be baptized, John at once recognizes him, and demurs at Jesus' request. "Nay," says he in substance, "it would be far more fitting for you to baptize me." "You are quite right," says Jesus, "but suffer it to be done." In the light of this obvious recognition by Jesus of his dignity the heavenly voice can no longer say—as Mark recorded it—"Thou art my beloved Son, in whom I am well pleased." Rather it proclaims to those who need the information, "This is my beloved Son." In Luke's account this process of subordinating John to Jesus is carried a step farther. Even before their births they had met. When Mary, in whom was the divinely begotten Lord, came into the presence of the pregnant Elisabeth, the latter's babe leaped in her womb, prompting words from Elisabeth which made Mary's *Magnificat* possible. In the Fourth Gospel the climax is reached. John is of a truth only the voice which proclaims Jesus. The author is familiar with the story of the baptism, but recasts it. How unfitting that the divine Word should have been baptized! Rather the Baptist sees him approaching and heralds him: "Behold the

Lamb of God, that taketh away the sin of the world! This is he of whom I said, After me cometh a man who is become before me: for he was before me." The dove is present, but not for Jesus. Well does the Lord, the incarnate Word of God, know his own identity. Rather the appearance is for John, the herald. "And John bare witness saying, I have beheld the Spirit descending as a dove out of heaven; and it abode upon him. And I knew him not: but he that sent me to baptize in water, he said unto me, Upon whomsoever thou shalt see the Spirit descending, and abiding upon him, the same is he that baptizeth in the Holy Spirit. And I have seen, and have borne witness that this is the Son of God."

A careful study of these four accounts leaves but little room for doubt that John the Baptist was thus transformed by Christianity from an independent preacher into the forerunner of Jesus. Nor is it improbable that his message has been similarly edited. It is to be observed that Matthew (altering the phraseology of his source, Mark) makes him utter precisely the same clarion call as did Jesus: "Repent ye; for the kingdom of heaven is at hand."[1] The special teaching of John which Luke alone records[2] is surprisingly like that later found in the mouth of Jesus (cf. especially, "He that hath two coats, let him impart to him that hath none; and he that hath food, let him do likewise"). The question arises whether, after all, the picture of John heralding the advent of the greater one who will baptize the nations in fire is not actually that of Jesus heralding the advent of the son of man, the final Judge, who, as we have already seen, was expected by many Jews to perform this function.

This explanation would appear to me supported by the one passage in Josephus in which John is mentioned.

Now, some of the Jews thought that the destruction of Herod's [*i.e.*, Antipas'] army came from God, and that very justly, as a punishment of what he did against John, who was called the Baptist; for Herod slew him, who was a good man, and commanded the Jews to exercise virtue, both as to righteousness toward one another, and piety toward God, and so to come to baptism; for that the washing [with water] would be acceptable to him, if they made use of it, not in order to the putting away of some sins, but for the purification of the body; supposing still that the soul was thoroughly purified beforehand by righteousness. Now, when many others came in crowds about him, for they were greatly moved by hearing his words, Herod, who feared lest the great influence John had over the people might put it into his power and inclination to raise a rebellion (for they seemed ready to do anything he should advise), thought it best, by putting him to death, to prevent any mischief he might cause, and not bring himself into difficulties by sparing a man who might make him repent of it when it should be too

[1] Matt. 3:2; 4:17.
[2] Luke 3:10-14.

late. Accordingly he was sent a prisoner, out of Herod's suspicious temper, to Macherus, the castle I before mentioned, and was there put to death.[3]

In this brief and intelligible account two points are striking: (1) the reason given for John's execution; (2) the entire absence of any mention of what in the gospels is a highly significant note, the advent of his greater successor. There is no need of an elaborate chain of reasoning as to why Josephus, although he mentioned John, was reluctant to mention Jesus or a mysterious "greater one" whom Christians were now confident was Jesus. The simplest and most likely explanation is that this was not an actual part of John's message. Josephus is not exercising editorial privileges; he is simply recording facts.

On the basis, then, of this critical sifting of the gospel account and of the testimony of Josephus there would seem to be little support for the modern conjecture that Jesus was started on his career through contact with the Baptist, and that he repeated the latter's message even after John's tragic death had sundered the bond of teacher and pupil. It would, accordingly, appear more probable that the paths of Jesus and John did not cross at all and that our gospel accounts preserve little or nothing of the actual history of this enigmatic man. As the years rolled by, John, although originally quite distinct from Jesus, was gradually brought into the Christian picture, if not into the Christian fold.

Nor is the reason for this transformation of the powerful wilderness prophet into the self-abasing voice far to seek. That John the Baptist had been in the early days a distinct hindrance to the rise of Christianity and that traces of this are still to be found in the early Christian records has seemed to many New Testament critics probable. In fact, the Fourth Gospel shows a clear animus against the disciples of the Baptist, and has for one of its purposes the complete and voluntary subjugation of John to Jesus, to be able to say to his followers: "Since your leader clearly recognized that our leader was the true Lamb of God, and gladly reckoned himself as but a voice to proclaim him, so you should cease your independent existence, and with us recognize and follow our common Lord." The occasional references to the disciples of John[4] suggest that his movement had by no means come to an end at the appearance of Jesus; nor is there any sign of a defection from his camp to that of his "greater successor." It is by no means improbable that the twelve individuals, whom Paul is said to have met in Ephesus,[5] who knew only the baptism of John and had never even heard of the Holy Spirit and who were accordingly rebaptized to remedy this lack, belonged to this group still in existence. The great influence that John exerted—

[3] *Antt.* 18,5,2.
[4] Cf. Mark 2.18; Luke 11:1; John 3:23; 4:1.
[5] Acts 19:1-7.

attested alike by Josephus[6] and the gospels[7]—suggests not only that the work of this preacher was no mere flash-in-the-pan, but that it might very well have tended to divert attention from the disciples of the other martyred leader. Furthermore, the famous testimony to John which Matthew and Luke attribute to Jesus—"Among them that are born of women there hath not arisen a greater than John the Baptist: *yet he that is but little in the kingdom of heaven is greater than he*"[8]—and which has never been satisfactorily explained on the basis of the traditional relationship between the two would seem to reveal a rivalry or at least a cleavage between the two groups.

Accordingly, it appears not unlikely that the incorporation of John into the Christian picture was a deliberate and studied attempt by early Christians to vanquish an embarrassing rival. The religions of antiquity provide numerous examples of a new god gradually supplanting an old and eventually being regarded as his son. The most effective way of getting rid of a rival is to align him with one's own cause. Accordingly, it would not be difficult to explain the rise of these stories, even though the tangents of Jesus and John never crossed. The story of the imprisoned Baptist sending his disciples to ask Jesus if he were the Christ[9] would not appear to indicate a cooling of John's ardour shown in such passages as Matt. 3:14 f. and John 1:15-42 but rather to reflect an earlier, less advanced, stage in their rapprochement.

Once John was in the Christian picture it is not difficult to see how the legend of Herodias' wrath might have arisen as an explanation of his untimely end. As has already been pointed out, Josephus gives a quite different and more plausible explanation. That a Herod should have been very much disturbed by an uncouth wilderness preacher's displeasure at his nuptials is perhaps less likely than that he should have trembled with dread at the thought of an increasingly popular movement, the burden of which was the collapse of established society. Rulers are not wont to take kindly such proclamations, even though the agent of the collapse be God himself. Antipas was probably keen sighted enough to realize John's aim was not political; none the less, he was canny enough to realize that such a message might well serve as the spark in the powder-chest of unrest toward Rome and all her hirelings. Naturally, such an explanation of John's demise would not prove acceptable to Christians, especially to those concerned with establishing the innocency of their movement in the eyes of Rome. How much more probable that this second Elijah, staunch advocate of pure morals that he was, had perished at the hands of this more formidable modern Jezebel!

Discussion of the significance of the baptism practised not alone by John,

---

[6] *Loc. cit.*
[7] Mark 11:27-33.
[8] Matt. 11:11; Luke 7:28.
[9] Matt. 11:2-6; Luke 7:18-23.

but by other sects in Palestine, and of their possible influence upon the externally similar rite which soon made its appearance in the Christian group, may profitably be reserved for a later page. The point of present importance is that the stories about him, regardless of their value for an understanding of later Christianity, would seem to throw far less light than is usually assumed upon the one who is popularly supposed to have designated and to have quickened his greater successor.

Chapter XI

JESUS AND THE GALILEE MISSION

For the beginning of Christianity we must look to Galilee, for it was there that Jesus "began both to do and to teach," for he must be seen as the point of departure for the movement which came eventually to regard itself as a new religion and to be called by his name. Regardless of the differences between his point of view and that of his early followers; regardless of the fact that many of the words attributed to him in the gospels were coloured if not actually produced by the outlook of the age in which they were written; regardless of the practical difficulties encountered in striving to apply these words literally in this twentieth century—none the less, Jesus is to be seen as the centre of the movement, and however he may be portrayed, however much we seek to prove that he was a first-century Jew in outlook and belief, this must not obscure the fact that it was his tremendous personality that gripped those first disciples, that wrested a man like Saul of Tarsus from the things formerly dear to him, and that has continued to the present day in unabated power. The emphasis of the Fourth Gospel is right: The living, deathless person of Christ is the ultimate force in Christianity.

This is not the place for a detailed study of Jesus' life or teaching. It is more than doubtful if either is possible of reconstruction, as is abundantly evidenced by the many attempts; certainly not without a thorough and exact knowledge of the literary relationship and problems of the gospels which must be reserved in this present volume for a later page. Accordingly, this chapter must be rigidly limited to a consideration of his direct influence, in so far as we may with reasonable confidence discover it, in the movement later to be called by his name.

Jesus was born and brought up in the hills of Galilee, in the quiet town of Nazareth, the very name of which is unknown to us in that period outside the gospels and Acts. The Bethlehem stories, regardless of their homiletic beauty, apparently rest upon no historical foundation, but must be regarded as pure legend. A critical examination of the two accounts—the one assuming the fixed residence of the parents in Bethlehem, the homage of Magi guided from the East by a miraculous star, the edict of a cruel king (strangely akin to that told of the infant Moses), the flight into Egypt, and subsequent return to Palestine, but to Nazareth, not Bethlehem; the other telling of a most unusual journey from Nazareth to Bethlehem, undertaken by the expectant mother in compliance with the requirement of a supposed census,[1] the inability to find lodgings, the resultant birth in a stable, the vision of angels granted to shepherds, and their visit to the manger—reveals that they are mutually exclusive, contradicting each other at every point. Their value is real; none the less, this value does not lie in the realm of history.

Nor do we know more of his boyhood or young manhood. At a very early date Christians were struck by these "hidden years" and sought to remedy the lack. The so-called Apocryphal Gospels, of which the Protevangelium of James, the Gospel of Thomas, and the various Infancy gospels are conspicuous examples, plainly evidence the utter lack of information that made the resultant grotesque and repellent stories possible. They simply depict a wonder child, endowed with limitless magical power but destitute of any ethical sense. In this connexion the one story which occurs in the accepted gospels[2] is significant. Due in part to the fact that it occurs in a *canonical* gospel, in part to the chasteness and restraint of the account in contrast to the tales of the malicious and malignant little boy of the other narratives, this story of the visit of the twelve-year-old Jesus to the temple has been often accepted, but usually with the entire evacuation of its meaning. Attempts to understand it as the normal attitude of the respectful little boy, awed by his elders, and thrilled at the thought that he is now a "son of the Law," quite miss the point. In essence the story is of precisely the same character as those in the Apocryphal Gospels. It portrays a unique child, wise beyond his years, aware of his vocation in life, asking his questions quite as a full-grown Socrates might have done, or as Jesus himself later did.

Attempts to probe back into the years before the ministry are utterly fruitless. The utmost that can be said has already been said by Luke, and said magnificently:

And the child grew, and waxed strong, filled with wisdom: and the grace of God was upon him.

And Jesus advanced in wisdom and stature, and in favor with God and men.[3]

More than this we can never know.

The gospel accounts begin with the story of the baptism of Jesus by John the Baptist. This story has been widely considered, even by critical historians, as resting upon an essentially trustworthy tradition of an actual occurrence, and many fanciful conclusions have been drawn from it: Jesus was started on his mission as a prophet by the Baptist—an explanation which

---

[1] Attempts to establish the accuracy of the Lucan account by postulating this earlier census, also conducted by Quirinius, as was the other one, definitely known to us (see above, pp. 67 f.) as one in a regular fourteen-year cycle, have been made, notably by Ramsay, *Was Christ Born in Bethlehem?* but have little probability and have not commended themselves to scholars generally.

[2] Luke 2:41-51.

[3] Luke 2:40,52.

would have scandalized the older conservative scholars, hard put to explain the inappropriateness of the sinless Christ deigning to accept baptism[4]—whose disciple he became. It was not until John's imprisonment that he started a really independent mission. He returned to Galilee to avoid encroaching upon the Master's territory. Thus the similarity of the teaching of the two was explained: Jesus' early message was essentially a repetition of the Baptist's. Such an explanation might account for the entrance of Jesus in the rôle of a prophet; however, it simply pushes the difficulty one stage further back by failing to provide a similar impetus for John.

Reasons have already been given in a previous chapter for viewing the whole story of the contact of Jesus and John as the creation of later Christian thinking. It is surely no less arbitrary to assume this relationship of master and pupil and to explain the similarity of teaching as due to the borrowing by Jesus of the message of John than it is to reverse the procedure and to consider the possibility that all the words found in the mouth of the Baptist in the gospel narrative are the result of Christian tradition and actually have as much right to be regarded as words, not of John, but of Jesus, as do the words actually attributed to the latter in the gospel pages. In addition to the reasons already suggested for hesitating to consider the account of the baptism of Jesus by John historical is the utter disregard of baptism, both in practice and in injunction, during the ministry and not improbably in the months—perhaps years—which followed.[5] As the account stands in Mark it was a critical experience for Jesus, a turning point in his career. Then it was that God's Holy Spirit descended upon him, transforming him into God's own prophet, commissioned from on high to sound the clarion call to repentance in preparation for the new age soon to dawn. It is astonishing that an experience of such moment to himself should not have commended itself to him as valuable for others as well. Finally, there is the problem of the source of knowledge of the event—and this applies equally to the subsequent narrative of the Temptation. According to the narratives of the Synoptic gospels—and probability bears them out—Jesus' first contact with followers was in Galilee; the notion of a ministry in Judea with disciples recruited there who followed him into Galilee is sheer assumption. Accordingly the information, if authentic, must have come from Jesus himself. That such information was given by him is also sheer assumption, and, as Origen early pointed out,[6] out of keeping with the character of the one who "on all occasions avoided unnecessary talk about himself." The presumption is that no information prior to the ministry in Galilee was available when the first traditions began to take form. Nor

---

[4] Ignatius (ad Eph. 18:2) remarks that his baptism was "to cleanse the water."

[5] For a discussion of such passages as Matt. 28:19; Mark 16:16; John 3.22; 4:1-2; Acts 2:38-41 which are in apparent contradiction to this statement, see below, pp. 194 ff.

[6] c. Celsum i,48 (end).

is it surprising that there was an occasional early attempt to push the pre-history farther back into a period before the time the central figure had come into the public eye. Flat and arbitrary denial of the possibility of the narrative being historic would of course be rash. But in history, as in engineering, one can never be too critical towards bricks destined for the growing edifice. Traditions which we can safely consider reliable do not appear to antedate the preaching in Galilee.

That something occurred in the course of the years before his appearance by the lake that led him to assume the rôle of prophet, confident that he had insights into the heart and purposes of God that the rest of Jewry did not have; confident that when he revealed the coming of the Kingdom—God's most precious boon for men—they, like him, would lay their tasks aside and prepare themselves for the blessed day—all this is perhaps intrinsically possible. But what led to that conviction—sudden or the result of years of reflection—we shall never know. That following this conviction, like the prophet of old, "As Jehovah liveth, what Jehovah saith unto me, that will I speak," he passed through a reaction of doubt and questioning from which he emerged to speak with a confidence which could not be daunted is also not unlikely. This we can assume from the common experience of mankind, not because of the conventional narratives of this period of initial temptation through which the heroes of both legend and history were supposed to have passed. Not only does the balanced structure of the triad of trials found in Matthew and Luke with their apposite quotation of Scripture appear the product of Christian meditation, but the simpler narrative of Mark appears designed for a distinct and practical end. The wild beasts with whom he spent forty days apparently would signify to the Jewish reader evil demons. These Jesus had conquered at the very beginning. Their power was broken; they alone, of all whom Jesus later approached, knew who he was, and feared but must obey him.

With his public appearance in the towns of Galilee on the shore of the lake our information about him begins, although it is far less definite than could be desired. In a curiously obscure phrase,[7] which has caused difficulty from the earliest days, Luke apparently says he was about thirty at the start of his ministry. Whether that rests upon a definite tradition or is a conjecture that when he started his work he was already a mature man is uncertain. Furthermore, although most scholars are agreed that his ministry was limited to Galilee until he "stedfastly set his face to go to Jerusalem," it is impossible to say how long this ministry was. The traditional view that it occupied three years rests upon the Fourth Gospel, which arbitrarily transforms this ministry into a series of visits to attend feasts. The Fourth Gospel is invaluable for an understanding of later Christian thought; it is valueless to the historian seeking information regarding the nature or the

[7] Luke 3:23.

length of the ministry. The other three gospels set no time. Their failure to mention any going to Jerusalem prior to the one ending in his crucifixion would perhaps heighten the probability that the ministry was limited to a few months, scarcely more than a single year. It is to be observed that many of the early writers, including Clement of Alexandria and Origen, reached the same conclusion, although on other grounds.[8] Jesus' words were such that opposition soon flared up against him. All the data preserved by our first three gospels could easily fall within a twelvemonth period. The elaborate synchronism of dates (Luke 3:1,2) apparently suggests 28 A.D. as the time of his public appearance; the spring of 29 A.D. is perhaps the most probable date for the crucifixion.

His message was simple. Mark summarizes it: "The time is fulfilled, and the kingdom of God is at hand: repent ye, and believe in the gospel;" that is, believe that this good news that the Father's greatest gift to men is at hand is true. It can scarcely be doubted that he sounded his message with full confidence that the nation would hearken and rejoice. It was all so clear to him; nothing else in life mattered. The Father had spoken. Of course God's children would obey as soon as they heard his voice. As the weeks went by and as he saw the initial enthusiasm giving way first to apathy, then to bitter opposition, he became quickly disillusioned; soon it was borne home to him that so strait was the gate and narrow the way that few would enter in. By the kingdom of God—Matthew alone prefers kingdom of heaven—he did not apparently mean the gradual amelioration of society, as is often imagined today. His message was pitched in terms of the first century, not the twentieth. The kingdom of God, soon to appear, was the Age to Come, the new age which would suddenly and spectacularly follow the cataclysmic end of the present age. Attempts to soften or alter his message to make it more acceptable to our way of thinking and to make it conform to the verdict of history are utterly superfluous. Much confusion has been caused by the endless debate as to whether the kingdom is present or future. The evidence of the gospels as well as the outlook of early Christianity, as revealed not alone by the opening chapters of Acts but by the letters of Paul, would appear unmistakably to indicate that in his thinking the kingdom was still in the future, but that it would appear at any moment. It was present only in the sense that the coming clouds in the heavens cast their shadow upon the earth. Israel was incessantly talking about God, deluding itself that it was obeying his commands. They must cease this playing at life; must turn back to the Father and recognize his sovereignty at once. Life must be made to conform to the pattern that soon would be introduced. Men must start now to live the kind of lives they would live in the coming kingdom—if they were fortunate enough to have

[8] They understood the phrase, "the acceptable year of the Lord" of Luke 4:19 (Isa. 61:1 f.) literally.

a share in it. "The kingdom of God is among you"[9] does not signify an "inward and invisible power in the hearts of men" wooing them to a growth in righteousness. It is a vivid announcement of the immediacy of the approach of this kingdom and its attendant judgment. It is so near at hand, that for added vividness it may be spoken of as actually here. The purposes of God are inevitable; he has spoken and will fulfil. The shadow of the approaching cloud is even now upon the land. The parable of the Seed Growing Secretly,[10] which has often been interpreted in the sense of the present kingdom, appears to yield exactly the opposite meaning. The seed has been sown; nothing that man can do to thwart it will avail; the harvest must come.

By the word "repent," Jesus meant, as did every other Jew, change of conduct as well as of heart. Everything incompatible with the kingdom— this new age soon to be set up—must be laid aside resolutely. As the merchant gladly sells all his other pearls to purchase the one of great price, or the man who has discovered a treasure hidden in a field sells all his possessions to gain that treasure; so the wise man will consider everything in life, not alone his immediate comfort, but his actual physical well-being, of secondary importance. What is an eye or a hand—parts of a perishable body—worth in comparison with acceptance or rejection by Almighty God at the Judgment soon to be set up! Words which must be watered down when the teaching of Jesus is forced into terms of modern thought are perfectly intelligible without appeal to "oriental hyperbole" when he who lived in the first century is allowed to think and speak as such. Thus there are few matters connected with the gospels clearer or more certain than that Jesus believed in the near approach[11] of this universal sovereignty of God, that is, the near approach of the apocalyptic Age to Come. This was the good news which he and his helpers were to proclaim.

As he proclaimed his message like one of the prophets of old, crowds flocked at first to hear him. Reputed miraculous cures attracted attention. His insistence on the purity of family life, his hatred of sham and pretence, his sympathy for the downtrodden and his depth of understanding, above all, his practical common sense and unflinching bravery, won him a hearing. Apparently some of the listeners stayed with him; soon there came to be a fringe of followers about him as he went from village to village proclaiming God's will and purpose as he believed God had revealed them to him. With some of these followers tradition says he became more intimate, that soon there was an inner circle of disciples with him whom we know as the Twelve. That he formally called twelve men and then conferred upon them especial powers is perhaps doubtful, but that in the course of

[9] ἐντὸς ὑμῶν —Luke 17:21.
[10] Mark 4:26 ff.
[11] See also pp. 165 f. below.

time some of his hearers came into more intimate fellowship is most probable. Not only were they to multiply his usefulness, they satisfied the desire for comradeship and for friends of this man who would gladly have taken the whole nation to his heart, but it would not. Then the opposition increased. As he failed to satisfy the turbulent and rebellious Home Rule Party, hundred-per-cent Jews with their strong anti-Roman attitude and their eagerness for rebellion, who must have appeared to him conspicuous examples of the folly of centring one's gaze upon any object save God's kingdom soon to appear; as he came into open clash with the Pharisees because of his complete disregard of their prized interpretations and his cavalier treatment of them personally: it is but natural that he should have been closer drawn to the group which followed him, and should have come to see in them the only hope for the nation. Truly, the way was hard; few seemed able to walk in it. But when this truth was forced upon him and the waves of temptation beat upon him, he refused to yield an inch but accepted the issue and reaffirmed his challenge. Like Seneca's seaman, he could say: "O Neptune, thou canst sink me; thou canst save me if thou wilt. Whatever comes, I will keep my rudder true."

In the gospels there is a very distinct opposition to wealth. Not only the more primitive form of the beatitudes in Luke,[12] but the story of Dives and Lazarus,[13] or the story of the Rich Young Ruler[14] are unmistakable in their teaching, and most naturally reflect the attitude of Jesus himself. It is not that Jesus approached his mission with clear-cut views in this regard, as modern socialists fondly but absurdly maintain. Rather his attitude appears to have come as the fruit of his experience. Those who were wealthy and in seats of power not unnaturally looked askance at the teaching of an impending cataclysm, even though it was to be brought about by an act of God. Those, on the other hand, who had nothing to lose and everything to gain by such an overturn naturally found the teaching more acceptable. Accordingly, it appears probable that this is the reason for Jesus' reported strictures upon wealth. This, he felt, and not unnaturally, was the stumbling-block for those who would otherwise have hearkened to the Father's voice. Riches, his experience led him to feel, were an insuperable bar to an attempt to gain the boon of life—entrance into the kingdom. Since all things were possible for God, it was possible that there might be an exception, but it would require as great a miracle to drag a rich man into the kingdom as to drag a camel through a needle's eye. Attempts have been made to tone down this clear word and to make it a special diagnosis for this particular man, but the evangelists give no support to this attempt to side-step an unpleasant teaching. Matthew recognizes the severity of the word and tones

---

[12] Luke 6:20-23; cf. Luke 6:20b and 21a with Matt. 5:3 and 6.
[13] Luke 16:19-31.
[14] Mark 10:17-31 and parallels (Matt. 19:16-30; Luke 18:18-30).

down the uncompromising "One thing thou lackest"[15] into "If thou wouldest be perfect."[16] This is perfectly obviously an early attempt to adapt the earlier uncompromising teaching, which was not intended as a social panacea in a society long to continue, but was a means of gaining admittance into the fast-approaching kingdom, into a workable dictum of morality in the early church which was now numbering wealthy men among its members. Precisely the same sort of attempt by Matthew to make uncompromising teachings more workable is seen in his treatment of Jesus' words regarding divorce. In direct clash with the tradition preserved by Paul, Mark, and Luke[17] that there is no ground for divorce, Matthew twice inserts the qualifying clause, "saving for the cause of fornication."[18] Yet he is not to be regarded as an ascetic, as John the Baptist is pictured. On the contrary, his opponents called him "a gluttonous man and a hard drinker."[19] Far from holding himself aloof he appears to have mingled with men and women and to have shown such sympathy with their problems and sorrows—especially in the case of the downtrodden—that he received the nickname "friend of publicans and sinners."

Did Jesus feel that he was the Messiah, the son of David destined for Israel's throne? In recent years this question has been hotly debated. The answer to it is by no means as simple as has often been supposed. The conventional answer has been, Yes; but it rested in no small measure upon the mistaken notion that all popular Jewish thinking in the first century centred about the person of the Messiah. Accordingly, it was argued: Any one to gain a popular hearing must pitch his message in these terms. Thus, although Jesus was by no means satisfied with the conventional thinking on the subject, he must for want of a better designation make such claims for himself. But if, as has been argued in a preceding chapter, the figure of the Davidic King Messiah did not bulk so large in popular thinking, there seems little reason to assume that Jesus felt compelled to accept the rôle unless it was perfectly congenial. As soon as this cardinal point is observed, it becomes highly significant that Jesus appears to have laid his emphasis upon the coming kingdom, not upon the one who was to be king in it. It is the Fourth Gospel which represents Jesus as habitually discoursing at length about himself, the king. That the representation in the Synoptic gospels is more primitive and more probably historic is almost universally conceded. That Matthew and Luke felt that Jesus was the Davidic Messiah is clear. However such a passage as Matt. 11:25-30 was originally intended, it now stands as embodying distinct and unique claims in the mouth of Jesus. Luke is very particular

[15] Mark 10:21.
[16] Matt. 19:21.
[17] I Cor. 7:10-11; Mark 10:11-12; Luke 16:18.
[18] Matt. 5:31 f.; 19:9.
[19] Matt. 11:19; Luke 7:34.

to make clear that Jesus' death was due to this claim alone. On the contrary, Mark 12:35-37 (‖ Matt. 22:41-46; Luke 20:41-44) can only be understood as denying that Jesus, although anointed, was the scion of David. Such a denial must have been primitive; it clashes too directly with early Christian thinking. The most natural interpretation of it is that it reflects Jesus' own attitude. Although he conceived himself anointed by God for his service, he rejected the notion that this meant that he was the anointed Davidic king.

Nor is it by any means certain that he claimed to be the supernatural figure, destined to be the Final Judge of men, namely the son of man, although his followers soon after his death were confident that he was that figure and had claimed to be. Indeed, the evangelists are so confident that he had made this claim for himself that they use the phrase as a substitute for "I." A striking example of this editorial revision is afforded by Matthew's alteration of Mark 8:27. In Mark the query reads, "Who do men say that I am?" Matthew (16:13) has "Who do men say that the son of man is?" Again, such passages as Mark 2:10 f.; 27 f. can scarcely be understood save as mistranslations into Greek, where the original Aramaic *bar nasha*, that is, human being,[20] has been mistakenly rendered "son of man," thus giving a specific application to Jesus not originally intended. The second of these passages is particularly clear. Jesus says, "The Sabbath was made for man, and not man for the Sabbath: therefore *man* is lord even of the Sabbath." This is balanced and intelligible; substitution of *son of man*, making a specific reference to Jesus, makes the "therefore" unintelligible. A third type of passage is illustrated by Mark 8:38—

> For whosoever shall be ashamed of *me* and of *my* words in this adulterous and sinful generation, the *Son of man* also shall be ashamed of him, when *he* cometh in the glory of *his* Father with the holy angels.

There would seem to be no compelling reason to identify here the "me" and "my" with the "son of man," "he," and "his." Indeed, it is not failure to believe in or to adopt a correct attitude toward him (Jesus) that Jesus is here condemning, but the rejection of the message which he is sounding. This rejection can only result in condemnation when the son of man appears in the very near future to sit upon his judgment throne.

That the phrase "son of man" was constantly upon Jesus' lips is highly probable. That he meant himself by the phrase is far less certain. That his disciples eventually came to the conclusion that by the enigmatic phrase he had meant himself is certain; that they made this identification after his death rather than during his ministry would appear not unlikely. Thus primitive tradition which revealed too clearly for the growing theological estimates of Jesus' person that he, as God's prophet, had heralded the coming of the

---

[20] See above pp. 141 f.

supernatural son of man, his successor, soon to appear to set up the Final Judgment and inaugurate the Age to Come, gradually came to be put into the mouth of John the Baptist. The whole imagery of final judgments, of supernatural figures coming on the clouds of heaven, was as natural to the first century as it is unnatural to ours. A man in those days could hold such views without raising the suspicion of mental disturbance. None the less, it is one thing for a first-century Jew to have expected such a figure soon to appear; a totally different thing for him to believe that he himself would be miraculously transformed from a flesh-and-blood man into this figure. With all allowances made, it is hard to conceive how such a view could have been held save at the expense of mental sanity. There seems no reason from the accounts to postulate this last conclusion. But views, which if held by himself before his death can scarcely be understood of a sane and balanced man, are easily understood for the disciples after his death. Then the obstacle was removed. He was now, they were confident, in heaven. There was now no reason why he might not come from heaven on the clouds.

But although it is thus by no means certain that the "Messianic authority," popularly supposed to have been claimed by Jesus, rests on any firm historical basis, the fact that he spoke with authority is constantly stressed in the gospels: ". . . the multitudes were astonished at his teaching, for he taught them as one having authority, and not as their scribes."[21] Although he had the most profound respect for the law, as did every true Jew, and never opposed it or hinted that it would ever pass away, he seems always to have sought to get at the spirit of it, to stress what true obedience to it entailed. He apparently was not concerned with making it either easier or harder. Reference has already been made to his words regarding divorce and the Sabbath. In the former, the law, he maintained, was far more stringent and uncompromising than the contemporary practice: "Moses for your hardness of heart suffered you to put away your wives; but from the beginning it hath not been so." On the contrary, a common-sense interpretation of the purpose of the Sabbath led him to a far more lenient position. In a word, his was essentially a layman's approach, which led him to a disparagement of the traditions of the elders which, he complained, had made void the word of God. This sort of teaching may well have been as popular with the unlearned as it was distasteful to the Scribes and their supporters who looked with contempt at this preacher, destitute in their eyes of any real knowledge of God's law and will, who yet assailed them for precisely those qualities and interests which they believed God had commended to them.

There was a freshness and force to his teaching. The short cut appeal to reason, not precedent, could not fail to attract attention. When charged with doing his healings by the power of evil,[22] he retorted: If the healing of

---

[21] Matt. 7:28,29 and frequently.
[22] Mark 3:22 ff. and parallels.

men's bodies is a worthy deed, how can the devil sponsor it? He would then be fighting himself. When asked as to the practice of paying taxes to Rome,[23] his answer was equally direct. There was no appeal to precedent. You are enjoying Roman protection, using Roman money; you are under obligation to be loyal to the government whose blessings you enjoy. To the charge that he spent too much time with publicans and sinners, his answer was apposite: "They that are well have no need of a physician, but they that are sick."

The novelty of such a method is revealed by an anecdote told of Hillel. In a remote village the elders were perplexed as to the proper procedure when the fourteenth of Nisan fell on a Sabbath. Was the obligation to slaughter and prepare the victims for the Passover superior to that which forbade labour on the Sabbath? Hillel, who had been a pupil of Shemaiah and Abtalion, was recommended to them as one able to give them the tradition on this point. By three lines of argument he sought to prove that the Passover requirement was the greater. In contempt for his opinion they exclaimed: "How could we expect anything of a Babylonian?" But when after fruitlessly arguing all day he fell back on tradition, "Thus I heard it from Shemaiah and Abtalion," their opposition ceased and they elected him their president.[24]

Such independence of tradition on the part of Jesus must have seemed the height of impudence to the outraged Scribes; to others, favourably inclined toward him, it may well have increased their interest. Surely one who would dare to speak so confidently and without respect for the opinions of the great must be very sure of himself; otherwise how would he venture on so reckless a course!

What then was the authority which he claimed for himself? The most obvious answer is not improbably the correct one, namely, the one preserved in the gospels themselves, that he was a prophet of God. This was apparently the impression he made upon his hearers. It is highly probable that this impression was due to his own belief. If this is the case, he must have believed himself to be inspired by the Holy Spirit, for in the thinking of Judaism the Holy Spirit is specifically the spirit of prophecy. "All the prophets spoke by the holy spirit. The holy spirit is so specifically prophetic inspiration that when Haggai, Zechariah, and Malachi, the last prophets, died, the holy spirit departed from Israel."[25]

Once more God was speaking to his people in the old and accredited way. The prophet like unto Moses long expected had now appeared. As the mouthpiece of God he uttered his clarion call, confident that it was not he but

---

[23] Mark 12:13-17 and parallels.

[24] Jer. Pesaḥim 33a; Pesaḥim 66a. For this old Baraita I am indebted to G. F. Moore, *Harvard Theological Review*, Vol. XVII, No. 4 (Oct., 1924) p. 366.

[25] G. F. Moore, *Judaism*, Vol. I, p. 237.

God who was calling men to repent and to watch for the appearance of the Final Judge who would baptize the nation with a baptism of fire. This passionate confidence may well have caused him to appear "beside himself."[26] To his opponents it was the frenzy of a man possessed by an evil spirit; to his followers the mark of that divine madness that proclaimed the power of God. To folk accustomed to explain everything out of the ordinary as the result of the presence of a *daimon*, good or bad, Jesus with his scathing denunciations and his impossible demands, his power to quiet the insane, his genial attitude toward children and those in distress, his absolute self-confidence, may well have seemed a most unusual and amazing character, one from the past sent by God to herald a new age.

And this catastrophic end was near at hand. It might come at any moment; when, he did not know. It could not, however, be long delayed. It would come before the present generation had died.[27] It is useless to try to smooth this difficulty away. To attempt to explain this as a misunderstanding of his meaning by his hearers or as a view later developed and attributed to him is most unfortunate. On the one hand, this would demand such an amazing lack of intelligence on the part of his hearers or inability on his own part to express himself clearly on a point of vital importance that we would be justified in doubting whether any reputed recollection from such sources could approach historical probability; on the other, each succeeding year made the difficulty of the expectation more acute, for the generation was dying. Why should his earliest followers have come to such an expectation and have believed he had taught them so, had their leader not so taught?

More impressive, however, than an appeal to any specific passage, which after all may be open to legitimate critical doubt, is the consistent tone and undercurrent of his reported teaching. Were men to follow implicitly the instruction not alone to the rich ruler but as recorded in the Sermon on the Mount—"And if any man would go to law with thee, and take away thy coat, let him have thy cloak also. . . . Give to him that asketh thee, and from him that would borrow of thee turn not thou away. . . . Resist not him that is evil: but whosoever smiteth thee on thy right cheek, turn to him the other also"—it would mean the collapse of society. It is possible to water these words—and there are many more like them—down into more or less innocuous admonition to be generous and even-tempered, but the result of this popular means of justifying present-day ideals by the appeal to the fancied support of Jesus are, to say the least, not impressive nor particularly convincing. The demands *are* impossible if life is to continue as it is. But in the thinking of Jesus this is precisely the point. Life was not to continue. The end was at hand. This might well be an ideal preparation for the Age to Come. Thus it would seem wiser not to call these teachings an "interim

[26] Mark 3:21.
[27] Mark 9:1 and parallels (Matt. 16:28; Luke 9:27).

ethic." Rather they are a "kingdom ethic." This is to be the kind of life lived in the new age soon to appear. To achieve entrance men must begin to live as though the change had actually taken place. In the short time of waiting matters which have seemed of so great concern pale into insignificance. Why concern oneself about wealth, clothing, position, bodily comfort, dignity, national pride which is affronted by subjection to a foreign power? The time is too short for indulging in such idle trivialities. Certainly his earliest followers in Jerusalem, who pooled their property in confidence that before it was expended the kingdom would dawn, appear to have understood him in this sense.

All this should make clear that the view, which still persists in some circles that Jesus' aim was to found a Church, distinct from the Synagogue, is quite improbable. The gospels themselves bear little trace of such a view. The word church (ἐκκλησία) occurs but twice in the whole gospel tradition, and both times in passages which are generally regarded as comparatively late and most improbable as genuine words of Jesus.[28] His message was not for a group of men who were to carry on in an unending world; on the contrary, his followers were to go out and to proclaim the same message that he, as God's prophet, was heralding. Prepare yourselves for the coming day. Live in such a manner toward God that regardless of the time of the coming of the kingdom you will not be caught off your guard. It will come as a thief in the night. Thus attempts to picture Jesus as breaking away from Judaism, of conceiving a new religion in which the Jew and gentile stood alike, equal in the sight of God, would appear to be in flagrant contradiction to probability. To be sure, there are frequent traces in the gospel of this new view, the most conspicuous of which is the so-called Great Commission;[29] but without exception they appear to reflect the later views, and to come from a time when his followers had been forced from the Jewish nest and had gone out into the highways and byways of the gentile world. Once this vision of the wider field had been glimpsed, the early Christians, confident that their movement was being blessed by God, were of course convinced that their Master, fully aware of the purposes of God, had intended it and had blessed it. Accordingly, such rites as baptism and the Lord's supper appear to have arisen when it became evident that the end was not so near as they had expected but that an interim of waiting was to be experienced.

After a time of itinerant preaching in Galilee, he turns south to the nation's capital. In Luke's fine phrase, "he stedfastly set his face to go to Jerusalem." Why did he go? The answer is by no means easy. It may well be that the

[28] Matt. 16:18; 18:17.
[29] Matt. 28:19,20.

increasing opposition had convinced him that his earlier dreams for the nation were not to be realized, that, like the prophets before him, he must fall before the blind prejudice of those to whom he had been sent. But if he were to die, he must first stand in Jerusalem and herald God's word in Zion. A prophet might not die save in Jerusalem. So he turned to the south. But this is easily over-emphasized. From the time of his transfiguration near Cæsarea Philippi the gospels represent him as speaking openly of his death, but invariably appending the mention of his resurrection three days later. This view obviously reflects the thinking of Christians at the time the gospels were written. That it accurately portrays the actual fact is far less certain. The stubborn fact of the dismay of his disciples, their flight back to Galilee, their feeling that the last word had been spoken and that that word was failure make very difficult the view that he had foreseen and openly predicted an event which was to vindicate in so startling a manner his mission, and which could scarcely fail to arouse joyful anticipation, not abject terror. As suggested on a previous page, such a view can scarcely fail to reduce the intelligence of his closest followers to the vanishing-point or to necessitate seeing him speaking in riddles, intelligible only to a later age. It is far wiser not to endeavour to give a fictitious clarity to those days known to us at best at a far remove, but to allow them to remain hidden. Whatever the motives which led him to leave the Galilean hills for the nation's capital, he apparently turned to the south with the confidence that, though he could not see the end from the beginning, God was directing his steps; God's will could not be·thwarted; so long as it was day, he would do the will of him who had sent him.

He enters the city of Jerusalem. The gospels represent the pilgrim throngs hailing him joyfully. But any such enthusiasm was at best short-lived. His preaching soon disillusioned them. The opposition in the nation's capital was far more intense than in Galilee. Those in control saw in him a most dangerous figure, the potential source of all sorts of difficulties, a disturber of the *status quo*, a troubler of Israel. With his eye fixed on the coming kingdom, impatient toward any such makeshift remedies as the Home Rule Party were crying for, he dashed any hopes they might have had for him to the ground. His outspoken attitude, which made possible the story told of the cleansing of the temple, sealed his doom. His life was forfeit. A short time—how long we do not know, for there seem to be hints in the gospels of a longer stay in Jerusalem than the traditional week—and he died on a Roman cross. His friends who had accompanied him scattered in dismay and fled back to their old homes. They had hoped in vain that it was he who should restore Israel. But the comradeship of the months with him could not be so quickly broken. He had built himself too vitally into their lives for that. Their first grief gave way; they experienced him again, became convinced that he had not been defeated, and returned to Jerusalem in joy and confidence. The true triumphal entry into Jerusalem was not on the ninth of Nisan but sometime later when these men, in whose hearts had dawned a new confidence, without display reëntered the city that a little earlier had seen the downfall of the prophet of Galilee.

Chapter XII

THE DAWNING CHURCH

THE first period of Christianity[1] was over; the second now under way, and for a time Jerusalem holds our attention. The story is a veritable snarled skein, at best but very imperfectly known to us. The temptation is to look first at one locality, then another, in systematic order, as evidencing the progressive stages reached by this new movement: first, Galilee—there it was that Jesus had proclaimed his message; then, Jerusalem—here the earliest work by his first followers had been accomplished; then, Antioch and the other places mentioned in the account in Acts—in short, to feel that these were, so to speak, successive acts in a drama; that when the curtain rings up each time the preceding scene is completely swept away.

This is all quite mistaken. The account in Acts begins with the Twelve in Jerusalem, and it is with their activities that the first half of the writing is concerned. From then on the account is limited rigidly to the activity of Paul. Other groups and their activities are mentioned only as their paths cross those of the author's chosen heroes. That the author was justified in selecting those incidents that appeared to him of chief importance in the unfolding story of the new movement, which in scarcely more than a single generation had spread from the remote shores of the Galilean lake to the capital of the Roman empire, and in limiting himself rigidly to them, is not to be denied. None the less, the student must not forget that there were other Agamemnons who never found a Homer. For example, there must have been many in Galilee who had felt the force and power of the strange prophet from Nazareth. That all who were affected by his ministry had accompanied him on his fateful journey to Jerusalem or had shared the new-born confidence of a Peter a little later that they were to leave their homes and remove to the nation's capital is most unlikely. None the less, that they had acted, quite unofficially, as informal witnesses to the power of the one who had strangely moved them, and that as they came in contact with other people they had told the story of the prophet who had made his appearance only to fall before the leaders' ire can scarcely be denied. Some such explanation is required to account for the appearance of little groups that we suddenly find existing in districts far from Jerusalem. It would be rash to point

---

[1] Of course, the term Christianity is not strictly appropriate at this period nor for many years. Usage and the avoidance of roundabout phrases as "the movement later to be known as Christianity" perhaps justify its use here.

to any particular group, for example, those in Damascus against whom, it is claimed, Paul had early proceeded[2] or those in Ephesus whom Paul there discovered, whose knowledge was restricted to the "baptism of John,"[3] as evidence of the activity of those in Galilee. None the less, this group should not be utterly overlooked, even though they may have left few marks in the early tradition.

That at the time of Jesus' arrest his followers fled back to Galilee in dismay would appear reasonably certain in spite of the silence of Luke-Acts which passes over this incident or, perhaps better said, rewrites the account in such a way as to preclude it. Mark, to be sure, has no mention of this experience in Galilee, but clearly indicates familiarity with the tradition of resurrection appearances there: "But go, tell his disciples and Peter, He goeth before you into Galilee: there shall ye see him, as he said unto you."[4] The traditional final parting of the risen Jesus from his disciples[5] and the moving story of the restoration of Peter[6] evidence the fact that the Lucan view was not universally held, but was apparently later and more conventional. Similarly Justin Martyr bears witness to the tradition of the flight of the disciples "who repented of their flight from him when he was crucified, after he rose from the dead."[7]

That behind these few obscure references lies a most significant incident for the history of early Christianity can scarcely be doubted. Would they go back to their earlier tasks with the feeling that the dreams had all been shattered by the hard facts of reality: "We hoped that it was he who should redeem Israel,"[8] or would their confidence in him be strong enough to face the problem of his apparent defeat and to transform it into a new ground for confidence in his eventual victory? Many attempts have been made to explain how the latter conviction was achieved. One thing would appear probable. Before the band of erstwhile followers returned to the nation's capital they had achieved a confidence that their leader had not been defeated by death which did not need to be bolstered up by the discovery of an empty tomb. Underlying the later conventional explanation of a series of supernatural appearances of the risen Lord which nerved them to their new task is the persistent reference to an appearance to Simon or Cephas or Peter.[9] That the most primitive element in the resurrection stories is the enigmatic "The Lord is risen indeed, and hath appeared unto Simon" has commended

[2] Acts 9:1 ff.

[3] Acts 19:1-7.

[4] Mark 16:7; cf. Mark 14:28. Luke alters Mark 16:7 to adapt it to his view (Luke 24:6) and omits Mark 14:28.

[5] Matt. 28:16-20.

[6] John 21:1-23.

[7] Justin Martyr, *Dial.* 106; cf. *Apol.* i,50,12.

[8] Luke 24:21.

[9] Luke 24:34; I Cor. 15:5. Apparently all three are names of the same individual, although this has occasionally been doubted.

itself to many scholars as highly probable. In line with this the words "Simon, Simon, behold, Satan asked to have *you*, that he might sift you as wheat: but I made supplication for *thee*, that thy faith fail not: *and do thou, when once thou hast turned again, strengthen thy brethren*"[10] are highly significant. It is well worth considering whether the revived hopes of the early group are not to be accounted for by the initiative of this one disciple who in Acts appears at first as the leading figure in the Jerusalem circle, and about whom many traditions soon gathered, both as to his prominence during the days of Jesus' ministry and also of his denial and restoration. Coincident with this new confidence, however it had been first achieved, would appear, as has already been argued, the belief that the "son of man" of whom Jesus had so often spoken was none other than Jesus himself, now in heaven whither he had been translated by God, and that he would soon come to establish the kingdom and to take his seat upon the judgment throne.[11]

In this confidence they returned to Jerusalem. How long the stay in Galilee had been is not known, nor is it by any means clear what led them to feel that their work was henceforth to be in Jerusalem. In Jerusalem they appear to have settled down as a separate synagogue with no thought of cutting themselves off from Judaism or of going to the gentile world as crusaders for a world mission. According to the fragmentary evidence given in Acts they visited the temple as did their fellow Jews. That the opposition to them which eventually came was due to any laxity regarding the Sabbath or to any attempt of theirs to disregard the prized interpretation of the Pharisees and Scribes is not hinted. Apparently they soon came to be looked upon as disturbers of the peace because of their preaching of the speedy end of the age and of the excitement which accompanied some of the early meetings. The speeches in the early chapters of Acts, which, while they may not be verbatim reports of the speakers, yet probably give a fair picture of the tone of the early Christian preaching, suggest that these men were decidedly free-spoken with regard to the guilt of their opponents in executing their leader.

But though attempts to see these earliest followers as considering themselves members of a new religion are most improbable, there were differences between them and their fellow Jews. They had become convinced that not only was the end of the world at hand but that the agent of this impending change was their former leader, Jesus of Nazareth, whose return from heaven they were now awaiting. For many years this confidence seems to have remained alive and to have been the distinctive note of their preaching. But the months and years went by and the expected event failed to materialize. While the confidence remained sure that the time must come, it was

---

[10] Luke 22:31,32.

[11] See further "The Date of Peter's Confession" in *Quantulacumque—Studies Presented to Kirsopp Lake by Pupils, Colleagues, and Friends* (London: Christophers, 1937), pp. 117-122.

necessary to push the time farther and farther into the future. Not alone the pathetic word at the close of Revelation, "Come, Lord Jesus,"[12] but the note that the "bridegroom tarried,"[13] not to mention the petition, "Thy kingdom come,"[14] still evidence the wistful longing. Gradually this expectation, which had been the mainspring of the early disciples, drops from the forefront of the Christian preaching, although a sporadic trace of it now and then appears, as, for example, in the very late writing, II Peter. If, as seems probable, one of the purposes of the Fourth Gospel was to salvage this hope, so sadly tried, and to avoid the danger which menaced, namely, that the promise had been a delusion, by maintaining that the expected coming had already taken place,[15] this would be but one more witness to the central place this expectation had and to the impossibility of trying to understand the early history without understanding it.

But even more distinctive of the early group than this expectation of the coming of the son of man—for, after all, other Jews probably shared this belief—was the fact that they had identified their leader with this supernatural figure. This identification was the centre of the preaching. And its consequences were far reaching. From this simple beginning was to arise the whole complicated and imposing Christology of later Christianity. This can here be only sketched, for the story would carry us far beyond the early Jerusalem days. An interest in the person of Jesus, a desire to explain who he was and to interpret everything in terms of him, came gradually to obscure the fact that he had never made such claims for himself, but had been content to proclaim God's purpose for the nation and to call it to repentance. Thus Jesus became more and more one whose person was to be understood and explained rather than one whose teaching was to be believed and obeyed. And the fact that Jesus had never apparently considered himself a teacher but a prophet may very well have aided this development of thought.

But be that as it may, there can be no question that as the years went by title after title was added. Although the gospels reveal the result of this process, they provide but few clues as to the steps in the process. Although Jesus may well have considered himself anointed of God to proclaim his will, it is far from likely that he thereby conceived himself as the scion of David who was expected by at least some of Jewry to reëstablish national independence. As a matter of fact, the adjective translated by the Greek χριστός, although regularly used in the later Jewish writings to designate this expected king, does not appear to have been so limited in the earlier period.[16] Eventually this identification was made as is evidenced by the refusal of the Christians to rally to the banner of Bar Cochba whose Messianic

[12] Rev. 22:20.
[13] Matt. 25:5.
[14] Matt. 6:10.
[15] See below, pp. 242 ff.
[16] See above, pp. 138 f.

claim was sponsored by no less a figure than Akiba. The Christians could not support him, however much they might have so desired, for to do so would have been to deny their Christ. Whether the identification of Jesus with this expected figure was due to a revived hope in Judaism for an expected deliverer as the heel of Rome grew heavier, or whether it was, so to speak, spontaneous, is difficult to say. That the identification took place on Jewish soil is probable, for coincident with the gentile mission the title χριστός, "anointed"—intelligible only to the Jew, for he alone used oil for honorific purposes—became simply part of the proper name Christ Jesus or Jesus Christ and a new descriptive title or designation was necessary.[17]

By the author of Luke-Acts, but not by either Mark or Matthew, Jesus was identified furthermore as the "suffering servant" of Isaiah. That this identification was made before his death is utterly improbable. It comes from a time when men were searching the Old Testament for predictions and prophecies of the coming movement, confident that everything that had happened had been prophesied, and conversely that everything that had been prophesied had happened. The fact that Matthew, who was particularly expert in this procedure, failed to adduce Isaiah 53 as a prediction of Jesus' Passion can scarcely be explained save on the ground that this interpretation was unknown to him.[18] Accordingly, it is probable that the view was of comparatively late origin and by no means universally adopted when he wrote. Nor is this surprising. Isa. 53 is not to be considered "Messianic" in the sense that it was understood as a prediction for the future, most certainly not of the Messiah or son of man. Rather it was a statement of Israel's suffering in the past; at least it was so understood by first-century Judaism. Probably, although this is not absolutely certain, no historical figure, aside from the nation itself, was intended by the author or understood by his later readers. Israel was not only the prophet of true religion, but the martyr as well. Eventually, however, Christians were struck by certain superficial resemblances to the traditional story of Jesus' death in this noble description, and, by ignoring other phases of the description which were not so congenial, found in the suffering servant a picture of their crucified Lord. That this was done by Luke is certain. Just before the betrayal Jesus had expressly quoted from the passage and applied it to himself:

For I say unto you, that this which is written must be fulfilled in me, And he was reckoned with transgressors: for that which concerneth me hath fulfilment.[19]

Even clearer is the identification in the story of Philip and the Ethiopian

---

[17] See below, pp. 192 f.

[18] In Matt. 12:17 Jesus is identified, to be sure, with the servant (Isa. 42:1 ff.) but with no intimation of suffering. "Atomistic" interpretation of Scripture by Jew and early Christian alike was such that a particular word or verse might be quoted without any regard for its original meaning, context, or related passages.

[19] Luke 22:37.

eunuch.[20] The latter is represented as reading from the book of Isaiah with his book open at the words:

> He was led as a sheep to the slaughter;
> And as a lamb before his shearers is dumb,
> So he openeth not his mouth:
> In his humiliation his judgment was taken away:
> His generation, who shall declare?
> For his life is taken from the earth.

And in answer to the query, "Of whom speaketh the prophet this? of himself, or of some other?" Philip, "beginning from this scripture, preached unto him Jesus."

So this interest in Christological speculation went on apace. We shall have occasion later to see other identifications, some apparently later, others perhaps earlier. Thus in Mark we seem to have the view expressed that Jesus had become the son of God at the time of his baptism, a view later to be espoused by the so-called Adoptionists. For others he was born the son of God, his very birth being a miracle, since God, not any man, was his father. For Paul he was preëxistent, the last man, in contrast to Adam, the first man. He was human born, to be sure, but one who originally had existed in the form of God, but had not grasped at equality with God, but had humbled himself and had gone willingly to his death.[21] In the prologue to the Fourth Gospel—here the influence of the Stoic concept of the Logos, as interpreted by Philo is conspicuous—he is the Logos, the embodiment of the divine creative wisdom, the one through whom all things were made.[22] Of this only-begotten Son it is thus quite proper for Thomas to say, "My Lord and my God."[23]

Although this apotheosis of their leader, son of man though they now believed him to be, was far from the thoughts of the early disciples as they began their lives in Jerusalem, it was the direct consequence of this first characteristic which distinguished them from their fellow Jews—their conviction regarding the prophet who had not been holden by death, but who was momentarily to come to baptize the world with his baptism of fire, and to take his place on the judgment throne.

Then again they believed they were from time to time especially endowed with the Holy Spirit and thus enabled to do wonderful deeds. Jesus had publicly claimed this endowment for himself. His followers had believed his claim: this was what had turned him into God's prophet. Now this endowment was theirs. As Elijah's spirit had passed to Elisha, so the Master's spirit had come upon them. It was their Magna Carta.

[20] Acts 8:26-39.
[21] Phil. 2:6-11.
[22] John 1:1-18.
[23] John 20:28.

There are at least two different stories in the New Testament by which later Christians sought to explain this confidence that from the very first the early church had been so endowed. In Luke 24:49 and Acts 1:4 f., 8 ff., Jesus bids his disciples to wait in Jerusalem until they have received the Spirit. Just as John had baptized with water, they would be baptized with the Holy Spirit. Then follows the Pentecost experience in which in vivid fashion the descent of the Spirit upon the waiting disciples is painted. In John 20:22, on the contrary, a different version is given. On the resurrection evening Jesus fulfils his earlier promise[24] that they would not be left alone. He breathes upon them, and says, "Receive ye the Holy Spirit." The belief that the Spirit had come to them directly from Jesus and that it was to be their authority, as it had been his, would appear central in the early confidence of the church, although opinions differed, at least in a later time, as to the precise manner in which it had made its appearance.[25]

The history of the belief in spirit-possession is a story in itself. The underlying concept was that a spirit, possessing individual existence—thus by no means an attitude of mind—entered a man and dominated him for good or for ill. Thus what the "inspired" or "possessed" man did or said was actually the work of the spirit sojourning in him. Originally God had been regarded as the source of all acts out of the ordinary, good and bad alike. Later the evil manifestations had been attributed to the work of evil spirits, in whom the exuberant angelology and demonology of first-century Judaism saw the ghosts of the wicked people who had perished in the flood. The story of the Gerasene demoniac,[26] in which Jesus converses not with the possessed man, but rather with the many demons in him, provides a vivid picture of the attitude of first-century Judaism. Just as it was a terrible affliction to be possessed by an evil or malevolent spirit, it was a great blessing to be inspired by a good spirit, preëminently by the Spirit of God.

One of the most striking examples of possession is to be found in the so-called glossolalia or ecstatic speaking with tongues. Paul provides a clear picture of this phenomenon in the early group at Corinth.[27] It was an ecstatic utterance or gibberish due to the religious frenzy of the one possessed. Words became unintelligible. Many of the Corinthians were boasting of this ability which they concluded was the sign that God had communicated to them his Spirit. Those of their number not so gifted they were inclined to despise. Paul's attitude toward this phenomenon gives a clear insight into its nature. Although he did not question its validity—he was able to surpass them all

[24] John 14:16; 16:7,13.

[25] That this view actually was that of the early Christians and not a later view, that in the early days the heroes had been so endowed, would appear established by the Pauline epistles. He evidences this confidence for himself and his fellow Christians.

[26] Mark 5:1-20 and parallels.

[27] I Cor. 14.

in this ability![28]—it was of but little value to the other Christians unless interpreted. It tended to breed disorder and confusion and could easily bring the
early group into disrepute and contempt. Nor was this merely a local
phenomenon in early Christianity. The roving bands of religious enthusiasts
who worked themselves into a frenzy by music and bodily contortions,[29] the
whirling dervishes, the extreme emotionalists of the present day, as the Holy
Rollers or the folk in the more backward communities "getting religion"
under the spell of a revivalist—all these provide the background of the story
of Pentecost, ancient explanation as it is of the first coming of the Spirit
to the early followers of Jesus.

For the author of Acts, Pentecost was of the greatest significance for the
early group. It was the moment when the promised spirit had descended in
power and had made the first great advance possible. From that moment
on the movement was to spread in ever-widening circles. Although the account is highly embellished and rewritten—probably deliberately—to make
clear its significance, there does not seem any just reason for considering it
pure fiction. On the contrary, it is highly probable that an initial period of
high emotional excitement had characterized the group and had convinced
them that the outpouring of the Spirit by the prophets long foretold had
actually come. The primitive character of the day has been obscured in the
Acts account. Speaking with tongues has arbitrarily been interpreted in the
sense of miraculous proficiency in foreign languages. None the less, traces
of the more primitive tradition are preserved. Some of the skeptical by-
standers gibe, "They are filled with new wine,"[30] to which Peter is made
to retort: "Since it is only the third hour (9 A.M.), it is far too early for them
to be drunk." Why proficiency in foreign languages should have aroused
such a charge is not clear; in the case of the inarticulate glossolalia, however, it would have been most apt. Editors may rewrite narratives; fortunately for the later historian they usually leave some clues behind them.

Nor was this rewriting due to misunderstanding his source through failure
to interpret what speaking with other tongues meant. Not improbably the
old legend of the Tower of Babel (Gen. 11) is in his mind, and its explanation of the multiplicity of languages that had arisen as the consequence of
sin. This sign of God's displeasure was not destined to last forever. The
view, if not universal, was certainly known at this time that in the future
this confusion of tongues would cease. Thus it is expressly said: "And ye
shall be for a people of the Lord *and one tongue* and there shall not be a
spirit of deceit of Belial."[31] It is probable that this view is in the mind of
the author: Pentecost gives a quick glimpse of this future blessed state.

---

[28] I Cor. 14:18.
[29] Cf. I Sam. 10:5-13.
[30] Acts 2:13.
[31] *Test, XII Patr., Jud.* 25:3.

Hence the host of men from "every nation under heaven"—the reading "Jews" in 2:5 is improbable both on the grounds of text and for internal reasons (cf. its clash with v. 10b)—is most appropriate. At this moment when the veil is for the instant torn aside and the future success of the movement is revealed, gentiles are (proleptically) introduced, although the gentile mission as such does not start, in his judgment, until the time of Stephen's death.

With all due allowance for later embellishments and revision of the story, it would still appear probable that not only did the early Christians believe themselves possessed of the Spirit, but in the early days of the movement they began to attract attention and win followers. That three thousand converts flocked to their banners is improbable. That the police authorities would have permitted such an activity on the part of men whose leader had been recently executed is unlikely. Even in modern times exaggerations in the report of the numbers of converts occur. The question as to whether baptism made its appearance as early as the Acts' account maintains is best reserved for a later page.

A third distinguishing characteristic of the group may be mentioned. It would appear from the early narrative of Acts that for a time the early Christians adopted a kind of communism. This has been heatedly denied, but apparently with little reason, for even the most conservative political economists can scarcely fail to be satisfied with its disastrous failure. Two parallel accounts of the experiment are given.[32] In keeping with their view of a speedy termination of the age and in strict compliance with the teaching of Jesus they pooled all their resources and lived on the resulting capital. However admirable such a policy might have been as a brief interim practice, it could have but one result if life were to continue. They spent their capital and got into difficulties. Their number was growing; needs always grow with income. Soon the time came when there was not enough to go around. The last chapter in this little story would appear to be the feeling of responsibility which some of the neighbouring churches felt for sending aid to the now pauperized, or at least embarrassed, Jerusalem group. Other consideration may have influenced Paul at a later time in his well-known desire to bring a peace offering from his gentile churches. It is tempting to wonder if this early page of apparently authentic church history may not have led him to feel that the gift would be most appropriate.

Although the authorities are pictured as being suspicious of these Galileans and to have attempted from time to time to restrain them—or at least their leaders—the community as a whole regarded them with no unfriendly air. They were pious Jews and showed no trace of breaking away from the Judaism that had mothered them. Eventually, however, came a change. Jeru-

[32] Acts 2:44-47; 4:32-5:11.

salem no longer remained the scene of their preaching, but they begin to push outside the city into adjacent territory, and soon, as the book of Acts continues its story, a distinctly gentile mission makes its appearance. Too often it has been overlooked that the account in Acts is but an epitome of the story; the incidents preserved serve as stepping-stones between the earliest days and the time in which the author himself was living. Whatever sources the author had at his disposal, it can scarcely be doubted that he used them, excerpted them, arranged them, and probably often rewrote them to portray vividly the truly momentous changes that had taken place. It is perhaps fair to say of the incidents selected—and this is particularly true of the early chapters—that they are evaluations of the changes that were taking place rather than actual photographs of specific historical events. It may be, as in the case of Pentecost, that an actual event served as the basis of the story; it should not be neglected that the narrative as we have it is vastly more an interpretation of the significance of that event than a mere chronicle of it.

Precisely the same is to be said of the story of the death of Stephen. This for the author is a highly significant moment. As a result of Stephen's death the whole policy of Christianity was shifted. "They therefore that were scattered abroad went about preaching the word."[33] This was the start of the gentile mission. Many attempts have been made to explain the precise cause of the outbreak of wrath against Stephen. The conventional explanation is that Judaism, while tolerant of these men so long as they remained orthodox in their attitude toward the law and contented themselves with peculiar views about their dead leader, felt outraged when Hellenists came to be of their number. Recently it has been convincingly argued that the word "Hellenists" did not signify "Grecian Jews," but simply gentiles.[34] The difficulty with this explanation is not the incidental, almost casual way, these Hellenists are introduced into the story,[35] but that according to the story the opposition broke out in the synagogue (or synagogues) of the Libertines, Cyrenians, Alexandrians, and of them of Cilicia and Asia;[36] that is, in the synagogue to which the Hellenists most plausibly belonged. Accordingly, it could be argued that, far from orthodox Palestinian Judaism taking offence at this contact with less orthodox foreign Jews, it was the Hellenists themselves who were enraged to find their own numbers being infected. And emphasis could be laid on the fact that a more stiff and suspicious orthodoxy could be assumed for many Jews who had had to fight to preserve their religious heritage in a hostile gentile world, and who had returned to Jerusalem to spend their remaining years under the shadow of Zion.

[33] Acts 8:4 and again 11:19.
[34] Jackson and Lake, *Beginnings of Christianity*, Vol. V, pp. 59-74. In Vols. IV and V, H. J. Cadbury replaced Jackson as co-editor.
[35] Acts 6:1.
[36] Acts 6:9.

The most cautious conclusion is that the problem is not to be solved, since, to use the language of mathematics, we have fewer equations than unknown quantities. In the form in which we have it the story has been so conventionalized and revamped that reconstruction is hopeless. Stephen's speech has long been recognized as casting no light upon the problem. The burden of it is simply: "Ye stiff necked and uncircumcised in heart and ears, ye do always resist the Holy Spirit; as your fathers did, so do ye."[37] That this was the theme of many a Christian sermon of this period and in a measure accounts for the fact that a wider sphere of usefulness came more and more to appeal to the preachers is likely; that it is an actual page of Stephen's speech is as unlikely as that Pericles himself pronounced the magnificent funeral oration which Thucydides records of him. It is tempting to wonder if the seven "deacons" who were selected by the twelve apostles to serve tables, but who, surprisingly enough, soon forsake this particular service to become preachers themselves, do not correspond to the Seventy, whom Luke alone records Jesus had sent out.[38] That the Seventy actually were sent out is most unlikely. The story would appear to come from a later day, when the church was largely gentile. It was unthinkable that Jesus could have neglected these other sheep. As the twelve apostles had been sent to the twelve tribes of the house of Israel, so the seventy had gone out to the gentile nations, regularly represented as seventy in number. Is there, underlying this story of the seven deacons, an earlier account in which the Seven were not so completely subordinated to the Twelve?

The net result, therefore, of a critical appraisal of the story of the Seven, of whom Stephen was the most conspicuous, would appear to be that it is an explanation of the change of policy that gradually but eventually came to some of the group in Jerusalem. It is by no means unimportant that soon the position of leadership passed from Peter to James the brother of Jesus, who appears to have been of a distinctly conservative type. Opposition had taken the place of passive indifference or even mild interest which had at first apparently characterized the community towards the Christian group. In Acts 12 a vivid picture of this changed attitude is given without any explanation as to its causes. It can hardly be coincidence that Jerusalem tended more and more as the years went by to become the stronghold of the distinctly conservative and Jewish wing of Christianity; that other communities, notably Antioch, sprang up and gained in importance as the centres of more progressive and liberal thought, to which those who felt themselves unduly restrained in Jerusalem naturally gravitated.

In Antioch a distinct change of policy is to be seen. Although some in Jerusalem may have come to believe that it was as legitimate for them to

[37] Acts 7:51.
[38] Luke 10:1-20.

make proselytes to their form of Judaism as it was for their fellow Jews; in
Antioch affairs took a different turn. A thriving Christian centre soon
grew up with gentile converts apparently predominating. Soon a new figure
makes his appearance, Saul of Tarsus, later to be known as Paul, the Apostle
to the gentiles.

The early years of Saul's life are unknown. That he was a Jew of orthodox
parents, though possessing Roman citizenship; that he was born in Tarsus;
that he followed the teachings of the Pharisees in his interpretation of the
law, as did most Jews; that he was strict to the point of fanaticism in his
reverence for the Jewish law and traditions; and that he joined heartily in
persecuting the early Christians—this is the sum of our knowledge of his
pre-Christian days. Then came his right about face; he became convinced
—how we do not know—that Jesus, far from being accursed of God, had
but done the Father's will; that he had risen from the dead and was now
sitting at the right hand of God, and would soon come to judgment. From
persecutor he turned to become the ardent champion of the faith he had
once sought to destroy. Following a period of work in Arabia[39] he spent
many years in Syria and Cilicia, not improbably about Tarsus, and eventually becomes prominent among the Christians of Antioch. From this city
as a base of supplies, so to speak, he spent a decade or more in the hitherto
untouched districts of Asia Minor and eastern Europe (Macedonia and
Greece), in the course of which he wrote many letters to the churches he
had founded, some of which being preserved came later to be regarded as
sacred writings. Although Paul may well have been the most influential
of all the missionaries to the gentiles, he was surely neither the first nor
the only one. The presumption is that others were working in about the
same general way as was he. That is, from now on Christianity had come
to take its place definitely in the stream of world religions. Eventually—
when, it is impossible to say—its adherents came to realize that it was
impossible to be at once Jew and Christian. Some tried it, and continued
to demand that converts to Christ come by way of Judaism with its law
and requirement of circumcision. But this group—usually called judaizers
—soon became an almost negligible quantity except in the neighbourhood
of Jerusalem, although it is popularly believed that they carried on an
active campaign in Galatia. Save for their possible mention in Paul's sting-
ing letter to the Galatians, they do not appear in his correspondence, and
a century later Justin Martyr finds it necessary to apologize for his broad-
mindedness in conceding that "those who have been persuaded to observe
the legal dispensation along with their confession of God in Christ shall
probably be saved."[40]

Almost coincident with the rise of the gentile mission it became increas-

[39] So apparently Gal. 1:17 is to be interpreted.
[40] *Dial.* 47.

ingly apparent that Judaism was destined to turn a deaf ear to the gospel. The bitter disappointment of early Christianity can still be read in the words of Paul and also in the gospels as well. In fact, it was the opposition of Jews themselves to Paul, whom they quite properly regarded as a renegade, which forced him to the position, undreamed of by him when he had turned from persecutor to advocate, namely, that Christianity and Judaism were two hostile camps, and that the gospel and the law could not both remain objects of a man's allegiance. Nor was Paul's a unique case. The gulf between Synagogue and Church was constantly growing wider. The flight of the Jewish Christians from Jerusalem to Pella in obedience to what they believed to be a divine revelation during the awful war against Rome, which was the consequence of the growing Jewish unrest under the later procurators, was simply the last blow which separated mother from child. Within fifty years after the Crucifixion, Christianity had become to all intents a gentile religion. The churches still had members of Jewish stock, but they were of the past generation. New recruits must come from the gentile world.

This had not been achieved without a bitter struggle. Even in the book of Acts, which seeks to minimize the disputes between early Christians, the intensity of feeling between two such rival centres as Jerusalem and Antioch is plainly visible. In Paul's writings it is even less restrained. Each group had been suspicious of the other, but eventually the one which had come to see the world as its field, and had been willing to adapt its message to the needs of those whom it wished to gain as converts, won. Then it was but a matter of time until the church should become convinced that this was all a part of the unfolding purpose of God. Was not the gentile mission being visibly blessed by God? Were not nearly all who honoured the name of Christ of gentile stock? Surely this was no accident. God had so ordained it. Furthermore, since Jesus had had all knowledge and knew the end from the beginning, he had foreseen and intended that the religion which was to bear his name should go in these paths. Thus while his words, "Go not into any way of the gentiles, and enter not into any city of the Samaritans," might still be preserved, they naturally came to be interpreted as binding only in the days of his earthly ministry. When he had left the earth to take his seat on the throne on high, he had set for his church its solemn task:

Go ye therefore, and make disciples of all the nations, baptizing them into the name of the Father and of the Son and of the Holy Spirit: teaching them to observe all things whatsoever I have commanded you: and lo, I am with you always, even unto the end of the world.[41]

And for another nameless Christian, equally convinced that the church's

[41] Matt. 28:19,20.

history had run in the intended path, Jesus' hour for leaving the earth could not have come until gentiles turned to him.[42]

The results of these early years of preaching with an ever increasing field opening up before the Christian preachers were truly momentous. To choose but two examples. It is today perfectly obvious that there is a vast difference between the nature of the messages of Jesus and Paul. At times this has led to unsparing condemnation of Paul and his associates who perverted the simple gospel stream. The slogan, "Back to Jesus," has simply meant "Away from Paul." But although many of the early judaizers may well have shared this feeling, their opposition was as futile as Canute's attempt to hold back the waves. To make it concrete: Had Jesus been able to attend a church service in Corinth in the year 54 A.D., he would have been astounded, and might well have asked himself in amazement: Is this the result of my work in Galilee? But it is none the less certain, that had there been no change, there would have been no Christianity. Regardless of the intrinsic values of teachings, unless men know them they can exert no influence. The revolutionary call of Jesus had been especially adapted to the Palestine of his day. But it was not a message, in the form in which he gave it, to exert any considerable influence on the outside world. Judaism had been known for centuries. There had been a constant flow of proselytes to its synagogues. None the less, because of its very nature it was not a gospel for the Mediterranean world. It was the natural outgrowth of the hopes and longings of a distinct and different race. And because Judaism was an old and firmly established religion, it could invite —it would not seek nor change. Thus the challenge of Jesus with its insistence on repentance, with its content the impending change, pitched in terms intelligible to Judaism, would have fallen on deaf ears in any portion of the Mediterranean basin except Palestine. The Greek and the Roman, like Gallio, "cared for none of these things." Salvation, a feeling of security, hope amid the crumbling ruins of the older religions which had been hamstrung by the merciless criticism of the philosophers—after all these did the gentiles seek. And it was because this new movement was able to break away from—or be thrust outside of—Judaism that Christianity triumphed as it did. Unhampered by a traditional past, it was far-sighted enough under the guidance of such men as Paul to see that the aims and longings of every human heart were legitimate; that it was not necessary for gentiles to banish their hopes and longings or to express them in the terms of Judaism, but that the gospel of Christ was broad enough and deep enough to meet and satisfy the longing of every human heart. This was the profoundest lesson the early church could have learned. And then as now the pew moulded the pulpit fully as much as did the pulpit the pew. As the years went by, the nature of the message necessarily changed. The most

[42] John 12:20 ff.

convincing proof that Christianity did adapt itself to its new environment and came to provide in acceptable and intelligible form the assurance and security that men were questing for is that Constantine saw emblazoned in the sky a cross and heard the congenial word that his campaign would be successful. Had Christianity not finally won out over her neck-and-neck rival, Mithraism, it is not improbable that instead of a cross he would have seen a torch, or perhaps even a helmet.

Accordingly, any attempt to understand the development of early Christianity must recognize the fact that it is largely the story of the transformation and modification of the heritage from Judaism under the influence of the thought and practice of the Græco-Oriental world. To neglect the influence of either heredity or environment cannot fail to give a one-sided and essentially inaccurate picture.

Because of the fact that at the time when all the books of the New Testament except the Pauline epistles received their final form Christianity had become essentially a religion of gentiles, it is easy to neglect the basal Jewish elements in it. A moment's reflection should be sufficient to correct this misconception. The earliest Christian teachers and missionaries were Jewish to their finger tips. Even a man like Paul, who in later years could term as refuse and loss those things which he had previously considered of the greatest value, never lost his essentially Jewish attitude, however much he might seem to inveigh against the law. The Old Testament—Jewish Scripture—was his Bible; its ideals were his ideals. Judaism, he felt, had been false to its heritage; yet precisely the ideals which Paul had come to believe were to be realized only in the Christian and were demanded by the union of the believer with Christ, rather than through the command of the law, had been held as standards for centuries by the orthodox Jew.

What was true of Paul was true of his fellow missionaries. The Old Testament became the Bible of Christians, and remained such even when in the second century specifically Christian writings came gradually to be added to it. The significance of this Christian adoption of the Old Testament cannot be overemphasized. Actually the Septuagint came soon to be regarded as essentially the property of Christians, not Jews. Not only was it believed to be full of prophecies of Jesus, the coming Messiah, but that it had been actually written for Christians. It is highly instructive to remember that the second century saw no less than three successive new translations of the Hebrew Scripture into Greek for Greek-speaking Jews—those of Aquila, Symmachus, and Theodotion. It was not unnatural that after the Septuagint had been taken over by the Christians and was being used as one of the most telling weapons against Jewish antagonists, Judaism came to doubt the accuracy of this version and to crave others which should be truly its own. Gentile Christians found it perfectly natural to consider and refer to themselves as "sons of Abraham." In fact, it was not only natural but distinctly valuable for Christianity to assert that it was the true Judaism, for Judaism was one of the *religiones licitæ* of the Roman empire, recognized and protected by Rome. However aware Christianity might be of the real gulf between herself and her now bitter rival, it was natural for her to endeavour to come in on the wave of toleration.

Again, it is from the early Jewish followers of Jesus that Christianity received the tradition and stories of Jesus and his ministry. That the traditions were conventionalized and revamped, perhaps more drastically than is commonly realized, as early Christian preachers used them in their efforts to make new converts and to edify those already in the church is not to be denied. For the historic materials which are preserved we are indebted to early Jewish followers. But more important than this was the note that was stressed in the early preaching, namely, that the Christian gospel made ethical demands of the greatest severity; in short, that morality and true religion were indissoluble, if not identical. This was the sinew of the early Christian message and was directly due to the heritage from Judaism. The picture of the moral bankruptcy of the gentile world has been grossly overdrawn by Christian apologists. The teaching of Stoicism and the lives and examples of men like Socrates, Epictetus, and Marcus Aurelius can never be overlooked. None the less, the notion that religion and morality were essentially one; that the religious professions and practices of men of unclean lives were abhorrent to God—this notion was not native to the Græco-Oriental world, as is abundantly evidenced by the difficulty Paul found in teaching his gentile churches this lesson to him so obvious. Christianity learned many lessons from the outside world, but this was not one of them. For this outlook, destined to be one of her greatest assets in enabling her to triumph eventually over her rivals, she stood indebted to the synagogue.

But, as has already been remarked, the transfer of this essentially Jewish message to the outside world involved startling and tremendous changes undreamt of by the earliest preachers. When the earliest disciples began to push out and to make proselytes they had no notion of the consequences of their action. To think that at some specific time they deliberately altered their practice—hitherto they had been unconcerned for the gentile world; now they would treat gentiles precisely as they had formerly treated Jews —is absurd. The proselytes they made were proselytes to Judaism. Gentiles might be fit objects to preach to; they were not fit table companions. The bars were by no means let down overnight. This important distinction is not always clear to the reader of the highly compressed account in the early chapters of Acts. A Peter might preach to a Cornelius; none the less, his qualms of conscience at eating with gentiles in Antioch might cause him to stand guilty of hypocrisy in the eyes of a Paul. In the course of long years of work in the gentile world, hampered and opposed by orthodox Jews,

Paul might come eventually to an open break: "There can be neither Jew nor Greek . . . ye are all one man in Christ Jesus;"[43] "circumcision is nothing, and uncircumcision is nothing;"[44] yet it is most improbable that had we a letter from his pen shortly after he had turned from persecutor to friend we would read these words. Eventually even the Christians who most vehemently opposed such latitudinarianism swung into line or else retreated into the shell of an ultra-Jewish gospel—more Jewish, if possible, than orthodox Judaism itself—and exerted no further influence in the movement as a whole. To write the story in detail of the gradual transformation of the early group awaiting the return of the son of man and proclaiming the message they had inherited from the prophet of Nazareth into an independent religion promising to the world salvation through the death and resurrection of the Lord Jesus Christ and made possible by baptism and a sacred meal is impossible. None the less, the general trend of the development is reasonably clear. We can still see evidences of the gradual fusion of such original contradictory views as those of the resurrection of the body and immortality of the soul, of a great final judgment at the end of this age and the immediate rewards and punishments to each individual at the end of his life, of the Galilean prophet anointed by God to proclaim his coming kingdom and the Saviour of the world.

[43] Gal. 3:28 f.
[44] I Cor. 7:19.

Chapter XIII

THE DEVELOPING CHURCH

THE Græco-Roman world in which the early church soon found itself was by no means as religiously bankrupt as has often been alleged. That many of the landmarks of the earlier forms of popular religion had crumbled before the criticism of the philosophers is true; that many men found themselves adrift in an unknown sea without chart or compass, anchors dragging and the familiar stars obscured by fog, is also certain. But that this means a confirmed and morally vicious atheism had taken the place of an exploded polytheism is no truer than would be a similar diagnosis of modern society. To cull salacious passages from Persius or Martial, or to fail to recognize that a Juvenal or Lucian was satirizing and hence deliberately choosing the most reprehensible elements available, results in a completely distorted picture. Furthermore, it is equally easy to point to Epicureanism and to emphasize that the removal of the gods from any intimate concern with the world must have resulted in an easy-going atheism, while the Stoic identification of the divine with nature could not escape a barren godless rationalism. Mature reading of Epicurus or of Epictetus and Marcus Aurelius by no means justifies such a priori conclusions. The readiness with which the provinces introduced a new goddess, Roma, into their pantheon in grateful appreciation for the coming of peace and security into their troubled world, and found it most natural to deify her emperors, first the dead and then the living, is by no means to be overlooked. Furthermore, the older hero cults of the Greeks, notably that of Æsculapius, which had been of such significance in the previous centuries, continued to exert an undiminished influence. And finally, to mention but a few, the so-called mystery cults, both Greek and Oriental, were providing the means of escape from present perils to a joyous and certain confidence, and were making converts at a rate which alarmed many a staid Roman. In short, the Mediterranean world, far from being immersed in indifference or hostility to religion, was showing itself most responsive. As has been acutely remarked, "Not because Gentiles were irreligious, but because they were so incurably and tenaciously religious, Christian propagandists actually made little headway with them at first."[1] Convinced as the early Christians were that their religion alone was true—again a heritage from Judaism—they bitterly opposed these other cults and practices as the stupid productions of wicked demons who were fruit-

[1] Willoughby, *Pagan Regeneration*, p. 2.

lessly striving against the one true God and his Son. Thus Paul reminds his Galatian converts that they had been in subjection to evil demons,[2] not that they had been religiously indifferent. The gentiles had "lords many" but were "without God" (ἄθεοι)[3] not because they were destitute of divinities, but because these divinities were demons or idols; this age had a god, but he was Satan![4] Accordingly the word attributed to Paul as he addressed his gentile hearers on the Areopagus, "Ye men of Athens, in all things I perceive that ye are very religious,"[5] is most apt whether the word, translated by some "religious," by others "superstitious," be considered a compliment or reproach.

As has already been emphasized, distinct changes had taken place between the message of Jesus in Galilee and that of his earliest followers in Jerusalem, even though the latter were quite unaware of the fact themselves. The *post*crucifixion experiences had convinced them that Jesus was more than the prophet of the impending kingdom. Actually he was the one who would momentarily return to earth on the clouds of heaven, himself to establish it. Thus was born the Christological speculations, destined to play such a large part in the triumph of Christianity. So even in the earliest days, while his followers were still on Jewish soil and without any thought of going into the ways of the gentiles, far-reaching changes had come. But the transfer from Jewish to gentile soil brought even more radical changes. Not only did the movement speedily become a separate religion, distinct from Judaism, but, as its message was translated into terms intelligible and appropriate to gentile hearers, it became gradually more and more like the other cults with which it found itself in conflict. By the middle of the second century—and probably much earlier—it had become one of the Græco-Oriental cults, and like the others offered salvation to its converts through its divine Lord. To understand and to appreciate this development a brief consideration of this type of religion is necessary.[6]

There were many kinds of mystery cults in the world at the time of the emergence of Christianity. Nothing is more misleading than to consider them all alike and to deduce from the characteristics of one the nature of them all. None the less, all of these cults appear to have had three characteristics in common: (1) All have some purificatory rite of initiation through which the initiate must pass. (2) All are essentially mysteries of communion with some deity who through this rite comes into union with his votaries.

---

[2] Gal. 4:3. The obscure στοιχεῖα, usually rendered "rudiments" or "elements," is apparently so to be understood.

[3] Eph. 2:12.

[4] II Cor. 4:4.

[5] Acts 17:22.

[6] In the following pages free use is made of an earlier study in my *The Ethics of Paul*, pp. 45-59.

(3) All look to the future life and secure for the initiate a happy reception in the world beyond the grave. This goal, the gospel of all the mysteries, is clearly expressed in the distich of Firmicus Maternus,

> Be of good courage, ye initiates; because the God has been saved;
> To us also shall be salvation from woes.[7]

Thus Cicero can say, "In the mysteries we learn not only to live happily but to die with fairer hope."[8] For the initiate the statement wrongly attributed to the Epicurean would be amended to, "Eat, drink, and be merry, for tomorrow you do not die at all—for you have been saved." This is strikingly illustrated by the word:

> As truly as Osiris lives, he shall live also; as truly as Osiris is not dead, shall he not die; as truly as Osiris is not annihilated, shall he not be annihilated.[9]

This goal was realized solely through the efficacy of the rites of initiation. It was through them that the secret of salvation became communicated. Much unnecessary confusion has arisen about the nature of these cults through the unfortunate title, "mystery religions." Actually the Greek word translated *mystery* ($\mu\upsilon\sigma\tau\acute{\eta}\rho\iota\upsilon\nu$) does not signify anything either mysterious or vague. Rather it was perfectly well known and clearly defined to the initiate to whom it had been revealed. It was thus a *secret*, known only to the members of that particular cult. This all-important secret had been communicated to him in the ritual of initiation by means of "the things done and the things said."

> Thrice blessed are they who have seen these rites and then go to the house of Hades, for they alone have life there; but all others have only woe.[10]

The cleft between religion and morality is evident. The two need not be antagonistic; none the less, salvation depended upon the efficacy of the vows, not upon purity of life. This gave point to the sneer of Diogenes:

> Pataicion the thief will have a better fate when he comes to die than will Epaminondas, because he has been initiated.[11]

But that this indifference to morality fostered immorality does not seem to have been the case. The cults were *un*moral rather than *im*moral. It is easy to stress the orgiastic excesses that apparently not infrequently followed the initiation rites, as, for example, the *Hilaria* in the cult of Attis, where feasting, masquerade, and often unrestrained ribaldry followed the frenzied mourning, flagellation, and even self-mutilation of over-enthusiastic aspirants for the priesthood. In some of the cults temple prostitutes were to be

[7] *de Errore* 22.
[8] *de Legibus* 2,14.
[9] Cumont, *The Oriental Religions in Roman Paganism*, p. 100.
[10] Sophocles, *Fgm.* 753.
[11] Plutarch, *Quomodo adulescens* 4, p. 21F.

found; not infrequently women were called upon to sacrifice their virginity to the god. Since many of the cults were based upon the perennial miracle of nature's fertility, the awakening of new life in the spring, it is quite possible that not infrequently "the things done and the things said" may well have been calculated to incite emotional extravagances in emulation of nature herself. None the less, it is very easy to exaggerate this phase; against the black picture it is to be remembered that the beautiful *Odes* of Pindar were penned by a devotee to the Orphic rites; that the one passage which we have that describes the initiatory rites of Isis[12] would seem to indicate that far from being degrading they were of a quite different nature; that much of our knowledge of these cults has come to us at second and third hand from those bitterly opposed to them, who, not themselves members of the cults, may accordingly be suspected of failing to differentiate between the nature of the rites themselves and the objectionable abuses of individual priests, adherents, or even outsiders. In the *Bacchæ* of Euripides we gain a real insight. Here the prophet with lofty unconcern retorts to Pentheus, "Dionysus does not constrain women to be chaste"; yet two lines farther on it is said, "Even in the Bacchic orgy the virtuous woman will not be corrupted."[13] That is, the cults were unconcerned with questions of morals. If a person were already virtuous, the cults would not corrupt him; if he were not virtuous, they would not tend to make him so. Crude and often repulsive legends were connected with all the cults and could only be explained away for the more cultivated devotee by some rationalistic effort or by a violent exercise of faith. Often the rites may, as has been already suggested, have been orgiastic in their nature and have incited the more easily excited spectators to acts of emotional extravagances and breaches of the mores (especially since in all the cults save Mithraism men and women were thus thrown together in these most intimate experiences), but that this was not the rule and that it was highly distasteful to the better type of adherent appears probable.

After all, the members of these cults were living in the world. Membership in this cult or that did not cut them off from their fellowmen. They heard the Stoic preachers in the marketplaces. The result is that while the cults themselves had nothing to induce either morality or the reverse, they gradually began to reflect the secular morality of their environment. The coarseness of the older myths and the obscene debauches that occasionally followed the ceremonies may well have appeared highly objectionable to many of the adherents. Nor is there any reason to suppose that every man or woman who joined the cults lost his desire for personal probity and uprightness of life. Thus gradually the cults began to reflect contemporary standards, and during the second, third, and fourth Chris-

[12] Apuleius, *Met.* xi.
[13] *Bacchæ* 314,316.

tian centuries came to contribute in no small degree to the higher moral and spiritual standards of the empire. In the Greek cults this had been to a measure true centuries early.

Each of these cults, as has been already remarked, had its own divine lord with whom the initiate came into union. The evidence is perhaps not absolutely certain, but it appears probable that while some of these lords may have been regarded as divine by nature, the majority were believed to have lived their lives upon earth as men (or women) and to have discovered through their own labours and suffering the way to victory. As a consequence, they had achieved immortality and had been rendered divine. Thus Cicero writes of Hercules: "Hercules has gone to the gods. Never would he have gone thither, had he not, while still among men, made for himself that road."[14] Later in the same writing he remarks that it was by his death that Hercules achieved immortality.[15] Nor was this true only of Hercules; it was believed of many others as well—Dionysus, Isis, or Mithras. It is also of importance to observe that those earthly heroes who gained the secret and power to become immortal while yet on earth were often regarded as children of heavenly parents. Thus the mother of Hercules was Alcmene, his father Zeus. Dionysus, too, was a son of Zeus who had cast loving eyes on Cadmus' daughter Semele. Though the hero had gone on high from the earth, he had left behind the secret; through the initiation rites other mortals became thus possessed of it. Like the god he dies (symbolically) and is made alive again or raised from the dead. Then finally when at the end of life the man actually dies, his spirit remains immortal. This is very clear in the story of Apuleius, already referred to.

By the second century Christianity had become one of these cults. Jesus was the divine Lord. He too had found the road to heaven by his suffering and resurrection. He too had God for his father. He had left behind the secret whereby men could achieve the goal with him. The convert was buried with Christ in baptism, was born again. That Christianity was so regarded is perfectly clear from the pains Justin Martyr takes to prove that these resemblances between Christianity and the other religions were all due to the malignity of the demons. These wretched demons had read the Scriptures and had realized, although imperfectly, what was destined to be. They trembled as they saw their coming overthrow and realized their helplessness to prevent it. To salvage as much as possible and to delude men they hastily concocted rites and ceremonies as near as possible to those they foresaw were to be instituted. Thus they hoped that when Christ appeared and instituted his worship men might be deluded into believing that the Christians were borrowing from older pagan ceremonies and beliefs. To the modern student this explanation of Justin may seem most

[14] *Tusc.* i,14,32.
[15] *Ibid.* ii,8,20.

naïve; none the less, it is highly important as incontrovertible evidence of the growing likeness of Christianity to the other cults which made such an explanation essential.

But though Christianity came to have many characteristics in common with these other older cults, due to the activities of her early missionaries one great difference is apparent. In Christianity morals and religion were one. Purity of life, stedfastness of character—these were never to be disregarded. This note Paul had sounded with all his might. The Christian was in immediate fellowship with his Lord. He had been baptized into his death, had died to the flesh, was a new man in Christ Jesus. But for Paul it did not end here. The Christian's life must conform to his new and exalted status of being "in Christ." He was assured of a place in the eternal destiny of the world. Death had lost its power over him. But this destiny was only for those who actually lived "in Christ." If he failed to live in a fitting way, to bear evidence in his life of this new relationship to God, this failure was proof positive that he was actually not "in Christ" at all. Every Christian would stand before the judgment bar. For those who were really "in Christ" and whose loves and characters proved it this experience would be the time of reward. It would mark for them not the day of wrath, but the day of salvation. To many of Paul's gentile converts this insistence upon ethical conduct sounded an alien note. Was not the efficacy of the rite of admission sufficient? What had matters of conduct to do with religion? For the gentile this was a perfectly natural attitude. It was Paul's lifelong task to try to show his gentile converts that morals and religion were one and the same.

This emphasis upon purity of life and uprightness of character so much emphasized by Paul and the other early missionaries—it was their heritage from Judaism—is almost certainly one of the principal reasons for the steady growth and eventual triumph of Christianity. Its Lord was no unmoral or immoral deity, as were so many of the "lords" of the other cults. No impure stories of his amours and activities needed to be explained or allegorized away. There was nothing in the ritual to cause men of moral refinement to hesitate to take the step. In the lapse of the years this ethical insistence of Christianity proved one of her greatest assets; it may have deterred some of licentious life who might otherwise have been attracted, but it drew to herself many others and welded them into a solid front.

That Christianity soon came to be regarded as one of the many mystery religions of salvation does not appear to be open to legitimate question. The problem lies in a different direction, viz., What caused Christianity to pass from the absolutely non-sacramental type of religion as revealed in the primitive tradition underlying the gospels and early chapters of Acts to a definitely sacramental religion? While many influences are to be seen in this transformation, one factor appears to have been of especial significance—the title which Jesus came to bear. As soon as the followers of Jesus began to strive for converts among non-Jews the question arose as to how he should be referred to. To speak of him as being the "Anointed of the Lord" ($\chi\rho\iota\sigma\tau\grave{o}s$ $\kappa\upsilon\rho\acute{\iota}o\upsilon$) was quite impossible, for this phrase was intelligible only to the Jew. To the Greek, who used oil solely for medicinal purposes—the relief of pain, not for purposes of consecration—anointed or *Christ* would signify only "the one smeared with medicated oil." Accordingly, we find *Christ* fast becoming a part of the proper name in the letters of Paul (Jesus Christ or Christ Jesus). As has already been remarked, the disciples of Jesus soon after his death came to regard him as the son of man. But such a title, while perfectly natural to Jews familiar with the apocalyptic speculations, would have been entirely unintelligible in Greek ears. It is not surprising that the phrase never occurs in the Pauline letters. The beliefs which these titles embodied must accordingly find expression in some other title.

As a matter of fact, the title Lord ($\kappa\acute{\upsilon}\rho\iota os$) soon became the common appellation ·for Jesus, as is abundantly evidenced by the Pauline epistles. Although the title is also freely used for Jesus in the gospels, a critical examination of the passages would seem to indicate it the Greek editors' own usage rather than their faithful translation of some Aramaic equivalent. Accordingly, it is highly probable that Jesus was not so addressed by his disciples during his lifetime. It is not improbable that after his death he may have been referred to in some Aramaic circles (apparently this was not the case in Jerusalem) as *Maran* or Lord. Some such assumption is apparently necessary to explain the puzzling *Maranatha* of I Cor. 16:22. Whatever the meaning of the phrase is, it certainly contains the word *Maran*, "Our Lord," and must reflect earlier usage, just as does the preservation of such Aramaic touches as *Talitha cumi, Eloi, Eloi, lama sabachthani* and perhaps *Abba*. But while this apparent (if limited) usage of *Maran* in some Aramaic-speaking circles may perhaps partially explain the employment of the Greek equivalent for Lord ($\kappa\acute{\upsilon}\rho\iota os$), the word in Greek had a vastly different connotation. This word was not only used in the general sense of master, lord, sir, but it was used specifically of the Roman emperors in the cult of the Cæsars, and was regularly employed for the divine heads of the different Græco-Oriental salvation cults. Whatever Paul and his fellow Christian missionaries may have meant by the phrase, "Jesus is Lord," it would signify just one thing to their hearers, namely, that Jesus was a divine redeemer-god, even as were the "lords" of the other cults. Whether this was what Paul meant them to believe is one question; that they did so believe seems clear. Accordingly, by this one fact alone, the Christianity which Paul was proclaiming was made to seem like the cults even though these cults may well have seemed to him hateful and creations of the devil.

Furthermore, the fact that this same word was used regularly to translate the divine name in the Septuagint may well have aided in securing for Jesus divine honours. The title Lord was now his. Christians were becoming convinced more and more that the Septuagint was their book, that it was full of prophecies of their Lord. Hence it was by no means unnatural for them to feel that many passages where the divine rights and prerogatives of the Lord, Jehovah, were mentioned were actually references to their Lord Jesus Christ.

Here another point is to be observed. Judaism was never unmindful of its painfully achieved monotheism. Jehovah alone was God. He could never stand one among many. This Jewish heritage at once makes its appearance in Christianity. Jesus and Jesus alone is Lord. In the other cults all the Lords were divine; to be sure, the devotee of a particular cult owed allegiance to his lord alone, yet he had no quarrel with his neighbour who was joined to another. As a matter of fact, it was by no means uncommon for a man to be a devotee of several cults at the same time.

For the Christian this was impossible. All the other cults were the creation of demons. His Lord, and his alone, was divine. All men must recognize him, "for he had a name which is above every name; to him every knee must bow, every tongue confess that Jesus Christ is Lord."[16] Such an intolerance could not fail to awaken a bitter opposition which otherwise the other cults would not have expressed. None the less, it was a distinct source of strength and of ultimate victory. Christian was drawn closer to Christian as they faced the common foe. Not only did it breed a genuine camaraderie, but the very audacity of such a claim could not fail to have a strange and compelling fascination for many who listened to these startling claims, and who would have turned a deaf ear to one content to be but one of many.

Thus the selection of this title Lord for the crucified Jesus was fraught with tremendous consequences. Not only did it contribute, probably unwittingly, to the entire transformation of the nature of the Christian message, but in addition it rendered it at once intelligible and highly acceptable to those who were longing for divine protection in a changing and terrifying world.

With this transformation of Christianity into a religion, which came more and more to appear like the other cults, promising salvation to its converts, baptism came to occupy a very important place as the initiatory rite, the way the convert became consecrated, set apart to God or Christ. In all these cults was a purificatory rite through which the initiate passed.[17] The candidate was

---

[16] Phil. 2:9 ff.

[17] It is never called baptism. In fact, βαπτίζω is never used in Greek writers for a ceremonial or religious purification, although it is used frequently in other senses: e.g., it is used of ships being *sunk*; of men being *plunged* into debt, *soused* in wine, *overwhelmed* in difficulties. Even among Greek-speaking Jews it was but very rarely used of a religious washing. None the less, Josephus' use of the noun βαπτιστής (baptizer) for John shows that while rare it was not

cleansed from guilt in water—or in blood, as in the taurobolium—and was thus born anew to communion and fellowship with the Lord whose he now was. The bitterness with which Justin Martyr and Tertullian—to mention but two of the early protagonists—inveighed against the demons for having counterfeited the Christian rite makes argument unnecessary that baptism had at a very early date come to be regarded as parallel to the initiatory rite of the other cults. Thus Tertullian writes:

We recognize here also the zeal of the devil rivalling the things of God, while we find him, too, practicing baptism in his subjects. What similarity is there? The unclean cleanses! the ruiner sets free! the damned absolves! He will, forsooth, destroy his own work, by washing away the sins which he himself inspires![18]

It has accordingly not infrequently been argued that Christian baptism was thus taken over bodily from the practices of the Græco-Oriental world, and was from the very first distinctly sacramental in its character. Against this suggestion the story of the baptism of Jesus, the baptismal command in the Great Commission, and the mention of the three thousand who were baptized at Pentecost have been urged as proof positive that far from this being the case baptism was practised from the very first by Jesus' followers. Between these two extremes a middle position appears probable. The antithesis, "I baptized you in water, but he shall baptize you in the Holy Spirit,"[19] is most naturally understood to mean that Jesus did not baptize with water, and accords with the entire absence of any mention of such an activity. In the Fourth Gospel, to be sure, it is said that Jesus and his disciples were making and baptizing more disciples than John,[20] yet at once the qualification is given, "Although Jesus himself baptized not, but his disciples." The most natural interpretation of these verses would not seem to be the contrast which the author draws, that although the disciples baptized Jesus himself did not, but rather that baptism was not a phase of the Master's ministry at all, for in all probability as Jesus preached and worked, so did his disciples. The author, convinced, as were all his fellow Christians, that baptism had been in vogue from the very beginning, but familiar with a tradition that Jesus had not baptized, simply drew a contrast where none was implied or legitimate. That even the story of Jesus' baptism at the hands of John is open to legitimate historical question has already been suggested.

About the Great Commission little need be said. As has been already shown, its whole tone reflects the later practice of the church, already involved on a world mission and is in decided contrast to the attitude of the first Jerusalem

---

unknown nor of Christian coinage. It is simply another indication of the wide gaps in our knowledge—linguistic as well as historical—of the early centuries.

[18] Tertullian, de Baptismo 5; cf. also de Præscriptione Hæreticorum 40, and Justin M., Apol. i,62.

[19] Mark 1:8.

[20] John 4:1; cf. 3:22.

followers who apparently shared Jesus' own view of the nature and purpose of his ministry. Furthermore, the command to baptize "into the name of the Father and of the Son and of the Holy Spirit" (the later orthodox formula of the Church as attested by second century writings and the only valid one according to Catholic law) runs directly counter to the early Christian practice, attested by both Acts and Paul, that Christians were baptized "in the name of the Lord Jesus" or some simple variant, as "into Christ Jesus."[21]

Accordingly there is no evidence of baptism before the return of the disciples to Jerusalem. This makes the mention of it in the Pentecost narrative the more difficult. Here it is introduced without explanation as the natural answer to the query of those who had been impressed by Peter's preaching. Had it been a feature of the work of Jesus and his disciples, one might have expected Peter to urge it and the people to receive it. But for an entirely new institution thus to make its sudden appearance is most difficult. Furthermore, it strikes an anticlimactic note. The Pentecost story is the fulfilment of Jesus' prophecy: "For John indeed baptized with water, but ye shall be baptized in the Holy Spirit not many days hence."[22] Baptism in the Spirit is not thus a consequence of baptism in water, but a substitute for it. The promise has been fulfilled, the Spirit has come. Accordingly the mention of the water baptism which followed seems a forced anticlimax and to reflect the latter view that possession of the Spirit and entrance into the Church were dependent upon water baptism. It is not impossible that the narrative of Paul's experience in Ephesus[23] may reveal this later view: Paul discovers twelve men who, though baptized "into John's baptism," had not received the Holy Spirit when they believed, nor had even heard of it. Paul considers their baptism defective, rebaptizes them "into the name of the Lord Jesus," and confers the Spirit. It is thus highly probable that the reference to baptism at the time of Pentecost rests upon nothing more solid than the author's conviction that from the very first it had been a universal custom.[24]

A far more probable clue to the actual rise of this practice is found in a later chapter of Acts; namely, in the work of Philip the Evangelist.[25] In this story we are in the third stage of Christianity, to continue the use of that convenient anachronism—first Galilee, then Jerusalem, now a gradual spreading out to Samaria and other territory not strictly Jewish. Here the situation is reversed. Philip baptizes various folk, Samaritans and the Ethiopian eunuch; later the apostles come down to Samaria—there is no further mention of the eunuch—and confer the Holy Spirit upon those already baptized. This representation of the apostles as a college of high officials who feel constrained to supervise and pass judgment on the work done outside Jerusalem should

[21] Cf. Acts 2:38; 8:16; 10:48; 19:5; Gal. 3:27; Rom. 6:3, etc.
[22] Acts 1:5.
[23] Acts 19:1-7.
[24] A similar situation is implied in Acts 10:44-48.
[25] Acts 8.

not obscure the probability that in this story is to be found the origin of the
Christian rite, for here for the first time is found a plausible reason for it.
As we have seen, the disciples in Jerusalem remained good orthodox Jews
for years after the crucifixion. They had unique views about Jesus and the
speedy culmination of the world's history. They had sensational ideas regarding Spirit-possession, may very probably have practised for a time a
most unfortunate financial experiment, but in all matters of practice they
remained zealous sons of Abraham. No record of any clash with the Pharisees
over points of belief nor of any rash words about the validity of the Sabbath
are found in the pages of Acts. The difficulties that came were of a different
kind. The group became stigmatized as a nuisance and menace to law and
order. If the speeches of Acts reflect at all, as apparently they do, the temper
and content of early Christian preaching, one wonders not at the clashes
when they did come, but at the long-temperedness of those who from their
high seats heard reports of what must have seemed to them dangerous millen-
nial nonsense.

Although at first they considered their task to consist in preaching their
message to their fellow Jews, they found themselves gradually, as the years
went by, forced to seek a wider field; but only gradually, and always with
trepidation. It may well be that this account of the work of Philip reflects
with accuracy this gradual start.

When these Jews began to preach in heathen territory, they naturally made
the customary demands of those who would be their proselytes. That baptism
along with circumcision was required regularly of Jewish proselytes at this
time is scarcely open to question, although the origin of the rite is quite
unknown. Many speculations are possible, but are fruitless. In contrast to the
other superficially similar Jewish baths and purifications this one was valid
only when official witnesses were present.[26] These early disciples may well
have used some such formula as "in the name of Jesus Christ" to show that
it was to a form of Judaism where the claims of Jesus were recognized that
converts were being bidden.

This would appear an adequate explanation of the start of the practice,
and would account for its early presence in the Jewish wing of Christianity,
as no explanation which would see it as an outright adoption from the
gentile cults of the empire could do. As the movement spread definitely into
gentile territory and thus came into the tideway of Græco-Oriental thought
and practice, drastic changes resulted. From a truly Jewish proselyte bath it
became a life-giving sacrament. That by the end of the first century this stage
had been reached is revealed—to mention but one case—by the reference to

[26] The candidate immersed himself. It is not improbable that this was true not only in the
case of the baptism by (in the presence of) John but also of early Christian baptism. On this
point see C. R. Bowen, "Prolegomena to a New Study of John the Baptist" in S. J. Case
(editor), *Studies in Early Christianity*, pp. 129-147.

the eight souls who were "saved through water: which also after a true like-ness doth now save you, even baptism."[27] That Paul believed, as the author of I Peter manifestly did, in baptismal regeneration is perhaps improbable; none the less, that even in his eyes it was vastly more than an act of obedience in testimony of an inward change of life cannot seriously be questioned. By it, on the contrary, the initiate was plunged into mystic union with the risen Lord, by the impartation of whose spirit a new life began.

The development in Christianity from its contacts with the gentile world is even clearer in the case of the Lord's supper or sacred meal. Whatever doubts may be felt with regard to Paul's view of the nature of baptism, it is scarcely open to question that in his eyes the Lord's supper was totally dis-tinct from any ordinary meal. He believed that it had been instituted by Jesus who had commanded its repetition.[28] It already had its liturgy, and it pos-sessed magical powers—at least for the misfortune of those who profaned it. The cup and the bread brought the partaker into a real relationship with the blood and body of Christ. By drinking the cup they shared his death. That Paul meant by the words, "This is my body . . . this cup is the new cove-nant in my blood,"[29] that the Christian actually ate the body and drank the blood of Christ as the heathen ate the body of their lords cannot be proved and is perhaps improbable, although the charge of cannibalism came soon to be made against Christians. None the less, that Paul believed that a direct and intimate union with Christ was achieved by the eating of this conse-crated food is undeniable. And herein lay its danger. To eat the bread or drink the cup in an unworthy manner meant to be guilty of the body and blood of the Lord. That this is no mere figure of speech is evidenced by his word: "For this cause many among you are weak and sickly, and not a few sleep.[30] It is impossible to free these words of their obvious meaning.

Furthermore, his comparison of the Christian meal with those in honour of pagan divinities is pointless unless it be conceded that both were capable of bringing about a distinct mystic union—in the one case with Christ, in the other with the demon: "Ye cannot partake of the cup of the Lord, and the cup of demons; ye cannot partake of the table of the Lord and the table of demons."[31] Sacred meals in honour of some divinity were very common in the Græco-Oriental world. They played a distinct part in the initiation rites of the cults. In the Mithraic rites the initiate ate the honey, at Eleusis drank the

---

[27] I Pet. 3:20,21. Cf. also John 3:5. For the place baptism had come to occupy by the end of the second century see Tertullian, de Baptismo, especially 1 and 12.

[28] I Cor. 11:23-26

[29] I Cor. 11:24 f.

[30] I Cor. 11:30.

[31] I Cor. 10:21. See my *The Ethics of Paul*, pp. 142 f.

sacred potion of meal and water and ate the food from the chest. From the cult of *Magna Mater* comes the oft-quoted:

> I have eaten out of the drum,
> I have drunk from the cymbal.

In the Dionysiac orgy the devotees had torn the living animal apart and eaten the bloody flesh. This scene was reënacted in the Orphic cult with the participants eating the sacrificial animal which represented the god himself. Papyri preserve invitations to dine with the Lord Serapis in his temple.[32] The unhappy experience of Paulina[33] in the temple of Isis suggests meals with the lord Anubis were also common. Thus it is not surprising to find Justin Martyr, in his description of the Eucharist, once more inveighing at the demons for their destestable copying:

> Which the wicked demons have imitated in the mysteries of Mithra, commanding the same things to be done. For, that bread and a cup of water are placed with certain incantations in the mystic rites of one who is being initiated, you either know or can learn.[34]

That the Christian meal soon took on a distinctly sacramental character is clear, but that this was the development of a more primitive meal totally free from such notions is highly probable. In the account in Acts of the life of the followers of Jesus in Jerusalem it is said:

> And day by day, continuing stedfastly with one accord in the temple, and breaking bread at home, they took their food with gladness and singleness of heart.[35]

There seems little reason to question this reference to a common meal. The intimate ties of fellowship of these early disciples are sufficient to account for such an act without reference to the common meals of the Essenes or Therapeutæ. Nor need we assume that these meals were intended to commemorate Jesus' death. None the less, they could not fail to arouse afresh memories of the days when he had been with them at table in Galilee; especially of that last time when he had sat with them in Jerusalem on the eve of his arrest and death. That as they had eaten they had spoken of his coming death, that the broken bread and poured out wine had been a natural description of it on the lips of one who had seen parables in all the homely facts of life, is far from impossible. To see in that sacred moment of friendship more than such a spontaneous act seems to deprive it of its real meaning. In the evening meals that followed the disciples could scarcely have failed to have spoken of him, to have felt themselves reliving those days with him. Thus without any

---

[32] Cf. *P. Oxy.* 110 and 523.
[33] Josephus, *Antt.* 18,3,4.
[34] Justin Martyr, *Apol.* i,66,4.
[35] Acts 2:46.

attempt to give them a formal or ceremonial nature they came gradually and spontaneously to be a continuous memorial to him. Confident that he was soon to come again, it is surely not impossible that the blessing at table was accompanied with a petition for his speedy return. Although, as the months and years went by, the number of the early followers increased and the original intimate fellowship with common meals became impracticable, an occasional meal in common in memory of him appears to have been held. How frequently they were held and whether at regularly recurring times is not clear.[36] That soon some sort of simple litany came to be employed and that by the sheer force of repetition the tradition soon arose that actually Jesus himself had ordained the repetition is perfectly clear from I Corinthians. Paul prefaces his rebuke of those who are profaning the meal with the words: "For I received of the Lord that which also I delivered unto you, that the Lord Jesus in the night in which he was betrayed took bread, etc."[37] The natural explanation of these words is that Paul meant he had gained through natural, not supernatural, means a primitive tradition of the institution of the ceremony by the Lord himself. It is highly instructive to observe that although this belief arose within the first twenty-five years—probably considerably earlier—it is not reflected in the accounts in Mark or Matthew, and that it is very probable that it did not stand originally in Luke. The omissions of the words

which is given for you: this do in remembrance of me. And the cup in like manner after the supper, saying, This cup is the new covenant in my blood, even that which is poured out for you[38]

from manuscripts whose tendency is to add not to subtract from the tradition, the obvious similarity with the Pauline word, and the double giving of the cup (if these verses are retained) have inclined many textual critics to regard these words as an early interpolation into Luke from I Corinthians.

Thus from a simple meal—at first no different from any other—in which the companions of Jesus found their thoughts going back to the one who had been taken from them but who would soon return in glory gradually arose a rite which was destined to occupy a very important place in the new religion. That the Lord's supper, as it soon came to be known, and baptism were deliberately transformed by the early missionaries—for example, Paul—into sacramental rites in order to rival the similar rites in the other cults is totally improbable. It is far more likely that the gentiles, to whom these men were preaching, saw resemblances where none were originally intended and that the process of transformation, while none the less steady, was from the bottom rather than from the top. Whatever the steps in the process be believed to be,

[36] *Didache* 14 and Justin Martyr, *Apol.* i,67,3 ff. would appear to indicate that in the second century it was weekly.

[37] I Cor. 11:23.

[38] Luke 22:19b-20.

it is hard to doubt that well before the end of the first century a new religion which promised salvation to its converts through union with its crucified and risen Lord and which had its sacred rites of initiation and communion had come to rival the claims of other cults promising precisely the same boon. Its claims were contemptuously dismissed. Its refusal to stand one among many, to live and let live; its insistence that it and it alone could bring the true and only salvation—this was to result in a baptism not of water but of blood for many of its adherents. None the less, within three hundred years from the death of its crucified Lord it, like him, had overcome the world.

Index I

Pages 1-200: *CHRISTIAN BEGINNINGS* (Parts I and II)
Pages 201-512: *THE LITERATURE OF THE CHRISTIAN MOVE-
MENT* (Part III)

NAMES AND SUBJECTS

In this index full-faced type indicates the title or theme of a chapter (*e.g.*, Acts, Book of, **413-425**); an asterisk indicates a principal or important reference (*e.g.*, Agrippa I, 75-77*). In the case of Greek or Latin writers whose works are cited frequently, only the more important passages are indicated in this index, but reference is made when the authors are referred to or commented upon rather than simply cited. In Index II will be found the complete list of such citations, together with all those from the biblical writings (including the Apocrypha and Pseudepigrapha), the Apostolic Fathers, and the Rabbinic writings.

Marcion, 264 ff., 275, 295, 303, 320, 424, 459, 462–466*, 469, 507

Mariamne, 43, 45, 48 ff., 57

Mark, Gospel of, **374–388**; nature of, 374 f.; chief themes of, 374–376; "Messianic secret" in, 376 f., 378 ff.; parables in, 375, 378; original language of, 380 ff.; place of composition of, 382; authorship of, 383–385*; date of, 385 ff.; alleged "lost ending of," 387 f.; relationship of to Q, 433; sources of, 435 ff.

Mark, John, 229 f., 322 f., 326. *See also* Mark, Gospel of (authorship of)

Marnas, temple of in Gaza, 84

Martyrium Andreæ, 370

Massebieau, L., 327

Mattathias, revolt of, 16 f.

Matthew, Gospel of, **389–402**, 459; nature of, 389; dependence of upon Mark, 389 f., 392 ff.; arrangement of material in, 389 ff., 396 f., 401 f.; historical value of, 392; non-Markan material in, 396 f.; interest of in prophecy, 397 ff.; anti-Jewish feeling of, 399; date of, 399 f.; authorship of, 400 ff.; place of origin of, 402

McGiffert, A. C., 229, 306, 346

Meat, consecrated, 251

Mekilta, 107, 109

Melchizedek, 310, 311

Melito, 469

Melkart, 245

Menelaus (Menahem), 13

Messiah, 68, 138 ff., 161 f., 173; "woes of," 143; preëxistence of, 364 n.

Messianic hope. *See* Future, views of

Meyer, A., 327

Midrash, 106 f.

Mishna, 106, 107 f.*

Mithradates of Pontus, 35, 224

Mithras, 189, 190, 198

Modein, 16

Moffatt, J., ix, 264 n., 265 n., 340 n., 343, 348, 424 n., 447

Moore, G. F., 92, 101 n., 102 n., 103 n., 107, 119 n., 127, 136, 139 n., 141 n., 164

Muratorian canon, 292, 320, 337, 347 f., 417, 451, 460, 466, 467

Mystery cults, 187–190*; three characteristics of, 187 f.; initiatory rite essential in, 188; unmoral but not immoral, 188 f.; reflect current morality, 189 f.; sacred meals of, 197 f.

Nazareth, rejection of Jesus at, 404, 414

Nebuchadnezzar, 3, 358

Nero, 365; N. Saga, 242, 365

Nestle, E., 487

Neutral text, 488, 490, 491, 504, 508, 509

New Testament, origin and nature of, 203, 204–206*, 213 ff.*, 455–474; first use of as title, 469; form of, 470; textual criticism (*q.v.*) of; manuscripts (*q.v.*) of; chapters and verses in, 507 n. *See also* individual books by title

Nicanor, 19

Nicodemus, 444

Nicolas of Damascus, 55, 59, 62

Noachian laws, 96 f.

Novatian, 312, 507

Octavia, 44

Octavian. *See* Augustus

Odysseus, 88 f., 325

Œcolampadius, 473

Œcumenius, 318

Old Testament. *See* Septuagint

Onesimus, 283 ff., 286 ff.

Onias II, 10

Onias IV, 12

Origen, 317, 320, 337, 471, 495 f.; on authorship of Hebrews, 312. *See also* Index II

Ormuzd, 356

Orpheus, 325

Orphism, 189

Osiris, 188

Palestine, under Egypt, 8–10; under Seleucidæ, 10 ff., and often

Palimpsest, 492

Panium, 10

Papias, 326, 349, 369, 383 f., 387, 400, 402, 431, 450, 458 f.

Papyri, 470, 475, 483 f., 486 f.*; Oxyrhynchus, 198; Chester Beatty, 265, 470, 475, 484, 486 f.*; making of, 483 f.

NAMES AND SUBJECTS

PASSAGES CITED

An asterisk after a page indicates that the passage is there quoted or explained.

PASSAGES CITED

PASSAGES CITED

RABBINIC WRITINGS